MW01142152

Raelene

Raelene

Sometimes beaten, never conquered

THE RAELENE BOYLE STORY

by Raelene Boyle & Garry Linnell

HarperCollins*Publishers*

HarperCollins*Publishers*

First published in Australia in 2003
by HarperCollins*Publishers* Pty Limited
ABN 36 009 913 517
A member of HarperCollins*Publishers* (Australia) Pty Limited Group
www.harpercollins.com.au

Copyright © Raelene Boyle & Garry Linnell 2003

The right of Garry Linnell to be identified as the moral rights author
of this work has been asserted by him in accordance with the
Copyright Amendment (Moral Rights) Act 2000 (Cth).

HarperCollins*Publishers*
25 Ryde Road, Pymble, Sydney NSW 2073, Australia
31 View Road, Glenfield, Auckland 10, New Zealand
77–85 Fulham Palace Road, London W6 8JB, United Kingdom
Hazelton Lanes, 55 Avenue Road, Suite 2900, Toronto, Ontario M5R 3L2
and 1995 Markham Road, Scarborough, Ontario M1B 5M8, Canada
10 East 53rd Street, New York NY 10022, USA

National Library of Australia Cataloguing-in-Publication data:

Boyle, Raelene, 1951– .
   Sometimes beaten, never conquered: the Raelene Boyle story
   ISBN 0 7322 7529 6.
   1. Boyle, Raelene, 1951– . 2. Runners (Sports) – Australia – Biography.
   3. Track and field athletes – Australia – Biography. I. Linnell, Garry, 1963– .
   II. Title.
796.422092

Cover and internal design by Melanie Calabretta, HarperCollins Design Studio
Typeset in 10.5 on 16.5 Sabon by HarperCollins Design Studio
Printed and bound in Australia by Griffin Press on 79gsm Bulky Paperback White

6 5 4 3 2 1   03 04 05 06

To my family and friends:
Thank you for your love and support
with all that I do.

To my cancer family:
Thank you for giving purpose to my life.

Contents

Preface

I HAVE KNOWN APPLAUSE. I HAVE STOOD IN THE WORLD'S LARGEST stadiums and received the plaudits of thousands. But I have never known such cheering as in the past six years. Through three bouts of cancer, I have been inundated with thousands of letters, floral arrangements and cards.

People write to say they are praying for me. Some believe my battles have given them strength to face their own struggles. Others simply want to let me know I am in their thoughts.

One of my great regrets is that I have never had the opportunity to respond. So this book, in a way, is a thank you letter to all those wonderful people who have encouraged and supported me during some of the dark and difficult times.

Writing this book has been an emotional journey. I have anguished over parts of it because my privacy is one of the few possessions I value dearly. But it's also been a rewarding experience.

It has given me an opportunity to reassess, recall and, most importantly, realise what a full and blessed life I have lived so far.

Apart from my running I've never been an ambitious person. But one of the main motivations behind writing this book has been a strong desire to make people understand that cancer is no longer a word that should be whispered.

When a good friend of mine who lives in a small country town was diagnosed with breast cancer, some of her best friends would cross the street to avoid her as a way of avoiding her illness. I don't want anyone to cross the street anymore. I want people to confront cancer, to talk about it, to understand it. Hopefully, this book will go some way in achieving that.

To those who have been alongside me for the battles, what can I say? To my brothers Ron and Rick and their families, to a large and supportive group of friends (you know who you are), to the doctors and their teams who saved me, my gratitude knows no limits.

And to Judy, who has lived the journey. Thank you.

PART I

ANNUS HORRIBILIS

1

My friend, the scalpel

LET ME SHOW YOU MY SCARS. TO KNOW THEM IS TO KNOW ME.

I should warn you that some of them are not pretty. But don't worry if you happen to be a little squeamish. The worst of them — the ones that run deepest — are the ones you cannot see.

Some people measure their lives by the amount of material possessions they have collected over the years. Ask them what they have achieved and they will point to a big house, a boat or an expensive new car. Take a look, they will say. That's my life.

Trophy collectors. As someone who won three Olympic silver medals, and no longer owns any of them, I hardly belong to their ranks. Don't get me wrong. I grew up so embarrassed with the peeling weatherboards and rundown appearance of our home in a working-class suburb that I would never dare invite friends home. I like my creature comforts. But trophies just aren't my thing.

I'm also not the curator of my own personal museum. I know plenty of people who can chart their lives through extensive photographic and video collections, whose homes are filled with mementoes and memorabilia. Many of them are former athletes and in a way I can understand their need to cling to the past. But I've never needed anything like that. The Raelene Boyle Photo Album is a slim volume — about the same size as the Raelene Boyle Book of Subtlety and Diplomacy.

No, it's my scars that record the life I have led.

Go ahead. Take a look.

Let's start with my heels. On the back of both of them are neat, thin incisions, fading purple with age. I like these scars. They are reminders of how my athletic career was extended at a time when the most important thing in my life — the ability to run fast — was threatened. As is the case with many sprinters, my Achilles tendons sometimes buckled under the strain and pressure I placed on them. Little wonder. Half my life was spent pounding up and down hard bitumen tracks and the stresses placed on those tendons were enormous. But every time they began to wear out and inflict pain on me, the scalpel was there to repair them and allow me to continue running.

How many places would I have not visited, how many people would I have not met, were it not for these scars? How can I not like them?

None of my scars embarrass me. There are parts of my body that resemble a country road map these days — jagged red and purple lines that represent journeys I would have preferred not to have taken. But they were all necessary. It's the reason why over the years I came to look upon the surgeon's scalpel as my friend.

At first it saved my career. Later it saved my life.

Look at my abdomen. The oldest scar there runs horizontally across the base of my belly, courtesy of a hysterectomy that finally ended my incredibly painful and long-running battle with endometriosis. It was a condition that caused such intense pain when I was a young woman that there were times when all I could do to cope was curl up in the foetal position. Sometimes I was more fortunate — I simply fainted.

That same scar is also a relic of my first battle with ovarian cancer: surgeons re-opened the wound from the hysterectomy operation to remove my ovaries and a large cancerous mass. That dark line now intersects with a long vertical scar, a memento of my second brush with ovarian cancer just a year later. It almost looks like someone has drunkenly tattooed an upside-down cross on my stomach.

Further up, my left breast bears the marks of my battle with breast cancer. Losing part of a breast can have a devastating effect on a woman. But I was fortunate. Because of my athletic career and my low body fat, I had never really had sizeable breasts and had never thought that much about them. I look at the scars now and recognise them for what they are — signposts that mark a significant turning point in my life.

It was through my experiences with breast and, later, ovarian cancer that I discovered a new passion in my life. I began to understand that because of my public profile I could play a role in helping other women — and men — confront and overcome some of the hurdles placed in front of them when encountering cancer.

Cancer. It's a powerful word. To be told you have it strikes at your basest fears. Suddenly, you are forced to confront the fact that your life is in danger and that you are not that powerful, immortal being you once thought you were.

Yet so many of us begin that battle with cancer without the one weapon that can truly help us — knowledge. Like so many before me, I had little idea what my doctor was trying to tell me when I was first given the news. I was in shock. But I was also totally unprepared for what lay ahead. Some of my later experiences did not help either. I have had some wonderful doctors along the way. But I have also encountered that cold, impersonal side of the medical profession where warmth and reassurance — the things a patient craves in those early, frightening days — are sacrificed on behalf of a clinical attitude that leaves you feeling lost and alone.

Excuse me if I sometimes sound a little abrupt, but patience has never been one of my virtues. And in the last few years during my battles with cancer, I have become more and more impatient with anything, or anyone, that stands between me and what I regard as the important things in my life.

It's all about quality, not quantity. If I were to suddenly confront the prospect of cancer again, to be told that I would have to endure another half year of chemotherapy, and still not be guaranteed that I would fully recover, then I would seriously think about rejecting the treatment. I might pack my bags and head to Africa, one of those places on this planet I have fallen in love with. There, I would find a place beneath a shady tree, settle back (with a drink in my hand, of course) and watch those beautiful animals of the open savanna — the cheetahs and the other big cats, the giraffes and the elephants — wander past.

But you cannot make those decisions if no-one has equipped you with the necessary knowledge. I have no time for people who waste mine by not giving me the information I need to make decisions about my life. I have suffered too many surprises during my numerous visits to doctors' surgeries and know the anxiety of not being prepared or informed enough about procedures or their consequences. The realisation that I was not in control of my life or the events around me came as a huge blow. For so many years I had been an athlete who knew the importance of preparation. I knew my opponents and anticipated their tactics. I trained until my body reached its peak. I tried to leave nothing to chance.

To not be in control, to not even fully understand the strength of my opponent, left a bitter taste in my mouth. And it was probably one of the reasons I sank into such a profoundly dark depression not so long ago that I considered suicide.

So now we come to the scars you cannot see.

Who is Raelene Boyle? I have had more than half a century to work it out. The answers do not come easily. But the scars I live with in my mind contain the key to who I am.

I am a mass of contradictions. But aren't we all? You could safely call me a conservative. I have old-fashioned views about many things. I hate drugs — I come from a family in which using aspirin for a headache was a sign of weakness. But I like a drink and I have participated in many memorable long lunches over the years.

In many ways I am also socially conservative. Yet there are aspects of my life, particularly in my long-term relationships, that have hardly been conventional.

I am a very shy woman. But I have often been the life of the party, too. The thought of having to speak in public in my earlier days used to leave me almost physically sick with fear. Yet I have a reputation for being outspoken and saying what is on my mind without worrying about the consequences. I've lost count of the times I have plunged myself into hot water by giving those around me brutally honest character assessments. Yet I hate it when someone does it to me, and my pride and ego can be punctured as easily as anyone else's.

I always take responsibility for my decisions and in many ways I am a loner. I don't make friends very easily. I keep my own counsel on many things in my life. Yet anyone who knows me will tell you how terribly afraid I am of being alone. Family and friends have always gathered and often even slept in my hospital room with me whenever I have undergone an operation because they know how scared I am of the silence. These days, as I travel the country speaking on behalf of various organisations and trying to raise funding and awareness for breast cancer, I find myself in many hotel rooms. The first thing I do after checking in is to look in the bathroom and make sure no-one is hiding behind the shower screen. There will be no shower scenes from *Psycho* in my life, thank you very much. After that, I check the wardrobes.

I don't like the dark places in my hotel rooms or my mind, and I try not to visit them. Some of it has to do with the clinical depression I have suffered from for years. I am certain it also has something to do with a strange and very frightening red-haired man who stalked me for more than twenty years, at times turning my life into a living hell.

I would like to think I can learn from my mistakes. But I am also stubborn and when I make a decision I often stick with it, no matter what the consequences. I had always been Daddy's little girl when I was growing up. I loved him without question, accepting his advice and words of wisdom as though they had been written in stone. Yet when my father died young of a heart attack in 1973, he and I had not spoken to each other in years. I never managed to tell him that I loved him. I never had the chance to thank him for everything he had taught me and given me. All because of my stubbornness. And his.

That stubbornness has cost me a great deal. But it has also given me the strength to keep going through difficult times.

Many people have commented on the ironies of my life. I was a sprinter who never quite got her timing right. I have no doubt that for a short time I was the fastest woman on the planet. But my athletic career peaked just when the East German sports factory began producing its assembly line of drug-fuelled athletes. On the one occasion when everyone thought I was destined to win a gold medal, and not even steroids could stop me, that lousy timing cost me again when I broke twice and was disqualified from the 200 metres at the Montreal Olympics.

I was also prominent as an athlete just before the explosion in endorsements and commercial contracts. So I could never bank on a secure financial future when my running career ended. Then, after spending several years trying to figure out what I wanted to do with the rest of my life, I finally found a job as a council gardener that I loved. But it lasted only until the new era in which executives worshipped the gods of "downsizing", "outsourcing" and "privatisation".

So maybe my timing was never quite right. But how could I ever feel bitter?

These scars of mine, both the ones you can see and the ones hidden from view, are my most valuable possessions. Maybe I am a trophy collector, after all. They have taken me to places that have scared me, that have sometimes overwhelmed me. But they have also introduced me to another side of life that I could never have imagined back when all I wanted to do with my life was run as fast as I could.

Through these scars I have met people who have taught me so many valuable lessons. I was lucky to find a wise athletic coach who helped reinvent my career. Later, I landed a job that introduced me to an array of characters I came to love and cherish as friends and confidants.

And now a day barely passes when I don't encounter someone in my large network of incredibly gifted and modest friends and acquaintances. They range from prominent public figures to doctors, from charity workers to humble old ladies facing death with dignity and style. All of them have changed and enriched my life in one way or another.

All of them have taught me valuable lessons. And along the way I have learned one of my own.

Not every scar fully heals. Some of them just cut too deep. But you can learn to manage them and get on with your life.

You may even come to love your scars, as I love mine. Because to know them is to truly know yourself.

2

Learning to say goodbye

HOW WE FACE DEATH IS EVERY BIT AS IMPORTANT AS HOW WE FACE
life. It's the ultimate test, a searching examination of character and
courage. And it makes a mockery of all the sporting clichés I have
heard over the years. And trust me, I think I've heard them all. No
doubt you know some of them just as well as I do. How many
times have you heard an athlete described as "brave"? How many
footballers have possessed hearts "as big as Phar Lap's"?

We hear and utter these bland, superficial statements so often
that after a while we blur the line that separates what is important
in life and what is not. I'm sure that when I was younger, when I
knew little else about the world around me, and cared even less
about anything much outside my running career, I was a big
believer in sporting clichés. I probably thought that an act of
courage was coming from behind to win a race.

I know better now, if only because I have seen so many people confront the end of their lives with dignity and class. It makes me wonder sometimes just how I will react when my turn comes, because the first time I came face to face with someone dying I failed the test. I fell apart, and the memory still haunts me to this day. Now I wonder: do I have what it takes?

It was 1976 and I had just returned home to Australia despondent and disillusioned with myself and athletics. The Montreal Olympics had been my greatest chance to win a gold medal. I had come close before, but had always seemed destined to end up second. Good old Raelene, went the thinking. Bloody good athlete. Just never quite fast enough to knock off those strapping East German girls. Mind you, everyone added, those girls had so much muscle. What the hell did they put in their breakfast cereal? And those voices ...

In Montreal, however, it seemed I had finally found my timing, and not even the steroid programs of the Eastern Bloc sports machine were going to beat me.

How wrong I was. I had won my first two heats in the 200 metres, my favoured event, and my form had been terrific. Everyone else thought so, too. While I was hardly under the same sort of pressure that Cathy Freeman confronted a quarter of a century later at the Sydney Olympics, there was no doubt that I was carrying a great burden. Australia was undergoing a lean period on the track. Those glory days of the 1950s and 1960s, when Betty Cuthbert spearheaded an amazing era for Australia's female runners, were well and truly over and I was one of very few medal prospects in the track and field team. In fact, at my third Olympics I was the strong favourite to win gold.

I was disqualified before I could even earn a berth in the finals.

The starter in my semi-final judged that I had broken twice. I was forced to leave the track. Television replays showed I had not broken the first time, but it didn't matter. Once again my career was embroiled in controversy. When the initial shock faded I was left with an aching, hollow feeling that so much of my recent life had been wasted. All those months of training suddenly seemed pointless, not to mention the painful injuries and even more painful recoveries.

By the time I arrived home I was still feeling sorry for myself. What I needed most was an opportunity to put my life in perspective, to reassure myself that I had not wasted the past few years, and that there was more to life than running quickly over 200 metres.

That opportunity arrived in the form of a sad phone call from the wife of one of my best friends.

Gwen Crimmins was married to Peter Crimmins, one of the finest rovers in Australian Rules football — a gifted player who had been captain of the Hawthorn team. I had worked alongside Peter for several years with the sporting goods manufacturer Puma. We had shared an office and quickly discovered we had many things in common, including the same sense of humour and love of a good time.

Peter was a beautiful man, physically and emotionally. But he was dying of testicular cancer and Gwen had rung to tell me that if I wanted to see him, now was the time to come and say goodbye.

I was living in Perth — I had moved there in the lead-up to the Olympics to refocus my running career, continue the healing process from my constant Achilles injuries and get away from the cold Melbourne winters, which played hell with my breathing. I grabbed the first flight available and headed east.

That flight across Australia gave me plenty of opportunity to think about Peter. I had never forgotten the look of absolute pleasure that seemed permanently etched on his face throughout the 1974 Commonwealth Games in Christchurch, New Zealand. He had gone to Christchurch as a Puma representative and every time I saw him he resembled a little boy finally realising a lifelong fantasy. He thought the Games were sensational. He relished the atmosphere — for a footballer whose career could never really take him out of Melbourne, being in the company of some of the world's best athletes was thrilling.

I was grateful he was there, too, and not just because I enjoyed having a laugh and a beer with him. It probably came as no shock to anyone that in Christchurch I was plunged into another high-profile debacle that created headlines back home. By then, no Commonwealth or Olympic Games was regarded as having run smoothly unless Raelene Boyle had gotten herself into strife. I'm sure there were several Australian team managers over the years who, having learned of their appointment, worried themselves sick at night — not about passports or visas or getting athletes to their events on time. No, there was only one word that could strike fear and exhaustion in their hearts: my surname.

This time there had been a dispute over my tracksuit. Yes, another world-shattering issue. Ethiopia was enduring another shocking famine and the Vietnam War was playing out its last tragic days. Richard Nixon was in disgrace and the entire American political system was in confusion. But all those events were momentarily put aside in order for everyone to focus on my size-10 outfit.

Puma had been loyal to me over the years and given me a job when I needed one. Naturally I wanted to wear their tracksuit while I was in Christchurch. There was just one problem. A rival company, adidas, had a deal with the Australian team. Naturally certain Australian officials decided I would not be allowed to wear my Puma outfit. The whole thing, as usual, quickly ballooned out of proportion — at one stage it appeared I would be banned from running for my country simply because of an argument over a piece of cloth covering my body.

It all blew over, of course. But Crimmo, as on so many occasions, had been a voice of reason and support. He became my spokesman and, in some ways, my de facto manager in Christchurch. I always think he understood me far better than most people. He knew I loved to party and have a good time. But he also knew I could apply myself when I needed to and get the job done.

The drive to Peter's home was a long one and I grew more nervous as we approached. I was just a young woman who knew and thought about little else except running. What would I say to him?

He had always been a remarkably brave person. When he was undergoing chemotherapy he would go to the Peter MacCallum cancer clinic in the mornings to receive his treatment. He would play with the young cancer sufferers who were receiving treatment alongside him — children who had little idea about the challenges in front of them — and crack jokes with them before coming into the Puma office. He'd try to eat lunch, but some days he just couldn't manage it because he was so overcome with nausea. Yet throughout that whole painful time he was always smiling. I never once heard him ask, "Why me?"

Peter was lying in bed when I arrived. He was clearly weak. But hell, the man had guts. Life had given him a few brutal kicks in its time. He had captained his side in 1974, and when his health had started failing he had been bitterly disappointed when Hawthorn dropped him for the 1975 grand final. He was only in his mid-twenties, and just days away from death. He was about to leave behind two beautiful little boys and a wife whose courage was something you had to see to believe.

Yet here he was, a frail figure knowing he did not have long to go, and the first words he managed to say to me were, "What happened?"

He was concerned about me. He wanted to know about Montreal. Why had I broken twice? Was it the official's fault? What had happened afterwards? Was I feeling all right?

I have replayed this scene again and again in my mind over the past quarter of a century. But it always ends the same way: Peter lying there, asking me what had happened, and me ... making a goose of myself. I couldn't comprehend what Peter was referring to. I wasn't listening. My mind was too clouded with emotion. I had a lump in my throat and I had to clench my teeth to stop myself from crying in front of him.

My reply was pathetic. "Yeah, it was a great Games," I told him. "I had a ball. It was great fun."

An awkward silence fell over the room. I felt like an absolute idiot. I only stayed for five minutes or so. It was clear he was tired and I certainly did not want to be a burden to him. I leaned over, gave him a gentle kiss goodbye and left the room. And then I broke down.

How could I have been so stupid? I kicked myself mentally. I had not even given him the respect he deserved by listening closely to what he was asking me. It was one of those situations where your mind comes up with thousands of replies and ways of handling the situation after the event. I felt humbled and extremely embarrassed. And those emotions have stayed with me to this day. Even now, looking back on that afternoon, I can feel my face flushing with embarrassment.

I cried like a child in the safety of the car. It was the last time I saw Peter. Not long after my visit, Hawthorn won the grand final and many of the players rushed to Peter's home to present him with the premiership cup.

He died a few days later. I didn't make it to the funeral. But on the day he was farewelled, I was thinking about him as I fell into a gentle, anaesthetic sleep in the surgery theatre of a Perth hospital.

I had discovered lumps in my right breast.

THEY WERE small, white bumps next to my nipple. I found them while I was in the shower one morning not long after coming home from Montreal. To be honest, they hadn't worried me. I was young. I was going to live forever, wasn't I? But as a precaution, and heavily influenced by Crimmo's deteriorating health, I had mentioned them to my doctor. He recommended I see a surgeon.

The surgeon poked around and ran a couple of tests. Nothing to worry about, he said. It was a phrase I would come to hear all too often in the years ahead. But he was adamant — they were nothing more than harmless cysts. It was up to me if I wanted to have them removed.

I shrugged. Surgery held no fear for me; the scalpel had already saved my running career by repairing my Achilles tendons back in 1974. I had been up and about very quickly after that operation. A couple of footballers were in the same hospital as me, having the same procedure in a bid to extend their careers, too. I'm not sure they looked upon it as quite the positive experience I believed it to be. In fact, I'm sure I heard their calls and cries to the nurses asking for pain relief while I was walking laps of my room.

So minor breast surgery held little fear for me. In fact, my grandmother was probably more concerned. I had moved in with her after shifting from Melbourne, and she had mothered me ever since. I was always fortunate that way. No matter how complicated or chaotic parts of my life became, there was always someone to help and console me. Since my father's death I had barely spoken a civil word to my mother. But despite the fragile nature of my relationship with the rest of my family, my grandmother was a doting figure who passed no judgment. I did not even tell Mum about the lumps in my breast, although I am sure my grandmother quietly kept her up to date.

As it turned out, the surgeon was right. The lumps were removed and they were harmless. I left hospital barely thinking about the experience. The world seemed a fairly simple place. It could certainly be cruel, and it was capable of inflicting enormous pain.

Peter Crimmins was dead and for what reason? How could such a wonderful and intelligent person be taken in such an unfair way?

Missing out on a gold medal, even in such humiliating circumstances, seemed trivial in comparison.

But at least I was healthy and fit. When a surgeon told me I had nothing to fear back then, I believed him.

When you're young, you'll believe anything.

3

Passion and death in the garden of desire

I HAVE ALWAYS HAD A PASSION FOR FLOWERS AND PLANTS. THERE IS something about witnessing the birth of a plant that thrills me. I love the way they can suddenly burst forth. Leave a seed buried in rich, fertile soil one evening and within days its first buds are pushing through the surface. Then a deeper fascination begins — watching the plant grow and the infinite ways in which it is fertilised and nurtured. Which birds and insects will it attract? How big will it grow? Will it survive?

It wasn't until I began working as a gardener for the suburban Melbourne council of Prahran in the early 1990s that I discovered I was not the only person with an unbridled passion for nature. In fact, the excitement and ardour some people seem to feel for even a humble strip of lush, green lawn beneath the shade of a towering gum tree is simply too much for them on occasions.

You wouldn't believe the number of people who have sex in public parks.

It is an issue I must admit I had never thought that much about before graduating from a series of horticultural courses in the 1980s. I just loved gardening, though I have no idea from whom I inherited my love for it. To Dad, greenery was the sort of thing that came in the shape of an iceberg lettuce in a summer salad. Mum certainly had a passion for plants, but with three children, her own health problems and a lack of resources — the Melbourne suburb of Coburg, a blanket of bitumen and concrete, was hardly filled with friendly, neighbourhood nurseries — the opportunities to garden were restricted. Somehow, though, the bug had bitten me at a young age. But it was only after being given responsibility for a public park of my own that I came to appreciate how many others enjoyed the calming scents of a flowering garden.

Victoria Gardens in Prahran are one of Melbourne's best kept secrets. They are tucked away in a relatively small block in a busy residential area of narrow streets and old working-class homes that are now worth a fortune. During my six years there I came to look upon the Gardens as my very own. I was more than passionate about them; I was fiercely protective. Some of the neighbours whose homes backed on to the park had created gates in their back fences and cultivated their own private pathways into the Gardens. Unfortunately for them, they had chosen to trample these pathways through *my* garden beds. It wasn't long before I stopped the practice by wiring up those gates. No-one walked over Raelene Boyle's seedlings.

On days off I would walk over to the park with my two dogs from my home in nearby Greville Street and keep an eye out for vandalism. Sometimes the odd local decided to spruce up their own front yard and took a few samples from *my* garden. But generally, people respected the Gardens and behaved in them. Well, at least when lust didn't get the better of them.

To me, there is something brutally raw and honest about a large garden. In that tumble of limbs and saplings and ground covering lies one of the truths of nature. Every plant is striving to force its way up to catch a glimpse of the sun and feel the warmth of its rays. They are like a roomful of schoolkids, all with their arms raised trying to attract the teacher's attention — *Look at me! No, look at me!* Some of those plants will survive. Others will shrivel and die. Maybe that's one of the reasons I was first drawn to gardening. Nature's law is also my philosophy of life. The strong survive, and win. The weak do not.

Of course, these were hardly the thoughts raging through the minds of many couples I and other park workers encountered over the years. They never ceased to amaze us — how they thought they could get away with making love in a public place unnoticed, I don't know. Some of them were quite good at it, I must admit. One couple performed sitting on a bench beneath one of the large elm trees. At first I and my colleague in the gardens, Mal Dean, hadn't paid them much attention. People sat on park benches all the time. Even on top of one another. It was only when we noticed a male cyclist out for a midday ride making the same detour, slowing down to almost a stop as he passed the couple, then coming back for another sly glance, that we figured something was happening.

Mal was a valued colleague back then. He is also one of the most intelligent people I have come across. On days when it was raining, or when a hot northerly wind was blowing hard enough to scatter my thoughts, I would while away the time in our shed listening to Mal talking about politics and religion and philosophy.

I learned a lot from Mal. It was fortunate that he shared my mischievous sense of humour, too. Having figured out what the couple on the park bench were up to, we sauntered across the park and turned on the automatic sprinkling system. It was the sophisticated version of throwing a bucket of cold water over them. But they barely seemed to notice.

That sort of thing happened all the time — secret liaisons and affairs in the corners of the Gardens, lovers who could not control their urges, and others simply trying it on for a dare. Mal and I believed we had a bestselling book on our hands at one stage. We were going to call it *People Who Make Love in Public Places*. With a title like that, we figured our futures were guaranteed. We only needed the same number of people to buy the book as we had caught having sex to ensure we made a fortune.

We had our vagrants, too, who used the park in the warm summer months as a place to sleep. We didn't mind most of them. Some were articulate men who had chosen a lifestyle of living simply under the stars and foraging for whatever they could. And there were the hard-bitten drunks, too. Others, though, had far more tragic backgrounds. I grew to know many of them. But if we thought there was a troublemaker or two among them — drug users who thoughtlessly discarded their syringes in the garden beds infuriated me — they were usually given a rude and wet surprise. What a rare experience it must have been for some of them when, at 3am, the watering system suddenly burst into life, giving them the opportunity to wash for the first time in a while.

I loved the plants in Victoria Gardens. But I also loved the people because they came in just as many varieties, shapes and colours. I liked them for who they were, and they liked me and treated me as a friend, and not just because they had some vague idea that I had run at the Olympics on one or two occasions.

I was drawn most to the dog owners. At certain times of the day Victoria Gardens resembled a dog show. The walking paths were like peak-hour traffic — most people in the area had small backyards and it made sense to take their dogs for a brisk walk through the Gardens. I didn't mind. I am a mad dog lover, one of those people who holds long conversations with their own pets, who constantly cuddles them and sometimes banters with them using the sort of baby talk that makes non dog owners cringe.

I had two dogs of my own, beautiful golden retrievers called Goldie and Ty. I treated them like princesses and they returned the favour. Some might say they were child substitutes. Maybe. Because of my severe endometriosis and, later, my hysterectomy, I was never in the position to have kids. And there had been a time in my life when I seriously thought about it. I think every woman goes through that urge. But it was never going to happen for me.

Every dog owner who came through that park had a tale as interesting, if not more so, as mine. I came to know them all and it did not take long before I was close friends with many of them.

Across the road from the park lived Nobby, a tall, shaven-headed man who would stand out in any crowd — even those in Prahran. He is one of the most creative and talented artists I have met. Then there were Peg and Norman, an elderly couple I still count among my closest friends. They were as protective of the Gardens as I was. If I was away on leave, Peg would provide me with a detailed report on the comings and goings in the park during my absence.

A group of local citizens even formed the Friends of Victoria Gardens lobby group. If there was something that concerned them about the Gardens — from a call for new seats to be installed to stricter rules on some of the strange people inhabiting the place — they were on the case immediately, making nuisances of themselves with the council. I thought they were wonderful. I loved the fact that in this day and age, when so many people seem to care so little for their neighbourhood or their surrounds, these people could become so passionate about a public space. I went to several of their meetings and was always cheering them on when it came to defending the Gardens.

It was a wonderful time in my life. To find an occupation that became a passion, a job that almost every day gave me an unbridled sense of freedom, was something I hadn't expected or dared hope for when my running career finished. Yet that job rewarded me with the same feeling of satisfaction and pride that I had experienced whenever I had run well, and fast.

I loved the days when there was no north wind — old sprinters never lose their dislike of wind. It was always the one thing that put me off balance, that lowered my times and gnawed away at my concentration. But on those warm calm mornings, before most people had risen, I loved to stroll through my Gardens smelling the lemon-scented perfume wafting from the park's two great eucalyptus trees. I would stop and admire the sun shining through the fork of one of the gums and watch how the light bounced off its salmon-pink bark. I could wander for ages beneath the enormous, swelling plane trees that encircled a small, sunken oval at the southern end of the park. They were more than 130 years old, yet they flourished because we cared for them lovingly and well.

But those years in Victoria Gardens weren't without their down periods. I always worried about the future — stressing about things over which I had little control was something I had definitely inherited from Mum. It would keep me awake, night after night. Because of my athletic career, I had not managed to begin a superannuation scheme until my early thirties. I worried about how I would take care of myself later in life; if anyone would be there to look after me. I owned my own home — I'd been smart enough to save hard and pay off my mortgage — but when I was old I wanted to be able to wander down the street and buy whatever it was I needed. I didn't want to scrimp and save and worry about how I would pay the next bill. Mum had never lost the sense that just around the corner disaster lay in wait. She always kept spare cash hidden away in the house, usually in small chicken stock containers. Like most people of her generation, she was conservative when it came to money and savings.

As I grew older, I was becoming more and more my mother's daughter. In too many ways.

I was lucky. I had a wide circle of friends, both in Prahran and from my old world of athletics. I had a job. I had my independence. Yet I never seemed able to shake off a growing sense of unease and disquiet. There was a darkness hovering at the edge of my world and every day seemed to bring it closer and closer toward me.

By the time I heard a man's piercing screams coming from the other end of the Gardens, the blackness had well and truly caught up with me.

IT WAS late February 1996, a normal working morning in Victoria Gardens. This was the time of year when the full furnace of a Melbourne summer usually arrived; scorching northerly winds could dry out the darkest and dampest area of a garden. Yet within a few weeks there would be a dramatic change. The leaves on the elms would start fading within a month or so and begin to curl, the first brown stains beginning to form at their edges. It was time to till the beds and begin organising my Gardens in preparation for the coming autumn and winter.

I was at the park's northern end, turning soil over and weeding, when I heard the screams. They came from the other end of the park, up near the water fountain that stands like a sentry in front of a series of shale steps leading to the sunken oval. I threw down my tools and ran.

The man was in his early sixties. He was a regular visitor to the park. Around the corner was a nursing home and almost every morning he would go there, collect his ailing ninety-year-old mother, and then push her in her wheelchair around to the Gardens. They would sit there and enjoy the tranquillity, sometimes talking, sometimes not. He was always immaculately dressed. Quite often, from the pocket of a well-tailored pair of trousers, he would produce a chocolate or favourite lolly for his mother. He was the dutiful son, a man who had never married, a man who had instead devoted his life to caring for Mum.

But this morning he was hysterical. He had been steering his mother in her wheelchair past the fountain when he stopped to look at some of the birds bathing and chattering in the water. The wheels on the chair were not locked, and while he was looking away the wheelchair began to roll toward the first of the stone steps. It hit it, and then crashed down the rest of them.

While he continued to cry out, I reached down to see how his mother was faring. I could find no pulse, and the fall had caused severe bleeding to her head. She was still strapped into the chair, so he and I undid the belt and laid her carefully on the grass.

"I won't be able to forgive myself if she dies," sobbed the man. He was a pathetic figure, alternating between cries of pain and waves of guilt. This tragedy, even though he was hardly to blame, was surely going to scar him for the rest of his life. I sprinted back to our shed, called for an ambulance, and then raced in my car around the corner to the nursing home to fetch one of the staff.

We were back within moments. By then, an ambulance crew had arrived and were trying to revive her. But it was too late. She had been too frail to survive the fall.

I was badly shaken, too. The coroner arrived and a small crowd gathered not too far off, watching the events unfold. I felt helpless. The woman's son remained inconsolable. There was nothing else I could do. So I collected my things and knocked off for the day. Ahead of me lay an uncertain week.

My doctor had called earlier that morning and asked me to come in. I had been to see her about a painful lump in my left breast that had been bothering me for some time. I was about to find out why.

4

The diagnosis

THOSE DARK CLOUDS THAT HAD BEEN HOVERING ON THE HORIZON OF my life for a few years had begun closing in towards the end of 1995. They were not, as it turned out, a passing storm. Instead, they would plunge my world into a year-long darkness that left me weak, vulnerable and, more than ever, afraid of the future.

I was hosting a quiet Christmas drinks party at my home — well, relatively quiet by my standards — when my mother's doctor called. Because of the noise, I took the call in the bathroom.

It would be a while before I managed to compose myself and return to the party. I could tell right away something was wrong — it's not every year your mother's physician rings to wish you the best for Christmas.

"Raelene, I'm afraid there's nothing else I can do for your mum," he said. "Irene's situation is terminal. I'm sorry."

I think I managed to ask him how long he thought she had to live. By this stage shock had set in and I had begun to cry.

"I'd say anywhere from between three to six months. I'm sorry. I suggest you really enjoy this Christmas as a family."

The task of telling my brothers, Ron and Rick, fell to me. They had always been close to Mum, particularly Ron, the eldest of the three of us. He was an airline captain with Cathay Pacific and was based in Hong Kong, but he had come home for Christmas to see Mum, the rest of us and the children from his two former marriages.

Naturally, Ron was devastated. So, too, was Rick.

We had known she was very ill with lung cancer. And probably deep down we suspected that she would never recover. Not long before, Ron and I had taken her to Africa. She had always had this thing for giraffes. She loved them — they were her favourite animal and it had always been her dream to see them in the wild.

Mum loved the trip. But she had been frail. One afternoon, as we drove through one of the magnificent game parks in South Africa, I suggested we pull on our plastic ponchos because the heavy rain clouds overhead looked set to burst. We put them on and then looked across at Mum. She had put hers on backwards and her face was covered by the hood. It broke us up as we bounced around in the open-top four-wheel drive taking us back to the compound.

She had a capacity to break into a conversation and say the most unexpected things, particularly in her later years as her hearing began to fade and she misinterpreted conversations going on around her. One morning in Africa while we were having breakfast, Ron and I were talking about what we were going to see later that day in the game park. Mum must have thought we were discussing something completely different. She interrupted the conversation to observe: "No matter how tight money was, I always made sure I bought myself a decent bra."

Ron and I looked at each other. The topic of brassieres wasn't one that immediately came to mind as you prepared to go out and see some of the world's greatest predators. But something had triggered it in Mum's memory, and she wanted to share the information with us. And if that made Mum happy, it was fine with us. Not long after she decided it was time to finally spend a bit of money on herself. So she embarked on what, for her, was a huge spending spree. She bought herself a new set of false teeth. And a hearing aid.

For all my problems with Mum — she had sided with Dad when I left home, triggering a lengthy Cold War between the two of us — we had grown much closer over the years. I began to understand her better — and see parts of her within myself. But she could still drive me mad at times. She had suffered oesophageal cancer in 1984 and had given up smoking. That was something that really pleased me. I have had a lifelong aversion to tobacco; both Mum and Dad were heavy smokers. They grew up at a time when it was regarded as trendy for both men and women to smoke. My mother forced herself to become addicted, putting up with months of nausea before finally "triumphing" and earning social respectability as a smoker.

Not long before she was diagnosed with lung cancer she had quietly resumed smoking. When I found out about it I was livid — with her and the whole damn tobacco industry. I can still remember the smell of our home when I was a child, the stains on my parents' fingers and that sickly yellow colour of our ceilings and walls. To have resumed doing something that was so deadly left me infuriated. I wasn't sure who was more to blame: Mum or the companies that traded in the poison.

Still, she was beyond worrying about my rants on the subject of smoking. If cancer had become her nemesis in her later years, depression had been her lifelong companion. She was a homebody —

she didn't like leaving her house for long stretches and her depression was one of the reasons. The condition went way back to her early thirties. She'd had a hysterectomy at about the same age as me, and at about the same age as her mother, too. But depression had always stalked her. When it became particularly bad she was hospitalised.

Rick and I rode our bikes over to the Royal Park psychiatric hospital one afternoon to visit her. We went everywhere on our bikes and we thought nothing of making the hour-long trek to the hospital. The nurse at the desk asked us who we belonged to. We told her and she went away, we assumed, to tell Mum we were there to see her.

But the nurse returned alone. "Sorry," she said. "Irene Boyle says she doesn't have any children." We were devastated. We were also too young to understand Mum's confused and depressed state.

I can only imagine what sort of therapy Mum suffered through back in the 1950s. Shock treatment was considered to be the appropriate cure for severe depression, and when Mum came home from hospital, sometimes glassy-eyed, it would take her several weeks before she was back on her feet — physically and mentally — sounding and acting like her old self.

Now, having just learned that Mum had only a few months to live, it became clear to me that I had inherited not only the gift of running quickly from my parents, but her depression as well. For no reason at all I would suddenly withdraw into myself, not wanting to talk to or see anyone else. I didn't know what was wrong, just that something in my life wasn't right. Depression has many names. Winston Churchill, the former British prime minister, probably coined the best description. He called melancholia the Black Dog. It's a phrase that instantly conjures up a vision of what depression is really like — menacing and ever-watching, stalking you constantly.

Christmas in 1995 was in Melbourne. We all knew it would be the last time we gathered together with Mum and so it was a special, if sad, period. We handed out the presents and made sure Mum was comfortable. We ate and drank and tried to make the most of it. Then it was off to Tewantin in Queensland, not far from Noosa. Ron had a house there and so we all flew up — Rick with his family, Mum, Ron and I. Again, it was a time for everyone to be together and cherish the days we had left with Mum.

But she was tiring and her health was deteriorating. She fell ill and it soon became obvious that she had to return to Melbourne. It was Ron's job to take Mum to Maroochydore airport for the flight home. But not surprisingly they missed the flight. I love my oldest brother dearly and he has been a constant source of strength and support over the years. But one of these days I'm going to get to the heart of one of life's greatest mysteries. How could a man who has never arrived on time for anything — invite him to dinner and stress it's for 7.30 and, sure enough, the doorbell is ringing at 9.30pm and it's a smiling Ron acting as if nothing is wrong — how could a man like that have responsibly flown international flights for so many years and arrived at destinations on time?

My mother was a stickler for punctuality, another trait I inherited from her. She must have been beside herself as Ron took her on a fast journey from Maroochydore to Brisbane to make the connection to another flight. They made it. Maybe that was how Ron delivered his planes on time — if there's a speed limit at 30 000 feet, my older brother must have a cupboard full of tickets.

We all made it back to Melbourne. I already had a sense that 1996 was going to be a tough year. But not even in my darkest moments did I realise just how hard it would be.

I ARRIVED at my doctor's rooms in the city late in the afternoon. I was still shaken by the death of the old woman in my park and my doctor, Magda Simonis, was concerned at how it had affected me. I trusted Magda; she was one of those doctors I always felt comfortable with. A few weeks earlier we had sat down and I had told her how Mum's condition had left me feeling more flat than normal.

There was another thing, too. I still loved my job in the Gardens, but it was becoming increasingly apparent that I might not have it for much longer.

The Kennett government had introduced a series of radical reforms throughout the Victorian public sector and its rippling effect had reached council level. Prahran council area had become the City of Stonington, and the council was in the throes of outsourcing most of its gardening and civic works programs to the private sector. All of which meant that my job and the jobs of others were on the line. I had taken part in a proposal put forward by a group of parks and gardens workers that would have seen our group take over the running and upkeep of several of the local parks. But we didn't like our chances. We knew how many people it would take to keep the Gardens clean and vibrant, and we knew there were many businesses prepared to sacrifice those sort of numbers in order to make a profit.

So it seemed I was about to lose my Mum and my job, probably at much the same time. Mum's condition had worsened since Christmas. There had been a brief period when Mum's brother and sister-in-law stayed with her and cared for her. They managed to convince her that she was in remission and that the cancer had gone. But it was only for a brief period. She was permanently hooked to an oxygen machine now — her lungs were filling with fluid and would, ultimately, be the death of her. They had been so badly burned by the radiation treatment that they could not function without the assistance of that extra oxygen.

Magda had put me on a course of antidepressant drugs in January and then recommended I see a psychiatrist she knew called Rozi Ana Udovicic. It was one of the best pieces of advice Magda had given me — and there had been plenty.

Rozi is a striking, dark-haired Croatian woman with an infectious laugh and deep, dark eyes that seem to peer right into your mind. I trusted her immediately — an unusual reaction for me, because it normally takes me a long time to consider and weigh up another person before deciding if I can trust them to become a friend.

I suspect Rozi was slightly taken aback at our first meeting. She was used to having to dig around in most patients' minds like a careful and fastidious archaeologist, excavating carefully before getting to the heart of the matter. With me, it was the opposite. This was one time when the old Raelene Boyle honesty and frankness would be of great assistance. I poured my heart out to her. She was given the full tour of every dark room I had kept locked from everyone else for so long. All my fears, all the insecurities that had nagged at me for years, came tumbling out.

I had walked out of her rooms feeling better. And I vowed that I would make my visits to Rozi a regular part of my life. I didn't want to end up like Mum, trying to tame the old black dog for the rest of my life. I needed an experienced trainer. One of my great regrets during my athletic career had been discovering the perfect coach a couple of years too late. I never wanted to make that mistake again.

I HAD shown Magda the lump on my breast the week before the old lady died in the Gardens. It was on the pectoral line and it hurt. It had been there for a few months but it had never really bothered me. Because it was painful when I pressed it, I believed there was nothing seriously wrong. I had heard the old adage "If it hurts, it's okay," but I had decided to show Magda, just in case.

Magda was more concerned than I was. She had known me for long enough, she said, to know that things never went quite right, or were easily diagnosable, when it came to the Boyle body. Back in 1994 I had had a lump removed from my left breast. It had proved harmless. The procedure to remove it had been the greatest complication. I was booked in for the operation on a Friday, but had a long-term commitment to go on a canoeing trip that weekend with a large group of friends. I was determined not to miss it.

By early that Friday afternoon I was up and about in the day clinic, packing my bag and checking out. Typical me. I figured it was just like having my Achilles tendon scraped and repaired. The lump they removed was just a benign cyst. But unfortunately, one of the blood vessels they had cut had not been cauterised before they sewed me up. The clinic probably should not have let me out that quickly. That "bleeder" became a real problem that weekend. I couldn't paddle the canoes because I had to keep a large wad of bandages and padding beneath my left arm to cope with the bleeding from the wound.

By the time the trip was over, I don't know who hurt more. My breast was black and blue. My friends were exhausted from taking over my paddling duties. So much for the scalpel being my friend.

But if that episode had proved anything — apart from my stupidity in going on a weekend expedition just hours after undergoing a general anaesthetic — it was that, health-wise, I believed I was safe. I had undergone two operations on my breasts, almost two decades apart, and both times I was free of cancer. Didn't that show something? I might have grown to become my mother's daughter more than I cared to admit. But at least the cancer gene had not been handed down to me.

Still, Magda was taking no chances this time around. She ordered me to take a mammogram, which I had done on the Friday. A mammogram is a relatively simple procedure which involves x-raying your breast. The x-ray is used to examine a lump, but it can also detect cancer before a lump is felt.

I should have known something was up when I had the mammogram. The radiographer took the pictures, went away and then came back and asked to take some more.

"Is everything all right?" I asked.

"No problems," she replied. "But maybe you should take a read of this." She gestured toward a wall poster that listed different sorts of cancer. One of the sections highlighted spots in the breast. Perhaps my mind had shut down for the day, or my subconscious was simply preferring not to hear what the radiographer was trying to hint at. But I didn't make the connection. When she returned with the second set of x-rays, I asked if I could have a look. I've always been interested in anatomy, particularly my own. And I regarded myself as a bit of a dab, if amateurish, hand when it came to reading and understanding x-rays.

The radiographer had circled a couple of small spots.

"What are they?" I asked.

"I don't know," she said, shrugging. "We're not sure." There was no diagnosis. And I was effectively told not to worry, so I didn't.

Ironically, Tess, the wife of my younger brother, Rick, was working as a medical courier at the time. She collected my x-rays, saw my name on them and grew alarmed. That night I received a concerned call from Rick, demanding to know what was going on. Was I seriously sick? Did I have breast cancer? Why hadn't he been told?

I laughed and put him at ease. "Relax," I told him. "I'll be around to annoy the hell out of you for a few more years yet."

MAGDA WASN'T at all concerned about the lump in my breast. But the spots, she said, needed to be checked quickly. She said she wanted me to see one of Melbourne's most respected surgeons, John Collins. He was renowned as an outstanding surgeon, a reputation he enjoyed for good reason given his remarkable skills.

But at first I was reluctant. Collins had been the surgeon two years before when my breast wound bled for days afterward. I knew he was one of the finest surgeons in Australia, perhaps in the world. But I just didn't feel comfortable with him. He was like a lot of other surgeons I had met — they were brilliant men who could achieve almost miraculous things. But when it came to warmth or getting close to their patients, they held back.

I didn't like that. To be treated with aloofness is not a great way to put a patient at ease. I can understand why surgeons are like that — to perform their jobs with the burden of being close to their subject is probably an additional weight they don't need. But I know from my experience, and the experience of hundreds of other women who have been through the same situation, that a little more tender loving care wouldn't go amiss. Doctors' rooms can be awfully sterile at the best of times. I'm not suggesting that we should all hug one another around a campfire in a surgeon's office, toasting marshmallows and singing "Kum Bah Yah". But a little bedside warmth would not go astray.

I agreed to see Collins a couple of days later. He placed my mammograms on a light box, examined the spots and told me he was 90 per cent certain they were fine. Fine, fine, fine. If I heard that word once during my battles with cancer, I heard it a hundred times. He gave me the choice as to whether I wanted to have surgery; he was sure the spots were all right.

I told him I'd rather have anything that was slightly suspicious taken out. The scalpel was the least of my concerns. I wanted to be certain, to know where I stood. I never considered the possibility of there being a problem. Not once. I was booked in for surgery in the Freemason's Hospital the following Monday, barely a week after my first visit to Magda.

SOME MIGHT suggest I am a control freak. But I doubt it. Over the years I have been more than willing to seek advice from a wide circle of people whose views I trust. But if there's one thing that upsets me, it is being placed in a situation where I have not been prepared.

You have to understand what it takes to get to the top of international athletics. It's like any other chosen profession — the commitment and application needed to be the world's best is enormous. I tried never to leave anything to chance. I had to know what I was up against. Was there going to be a headwind? Was the girl in the lane next to me susceptible to being psyched out if I stared at her in the change rooms before the race? What about the surface we were racing on? Was it likely to suit my shoes — or my style?

So you can imagine my state of mind the following Monday morning not long after arriving at the hospital for surgery. After showering and having an antiseptic scrub, I went down to the radiology department for what I thought was another mammogram. My left breast was placed in the machine, and on its side was positioned a triangular piece of plastic with holes in it. The holes were to help steer two thin wires into my breast. The spots in my breast were so small that it would take forever — and probably a decent dose of luck — for a surgeon to find them. So the wires would act as guides. Once steered to the point where my spots lay, the wires, which have small hooks on their end, would be anchored into the surrounding flesh.

Which would have been fine. Except I had no bloody idea what was going on.

A lot of women faint during this procedure. It is enormously painful. There is no anaesthetic. I kept thinking, "Why the hell didn't anyone tell me this was going to happen?" The pain was incredible, but had I been warned I could have psyched myself up for it. I can understand why they don't tell some people. They might not be able to cope. But I was angry because no-one had given me the option.

I survived the first wire. The assistants were lovely. But as they prepared to insert the second one I could feel myself losing it. The room started spinning.

And then I fainted.

It had been a long time since I had passed out like that. Apart from many severe cramping episodes with period pain and endometriosis, my last fainting episode had probably been back in 1978 at the Commonwealth Games in Edmonton, Canada. Then, I received a B-complex vitamin injection in my arm, when it really should have been stuck in my backside. I fainted on the spot, and it became the cause for much laughter for some time after.

When I finally recovered my senses in the radiology room, I had two wires jiggling out of my left breast. I went back to my room, and the operation went ahead not long after. By midday I was sitting up in my bed anxious to go home. I only had a small wound, and I felt fine. Within a few hours I was at home, convinced that I would shortly be back at work and getting on with the rest of my life.

5

Intrusions

I FELT WONDERFUL WHEN I WOKE THE MORNING AFTER THE PROCEDURE. I'd slept well and there was no pain. I spent a few seconds wondering if I should go into work, and then had a better idea.

The previous night I had looked around the kitchen and my eye had been drawn to my ramshackle collection of plates and cutlery. I'm one of those people who believe that if you sit down to dinner everyone should be eating off the same sort of plate, using the same cutlery and drinking out of the same type of glasses. It was something that must have nagged me since childhood, when we ate off different plates, drank out of vegemite jars and things were constantly being broken or misplaced.

There was a sale on in the city. Was there a better way to spend a sick day? I could buy a new set of cutlery, then go on to the official launch of that year's Stawell Gift, the richest professional sprint in the country and something I had supported for years. John

Toleman, a close mate of mine, had been involved in the organisation and promotion of the Gift for years. Each year he gathered the media together at a swish hotel in the city. He would usually announce some of the big names — both local and international — who had been secured for the event. Then he spent the rest of the day trying to fill the journos with as much alcohol as possible to get the publicity machine rolling for the event: a weekend-long festival of running that drew thousands to the small country town in Victoria's Wimmera district each year.

But that morning the phone rang. It was the surgeon's secretary. "Raelene, Mr Collins would like to see you today," she said. "Could you make it in this afternoon?"

I said I had a few things on. Was it possible to make it another day later in the week?

"Raelene," she said. "You're not listening to me. Mr Collins wants to see you today. Can you be here at 3.30?"

I started to stress. What was it Collins had told me before the operation? It would take time for pathology to send the results back. Sorting through the tissue to get to the spots might take three days, perhaps more. It was less than twenty-four hours since the operation. Clearly there was something wrong.

It was then that I began to fall apart. The tough barricade that I had set up in my mind, all that bravado I had displayed while talking on the phone to my kid brother a few days before — *Yes Rick, don't worry, there's nothing wrong, stop fussing will you?* — it all began to crumble.

I was lucky that my housemate, Barb Murphy, was home. She'd been a good friend for years, and had recently sold her home and finished a university degree in business administration. While she figured out what to do next, she had moved in to share my house. It suited me. She met the criteria of any Boyle housemate. She got along with my dogs and even appeared capable of putting up with me.

But the best thing about "Murph" was her ability to stay calm in the midst of any storm raging about her. As I began weeping and fearing what lay ahead, she remained composed. She was adamant she would go with me to see the surgeon. Another old friend, Fiona, also agreed to come.

We decided the best thing for me to do in the meantime was to go in to the city, buy the cutlery, attend the Stawell Gift function and carry on as normal. But when I arrived at the launch I was hardly my old self. Toleman came over, took one look at me and asked if I was all right. I muttered something about not feeling 100 per cent. I think I downed a glass of wine, said hello to a few old mates, including Neil King, who was then the chief executive of Athletics Australia, and left. Toleman was so concerned about me that he left the function midway through to walk me downstairs, an unprecedented move on his part. I hope none of the journalists sobered up during his absence.

I was a mess by 3.30pm when the three of us arrived at the surgeon's office. I couldn't stop crying. I was angry with myself, too — I was desperately trying to regain my composure because this was important. It might be the most crucial meeting I experienced in my life. I needed to be in control and to listen to what the surgeon had to say.

We sat down and Collins looked grim-faced. The results had come back from pathology, he said. The spots were cancerous. I found it hard to take anything else in from there. I remember him saying that he would probably have to operate again and take out a wider section of my breast. But he felt certain there would be no more problems.

Then he went on to explain what I could expect after the operation. I might have to undergo radiation therapy. There was a chance I might have to have chemotherapy, too, but at this stage he doubted that very much. Everything would turn out just fine.

He started talking about what was required over the next few days — the blood tests, the bone scans, further x-rays. It was important at that stage for them to obtain a "marker" — a full reading on my blood levels and overall health at the time of diagnosis. This would be important as comparisons would show what was happening inside my body as my treatment progressed. But I wasn't taking much of it in. I excused myself and asked Fiona and Murph to stay and listen. I had to get out.

Panic had set in. I rushed out of the office and caught the lift. I felt surrounded and desperately needed to be outside, to suck in some fresh air and look at the sunlight.

And so there I was standing on the footpath, red-faced and still crying, when a familiar figure strolled past. It was Neil King, the athletics supremo, on his way back from the Stawell Gift function. He said hello, walked past and then promptly did a full circle and came back.

"I'm really sorry," he said. "If there's anything I can do, let me know." He thought my mother had died.

"Neil, Mum hasn't died," I blubbered. "I've just been told I've got cancer."

He turned pale and stepped back, not knowing what to say. "This will go no further," he insisted. "I promise. This will not pass my lips. I won't tell anyone." He gave me a hug and then went off to visit his mother, who was also sick. As the long weeks and months wore on, Neil King was a man true to his word. He also became part of my large and incredibly loyal support team. Neil would often pop in to visit me during my sickest periods and bring his young son Wilson, who would climb into doona covers with one of my dogs, play with them and crack us up laughing.

Fiona and Murph eventually came downstairs. We drove home, pretty much in silence. And then we hit the phone. I had to tell my brothers and a couple of other close friends. But that was all. I wanted this kept quiet. This was an incredibly private anguish that I was suffering. I didn't want anyone outside a small circle of friends and relatives to know.

And most important of all, I did not want my mother to find out. After all these years I thought I knew her. She would blame herself for my cancer. There was no doubt about that. Mum would find some way of taking on the responsibility — it was something instinctive inside her.

I didn't want her to spend her last days on earth wallowing in guilt.

THE NIGHT of my cancer diagnosis saw the first of many gatherings at my home of Team Boyle, a collection of friends and family who would become my mainstays over the next few months. My brothers and their families had dropped in. I think the thing I like about Ron and Rick, more than anything else, is their willingness to show their feelings.

We're an emotional family and both Rick and Ron share a trait unusual in men. They were unafraid to cry in public long before it became fashionable and the term "sensitive, new age guy" became popular. Ron, particularly, is an emotional guy. It's one of the reasons I can easily forgive him when he rolls up late for a function.

Rick became my shadow. I don't recall him leaving my sight at that time. I guess I'd been very protective of my little brother when we were growing up — he is four years younger than me — and now it was his turn to keep an eye out for his big sister.

A few friends dropped in that night, too, including George Lawlor, a colleague from my working days with the sporting goods manufacturer Nike. Georgie is one of those people who seem to have a talent for knowing when things in your life are not going well — he has made a habit of calling me just when I need to hear his voice. He's ten years younger than me, and a real lad. I don't think anyone has made me laugh more than Georgie. He works in

Nike's marketing division and we hit it off the first time we met. I'd
worked as a promotions officer with Nike during the 1980s and
George took over from me when I left. He and I had a similar sense
of humour and, along with the rest of the Nike team back then, the
same passion for drinking and having fun.

I have vague memories after one memorable Nike Christmas party
of competing topless in an impromptu sprint down Victoria Crescent
near Nike's office in Abbotsford. The party itself had been staged at a
farm retreat on the outskirts of Melbourne, and the company had
provided a bus to return everyone to the city. George says I was one
of the first to "fling off the slingshot" (Georgespeak for taking off the
bra) and sprint down the street after getting off the bus. I don't see
how he could recall a thing given that he had turned a peculiar shade
of green by that stage and no-one had been too interested in sitting
next to him on the bus. But they were certainly raucous, hard-
partying days and I had kept in touch regularly with George and his
wife over the years. So when we opened the door that night and
Georgie was standing there with an armful of medicine for me
(Georgespeak for a six-pack of beer) he was warmly welcomed inside.

George's mother-in-law, Judy Gleeson, would end up playing a
crucial role during the next few months. A breast cancer survivor
herself, Judy lived in a small country town and after her diagnosis
locals would cross the road to avoid speaking to her. What they
were really doing was avoiding a confrontation with Judy's
condition. She made me aware that a lot of people I knew might
not be able to cope with my illness. Without Judy's wise counsel
and the comfort I also received from the wife of a Nike executive
who had endured months of chemotherapy, the year would have
ended up being far more difficult than it was.

With friends and family around me, I calmed down considerably
compared with my earlier state. I hated "losing it" like I had that
afternoon. But the old black dog was becoming a pretty close

companion of mine. My antidepressants were keeping it at arm's length but I could damn well sense its presence.

We had a round table conference, and we all agreed on the need to keep my cancer from Mum. Ron's first wife, Anita, had come down from Queensland for a while to take over the nursing duties with Mum. She was at my home that night, and she agreed it was better for Mum that she not find out.

By the time the last visitor left, I was exhausted, but feeling better. That evening had shown me, perhaps for the first time, just how important it was to have familiar faces near me.

The next few days were a blur. I underwent a series of examinations in preparation for my next surgery, which was scheduled for a Friday. There were blood tests to be performed, along with bone scans and a myriad of other tests.

The bone scan ended up being a bit of a laugh — as well as a revelation. Bone scans reconstruct your skeletal system. They show up breakages and other injuries that have happened in your life by using a temperature-based measuring system. That way "hot spots" that provide an indication of secondary cancers spreading into your bones can be detected.

I was lying on the table, the imaging machine scanning my body just centimetres above me. But it was hardly a smooth run for the poor guy running the scan. Every few minutes I'd hear him sighing or expressing surprise, and then his head would pop into view.

"Ever had an injury to your right shin?" he asked.

"Yep. I had shin splints when I was a kid. I did a bit of running back then, you know."

"You didn't have shin splints," he said. "You had stress fractures in your right leg."

Now that made sense. I had gone to the Mexico Olympics in 1968 as a young and naive seventeen-year-old girl. I was lucky to get there; Dad had worked overtime treating me for shin soreness. I had been in real agony with it. Now it turned out there was a reason for the pain. Fractures! I should not have even been running.

A few minutes passed. Then I heard another exclamation.

"Oh God, what's this on the top of your right foot?"

"I broke my foot dancing one night a few years ago," I said.

I started wondering if this was the first bone scan he had ever performed. He had more questions — what had happened to my knees? Just a bit of tendon soreness over the years, I said. And, of course, my heel bones were glowing — I'd had them scraped and cleaned up again in the previous twelve months so I could continue jogging and maintain my fitness.

I also had to tell Prahran council that I was ill and would require some time off in the next few days. We were in the midst of the compulsory competitive tendering process and our group was busily putting together its bid to try and win the contract from the council. I told a couple of trusted colleagues, along with my boss, of my diagnosis. I knew they would keep my condition quiet and they were all supportive.

Mal Dean was particularly shocked. He, more than most, understood how fragile I had been feeling recently.

Not long before, I had gone to the police to lodge a formal complaint over a man who had been stalking me for years. He had never physically touched me, but I was one of several high-profile athletes, I later learned, whom he had become obsessed with over the years.

I could barely remember a time when he had not haunted my life. He was like one of those shadowy figures you often see depicted in the movies — the creepy character who lingers just out of view. He was tall and red-haired, and I always thought he had a slightly disturbed look on his face. He would write letters to me: usually harmless, indecipherable scribblings that were good only for gaining an insight into his scrambled mind.

Quite a few people over the years told me not to worry about him; he was just one of those harmless weirdos, they said. He never drove, he was always riding a bike to some mysterious meeting or another. But there was something about him that used to put the fear of God into me. The strange thing was that he never pushed things too far. He seemed to know just how close he could come to me. I would appear at a function or, in the early days, at a track meet, and I could sense him in the crowd, watching. But he never approached me, never quite had the courage to confront me.

There were times when I simply forgot him; he was probably off pursuing another obsession of his and he faded from my life. But he always came back. By the mid 1990s he had discovered that I spent most of my time in the Victoria Gardens. There would be days when I would be planting rows of seedlings, or simply cleaning the beds, and I would get that strange feeling I was being watched. I would glance up and he would be standing in the distance, watching me. The rest of the gardening crew knew about him and they looked after me. I think he knew that if he ever came too close he might have to live with the indent of a shovel on the back of his head for the rest of his life.

One event, however, changed my view that he was just a harmless creep. One of my neighbours surprised him one afternoon. He had dropped around to my place to collect something. Walking up the side of the house, he heard a suspicious noise and found my stalker in the backyard trying to get in through the back door. I have no idea why my dogs didn't attack him as they were always very protective of me and the house, particularly Goldie. She would sit at my feet when someone was sitting opposite having a chat and never take her eyes off them.

Caught by surprise, the stalker took off over the fence and sprinted away. But by then the state of Victoria had introduced much stricter anti-stalking laws. I had spoken on and off to the police about him for years. They knew the guy, but because he had never come very close to me they always shrugged and said there was little they could do.

This time, however, I was determined that something be done. Not all stalkers are the same, but some share certain traits, and one of them is that they grow progressively bolder over time. His presence in my backyard marked a significant escalation in his intrusion into my life. Who knew what that chorus of haunting voices in his head would tell him to do next. I went down to the Prahran police station in a state of high anxiety and told the detective at the desk that something had to be done about this creep. Right now. We talked for a while and he said to leave it with him.

My problems with the stalker were over, at least physically. I understand that in the following few months my nemesis received several middle-of-the-night visits from the local police. I'm not sure of the discussions that took place, but I'm fairly confident he was given a pretty colourful explanation of what might happen to him if he continued harassing me. What did he think of a long-term future sharing a cell with a large, powerful, tattooed man who had decided he needed a new girlfriend?

So my stalker vanished. But in many ways he stayed with me, as they always do. I always looked twice at the dark places in the Gardens — those areas shadowed by trees and foliage — before entering. Even in a crowd I never felt absolutely safe, and still don't. You never quite get over the feeling that someone is watching.

6

The road to Gundagai

MUM'S HEALTH HAD DETERIORATED AGAIN AND IT SEEMED SHE DIDN'T have long. I went out to see her, gave her a kiss and said I would see her soon. I was going to Gundagai for a few days, I said.

It was one of life's little white lies, an understandable and excusable one. I had to give Mum a reason why she wouldn't be seeing me for a week or two. Why Gundagai? A friend had mentioned it to me not long before, saying it was a nice out-of-the-way place worth seeing one day. The name had just popped into my head. She nodded and seemed to accept this explanation. Time was passing differently for Mum — the cancer was eating away at her, and the oxygen and pain-killing drugs she was taking saw her occasionally drift in and out of reality. A week might pass like a day.

Mum and I were extremely close now. And we even shared something of which she was unaware.

In the previous couple of months I had made it my task to ensure that all her affairs were in order. The boys had been terrific when it came to being with her and caring for her. But confronting the other tough tasks that needed to be done was a job I had taken on.

I had done it a decade earlier when she was diagnosed with oesophageal cancer. Mum was never one to bother herself with details. "Am I going to live or die?" was basically all she wanted to know from her doctors. She also had an old-fashioned respect for even GPs that bordered on worship. She didn't think she should be there wasting their time. Quite often I would sit in a surgery and listen to her telling the doctor exactly what she thought he wanted to hear.

"Eating well, Irene?"

"Yes, doctor. Very well."

"Feeling all right are we, Irene?"

"Absolutely, doctor. I feel wonderful."

So I had always made sure to pull her doctors aside later on and tell them the truth. I would tell them what she was eating and what she was not. Some of the doctors seemed interested; those who knew her well understood what she was like. Others appeared not to care less.

One morning while she was lying in hospital after receiving treatment for her lung cancer, I asked her where she wanted to die. "Do you want to die here, or at home?" At that stage she wanted to die in hospital because she thought that if she passed away at home, no-one would want to buy her house. Mum was like that, even worrying about things that would take place when she was no longer there.

That conversation had been one of the most difficult in my life. I'd had to psych myself up for it. I didn't want to break down and turn it into a messy and emotional scene where nothing was really decided. But I was lucky. She was an incredibly dignified lady, particularly when she realised she was never going to recover. She was seventy years old, and even through her pain and probably her fears she was coherent and sensible, particularly when it came to organising the minutiae of her life.

She was very matter-of-fact about what she wanted. She told me where her will was, and her marriage certificates. (She had remarried a few years after Dad died, but it didn't last long. Her second husband was a loser who beat her. Mum was smart enough to get rid of him, even though, like me she hated being alone.)

She told me where she had hidden her valuables in the house. So I had gone and gathered everything together. Her will was handwritten, so I called a solicitor friend of mine who came in and sat next to Mum, reworded it and ensured it was a legal and official document.

She soon decided, however, that she would prefer to die at home. By the end of that first week in March, she was struggling. I left and headed home. I had a bag to pack. I was off to Gundagai.

THE SECOND surgery was more complicated than the first. The surgeon had to remove a much larger area of tissue from my left breast in what is officially called a partial mastectomy. As well, he had to perform an auxiliary node removal, taking out lymph nodes in the area near my armpit. Lymph nodes are small, bean-shaped structures that play the important role of helping to remove bacteria and other infectious organisms from the body. There are lymph glands situated throughout the body, all of them working hard to prevent infection. If cancer is found in the lymph nodes, it means a certain bout of chemotherapy.

This is because lymph nodes provide cancer with a super highway through the body. If cancer in a breast is going to spread, the first thing it will move toward are the nodes beneath your arms.

For the first thirty-six hours I drifted in and out of an anaesthetic haze. Every time I woke I saw Ron and Rick at the bottom of my bed. Murph came in early each morning, set up her laptop computer next to me, and did her work while keeping me company. I didn't want to be alone and so Team Boyle had organised that someone would always be there. It was a long weekend, and from my room in the Freemason's Hospital I could hear the whining, mosquito-like droning of the Grand Prix cars down at the Albert Park lake circuit.

I felt good. My spirits were up, no doubt due to the fact that my surgeon had not appeared. To me, his absence meant that the surgery had been a success. The scalpel would once again have saved the day.

I went for a walk through the wards the following Tuesday afternoon. When I returned to my bed, John Collins was standing there. By now I knew, just by looking at him, when he had bad news to deliver. He told me he was sorry, but the cancer had spread to three or four of my lymph nodes. I would not only have to undergo radiation treatment, but chemotherapy as well. I didn't know much about chemotherapy, only that it made people sick and caused their hair to fall out. I was knocked around by the news. This was a significant setback. But I was assured that it was unlikely the cancer had spread any further. So I quickly pulled myself together and said, "Okay, if it's going to happen, let's get on with it."

I rang my brothers. Rick flipped out. He was up at the hospital that night with a bottle of the liqueur Benedictine in his hand and we sat up late having a couple of drinks. It had always been a bit of a tradition. Whenever I went overseas, I always remembered to buy a bottle of Benedictine to drink with the boys. Ron arrived too, a little behind time, of course. It was that evening we first seriously began discussing what we would all do when Mum passed away. It was a strange feeling. Before long, even though we were adults, we would be orphans.

Ron had asked Rick if he would consider moving to Queensland. Rick was keen, it was a subject they had discussed before. "I'll come too," I said. "I've got no reason to stay in Melbourne anymore. I'm going to lose my job. When it gets cold down here in the winter I usually end up with bronchitis or pneumonia. If I've only got a couple of years left to live, I might as well enjoy them in the sunshine."

I had six months of chemotherapy ahead of me to worry about first, however. When I was discharged from hospital, I went home and began getting my affairs in order, just as I had done with Mum not so long before. I rewrote my will. I made sure someone would be there to look after my dogs. I confronted all those critical issues. I had always felt that if you had the chance you had to be responsible and lessen the pain your family might feel after your passing.

THE FUTURE. It was always on my mind. Now, with breast cancer diagnosed and the uncertainty ahead of chemotherapy, I grew concerned at how I would cope financially. I also knew that news of my condition would eventually have to leak to the media. I had been around journos enough over the years — I counted quite a few as good friends — to know that it wouldn't be long before stories of my illness began circulating.

So I wanted to control how that information was released, and perhaps do some good in the process. Breast cancer awareness had been growing in recent years, but as I discovered from my own experience, there was little information to prepare you for the changes that would affect your body. And your mind. Perhaps I could show others what it was like, using my public profile to draw attention to the illness.

I rang the former "60 Minutes" reporter Jennifer Byrne, whose family I had come to know because they had been frequent visitors to my Gardens. She told me who to contact at "60 Minutes". I set up a meeting in a local café with one of Channel Nine's producers, Kerryn Pratt. I told her about my condition and asked if the program would be interested in following me as I confronted the weeks ahead. I would, of course, be paid for the story.

We eventually worked out a fee that I felt would be worth both the intrusion into my life and would cover my medical expenses. I was, after all, in my mid forties and about to lose my job. Who was going to employ a woman that age whose health and future was uncertain? In the process, a twenty-minute segment on one of the most watched programs in the country would guarantee an instant boost for breast cancer awareness. For exactly the same reasons, I also organised a deal with the *Australian Women's Weekly*. By now I was a pretty experienced hand when it came to dealing with the media — after all, I had been speaking in front of their microphones regularly since my trip to the Mexico Olympics as a teenager. I knew that news of my cancer would be of interest. By going on "60 Minutes" and appearing in the *Women's Weekly*, I figured I would be reaching the widest possible audience. Hopefully, that would mean that the rest of the media would cut me a little slack and not bother me too much.

In the meantime, George Lawlor again popped in just when my spirits needed lifting. He dropped by for a couple of hours one night not long after I had undergone surgery. As he was leaving I accompanied him out to the footpath outside my home in Greville Street.

"Well," said George, "you reckon you've got problems. I've just had a vasectomy and I swear it feels like someone has stuffed a couple of basketballs down my pants."

"Really?" I replied. "You men are all the same. Wimps. Bet your scar is nothing like mine."

That was enough for George. The challenge had been issued. You show me yours and I'll show you mine. So there, in a busy suburban street, I gave Georgie a look at my recovering breast. He promptly dropped his dacks and gave me a glimpse of his swollen nether regions.

It was at that moment that a prominent Melbourne footballer, Alastair Clarkson, who happened to be a neighbour of mine, walked past. It's not an easy thing to embarrass a league footballer. But Alastair clearly didn't know where to look.

I did. And my scar was certainly worse than George's.

MY BROTHERS and Murph went with me to confront chemotherapy for the first time and ensure I didn't feel alone. I felt secure with them around; now I know how some of those pop and film stars feel when they go out in public with a handful of big bruisers lurking behind them in dark suits. Rick and Ron were determined to protect me. I was grateful for their company. I had psyched myself up for the day and felt quite strong. But it made a big difference knowing that Team Boyle was there as well.

To walk into the unknown, I took the lift inside the Freemason's Medical Centre in Victoria Parade up to the first floor. Down the hall was the chemotherapy room, just near the rooms of my haematology oncologist, Michael Green. I was focused, even though I had little idea what lay ahead. Would I vomit? Was I about to die? I'd never wanted to take drugs in my life. Throughout my athletic career I had hated the fact that I was beaten by drug cheats. Now, here I was having all these rotten chemicals pumped into me.

I sat back in a big, grey leather armchair. The nurse placed a cannula in my arm and made sure all my drugs were ready. Then she connected me to a saline drip. The saline would work its way through my system, she said, diluting the highly toxic drugs. She explained that as the drugs entered my system I would get an immediate sensation in my mouth, a metallic taste that would be accompanied by the feeling of pins and needles around my genital area. They ask you to suck on ice before this happens — the chemo drugs head straight to the vascular areas first, and numbing your gums helps slow down the reaction and reduce the chances of mouth ulcers. It turned me off having ice, even in a drink, for years.

Michael Green had already patiently explained to me how the chemotherapy course would work over the coming six months. On the first and eighth days of the cycle I would be given intravenous injections of two drugs: 5FU, or 5 fluouracal, and methotrexate. The rest of the time I would take oral tablets of cyclothosphamide. The names were as foreign and difficult to pronounce as those of some of my opponents from my athletic career. To me, like just about everyone else, they were simply my chemo drugs. And I would come to endure the same love–hate relationship with them that everyone does. You love them because they are saving your life. You hate them because of how they make you feel.

Chemotherapy does that to people. It gouges its way through your body in search of those powerful cancerous cells that multiply more rapidly than ordinary ones, and in doing so it embeds itself in your psyche as well. Some of it has to do with its side effects. Even though modern treatment has evolved a long way compared with the methods of two or three decades ago, nausea and lethargy are still two of several outcomes you experience. Hair loss is a common, but not uniform, effect. My hair would thin over the coming months, but fortunately I never lost it like some people do. But it is the psychological effect that I think is a far more powerful and lasting outcome of chemotherapy. Michael Green explained to me one day that he was the sort of medical specialist whose patients rarely came back to visit him. It certainly wasn't because of his bedside manner.

Michael had once treated a woman who, years after completing her course, could not drive past his rooms without vomiting. It would happen just like that; she might be in a cab in a rush to get to the airport. The cabbie would decide to take a shortcut and by the time the woman realised where he was going, they were driving past Michael's office and she was vomiting out the window.

Highly acclaimed in his field, Michael spent seven years working and studying in New York. He was in a local grocery store there one afternoon when a woman he had been treating bumped into him. She promptly vomited.

Let me add that he doesn't have that sort of effect on most people. But it helps illustrate just how powerful and lingering the experience of undergoing chemotherapy is.

I watched them push the drugs in, and almost instantly I could taste them. The drugs were doing their work immediately, but in seeking out cancerous cells they were also killing a few million of my tastebuds. What's it like? I have often explained that I spent half a year eating steam trains. Chemotherapy was metallic and invaded every tastebud, every pore of my body. I can taste it even now, just thinking about it. I can smell it, too. You cannot wash it out of your mouth, or off your hands. After a while, you begin feeling like one of those aliens in a science fiction movie — half metal, half flesh. It is an incredibly invasive feeling. Some people experience it differently, claiming they can taste everything from garlic to God knows what. Strange, isn't it, how no-one has ever reported the taste of lobster mornay or even the flavour of a cheeky little red with just a hint of cinnamon. Science has put men on the moon, but it has never been able to create something that is good for you that tastes nice, too.

The whole procedure only took a few minutes. Apart from the taste, I walked out of there feeling slightly triumphant. I'm going to manage this, I thought. This is not so hard, after all.

7

Goodnight Irene

ON SUNDAY, 21 APRIL 1996, I FELT LIKE STAYING IN BED ALL DAY. THE exhaustion had begun to set in and I knew I needed to look after myself. It was clear to me that my chemotherapy course would be a marathon event — a long, gruelling affair that would require me to pace myself and ensure I did not wear myself out. But I wanted to see Mum. I'm glad I went.

She managed to get up out of bed, and very gingerly I helped her make the long trek to the family room, her oxygen tubes trailing behind her. Her oxygen machine sat in the middle of the house, and its long cords allowed her to move around the house, although in the past few days she had pretty much stayed in bed.

She sat and chatted quietly, sipping occasionally from a cup of tea. My mother was very matter-of-fact about her condition. She knew she did not have long to go and as far as she was concerned there was no point dwelling on what might have been, or even the unfairness of it all. She tried to eat a small pikelet, but it required too much effort. Her appetite had been extinguished long before.

With that, she decided to go back to bed. I went in, made sure she was comfortable and said goodbye. "Love you," I said. And then I thanked her very much for being my mother, and for all the things she had done for me.

"I love you, too," she whispered.

The next morning I went to work in the Gardens. I was due to finish early that afternoon because I had a 3pm appointment for chemotherapy treatment. But Murph arrived mid morning in the park and said she'd had a phone call suggesting I get over to Mum's place as quickly as possible.

By the time we arrived, Mum had passed away.

I was distraught. That it was finally over — that Mum's suffering had at last come to an end — seemed slightly unreal. Rick arrived not long after, and we both decided to go out to the airport and break the news to Ron. He was piloting a Cathay Pacific flight and was due to pass through Melbourne airport late that morning. We informed the Cathay staff and they ensured another captain was ready to take over.

Ron saw us waiting for him and a big smile began spreading across his face. But when we told him the news, his face fell apart. He was devastated. But there was a lot to be done in a short space of time. The two boys began organising the funeral details, while I headed off to receive another chemotherapy treatment. The "60 Minutes" crew filmed me in there that afternoon as the drugs began to work their way into my system and my mouth began to feel like it had been filled with liquid steel.

The week didn't get any better. Two days later I went to farewell Sir Hubert Opperman. Australia's legendary cyclist had died at the age of ninety-one the previous week. Much had been made of the fact that he had died while riding an exercise bike in a retirement village at the foot of the Dandenong Ranges. I had known Oppy for many years; he had been a wonderful gentleman and I had never given up an opportunity to chat with him.

He had established his reputation in the 1920s. Such was his fame back then that he was the clear winner of a poll in a Paris newspaper to establish the most popular athlete in Europe. He was the Bradman of the bike, a long-distance specialist who smashed records everywhere he raced. He was only a small man, just 63 kilograms of wiry muscle that was wound so tight that it was little wonder his bike took off like a shot when he unleashed the power in his legs.

But it was not only Oppy's sporting career that impressed me. He had gone on to become an influential federal politician, and many believed it was his "Opperman Doctrine", which allowed non-Europeans with certain qualifications the opportunity to settle in Australia, that triggered the end of the White Australia policy. Sir Robert Menzies once said of him, "I will always think of him as the best and most courageous local member I ever met."

The railings outside St Paul's Cathedral in Melbourne were jammed with bikes. It was an emotional service, made especially so for me because I knew I would be going to another by the end of the week. I tried to concentrate and begin mentally preparing myself for what was to come.

THE ONLY task the boys gave me when it came to farewelling Mum was to locate a copy of the famous old song "Goodnight Irene". It had been a long-running family story. Mum's father, it is said, used to sing it to her whenever he had one or two drinks too many. It used to embarrass her at the time, but it was also a song that held many fond memories for her. We could think of no more memorable way for Mum to leave this world than to have that song playing as her casket left the chapel.

On the day before the funeral, Ron Reed, a Melbourne sportswriter I had been friends with for years, called to say he had seen the death notices in the paper for Mum. I had placed a simple notice in the paper that, for me, had summed it up: "Sleep peacefully Mum. Love you lots." Ron said he was sorry to hear she had passed away and if there was anything he could do, please ask.

Reed was a veteran journalist, known to everyone in the sporting world as "The Hound". I decided it was time to put his nickname to the test. I asked him if he knew where I could get a copy of "Goodnight Irene". I had no idea, time was running short and I was not feeling well enough to go on a search of the city music stores, but I didn't let on to him that I was sick.

"Leave it with me," he said. "I'm sure I can track it down."

He was true to his word. That night he left a recording in my letterbox.

A few friends popped around to lend support the next morning as I prepared for the funeral. Because we had a few minutes to spare, I asked someone to put the tape on so we could listen to it and see how long it lasted.

When the volume was turned up, we stood and stared at one another in disbelief. And then we broke up laughing. Ron Reed had delivered the bootscootin' version of "Goodnight Irene". It was hilarious — and just the thing to shake me out of the misery and dread I was feeling about the day that lay ahead.

Unfortunately, I hadn't time to tell my brothers that the song didn't quite capture the mood of the occasion. The service was a predictably sombre affair, and when Mum's coffin left the chapel to absolute silence my brothers looked at me questioningly. *Where's the bloody song?* I could picture them thinking. When I told them later, they broke up laughing, too. It was the sort of absurd thing Mum would have appreciated.

Smiling wasn't something I had done that much of in recent months. Since my own cancer diagnosis, Mum's last few months had left me wondering at times if I was simply looking at a mirror image of myself. Was that me in a year's time? We all tend to see ourselves in fairly heroic terms, no matter how modest some of us are. I wanted to be brave. I wanted to be strong. I wanted to be like Mum in so many ways.

But I also knew I didn't want to be like her when it came to understanding what this disease was that I was up against. Mum never really wanted to know, and I did. I knew my body pretty well, I understood its little chinks and creaks better than anyone else because I had listened intently to it throughout my athletic career. I also knew Mum must have suffered terribly mentally. Depression is an awful thing, but to suffer from it while you know you are dying must have tortured her.

We had talked about euthanasia during her fight with oesophageal cancer in 1984. She agreed with the idea. "You put a dog down when its time is up, so why wouldn't you do it to a human being?" was her view. But during her long bout with lung cancer the subject never came up. The only thing she had told me was that if she arrived at a stage where machinery was required to keep her alive, I was not to allow it.

We had a wake after the funeral, of course, and I told a few members of the family about my condition, if only to explain why I looked ill and worn-out. Then about twenty of us gathered that night at one of my favourite restaurants in Melbourne, the Jewel of India. We talked and joked and remembered Mum, talked some more about the possibility of all of us moving to Queensland, and then I said it was time to get home.

I was exhausted. But I walked the few blocks from the restaurant to my home because I felt like some fresh air — the aroma of Indian food had suddenly plummeted on my list of favourite stimulants. Everyone had protested, saying I should not be out walking when I felt so ill. But I wanted the opportunity to be alone, even briefly.

I went home and slept, grateful that one of the most stressful weeks in my life had apparently ended. I should have known it would not be as simple as that. Nothing in my life ever was.

THE PHONE call came through early the next morning. Had I seen the paper? It was plastered all over page one of the *Herald Sun*, Melbourne's tabloid morning newspaper.

"Athletics great Raelene Boyle is fighting breast cancer," announced the article. "The winner of three Olympic silver medals and hero of the 1982 Brisbane Commonwealth Games is having chemotherapy."

I was shocked. And then shock gave way to a burning anger. How was this possible? The newspaper had not even had the decency to call me before publishing the article. I had always prided myself on my availability to journalists. Over the years they had called me at all hours, and no matter what the issue I had always tried to do the right thing by them.

So that morning's article stung. Even worse was the third paragraph: "Yesterday she conceded she is battling the odds to survive."

I had conceded nothing. In fact, I had not even talked to a reporter. What also riled me was the fact that there was no byline on the article. Whoever had written it had not even had the guts to put their name to it — much less the courage to ring me. I was offended. There are lines you can and cannot step over in life, and surely the media had trespassed this time.

It didn't take long before a large media pack had gathered on the footpath outside my home. Reporters kept ringing the door bell and knocking on the door, while crews from the television networks poked their cameras over the fence trying to catch a glimpse of me. That really annoyed me. If there was one thing I had been protective about in my public life, it was where I lived; I had learned a painful lesson with my stalker that it was best to keep your public and private lives well separated.

This situation felt just as intrusive. I was close to pulling my hair out in frustration, but by then it had started falling out of its own accord.

One of the problems was that I had not yet told a lot of people I was close to that I had cancer. The phone just kept ringing — upset friends were leaving messages asking if it was true, reporters kept calling to see if I would comment ... I hope whoever it was who invented the answering machine made their fortune, because it certainly saved me that day as Greville Street turned into a circus.

I stayed inside and said nothing. Once again Barb came to the rescue, ensuring I was cocooned away from the throng and kept as stress-free as possible.

The producers at "60 Minutes" were none too happy with the article in the *Herald Sun*, but there was nothing they could do about it. In my deal with them I had made it a condition that they could not put my story to air until my mother died. Of course, with the story of my condition now out in the public arena, they were keen to air the interview as quickly as possible. It was given a big run, and the response was remarkable. I was inundated with letters and faxes from people I had never met. The most touching messages were from a section of the community who understood what I was going through.

Women who have suffered breast cancer have a unique bond. We are almost like sisters in our ability to empathise with each other. We understand what it feels like to face the demons of not knowing if you will survive. Many of us develop a morbid sense of humour: if we suffer a slight ache in our backs, breast cancer conquerors will often remark, "Oh God, it's back. And it's in my liver ..."

Those messages of support helped keep my confidence up and my determination steady.

It was about that time that I noticed something outside my window. I woke up early one morning at about 5.30 am. It was 24 June, my forty-fifth birthday. Sometimes at night I would doze off before waking again, my head filled with the clutter that only stress and depression can create. I would worry over the simplest of things. Sometimes I just lay there and wept.

That morning I looked out my window and noticed a bright star, seemingly fixed in the sky. It sounds incredibly corny, but I started looking upon that star as a sign of my mother. I had a tear in my eye when I first saw it. It gave me an enormous amount of comfort. Mum was out there, watching over me. I was a little girl again.

Chemo has no regard for birthdays. As a surprise the nurses in the day clinic had a cake for me — it was bright green. As lovely as the thought was, I took one look at the cake and started vomiting. Unfortunately, this turned out to be one of the toughest infusion days that I had.

Of course, the next day soon arrived. And with it came what had now become my rituals — work when I felt well enough, chemotherapy, nausea and the black dog that still followed me. My visits to Rozi continued; in a way they were a godsend. Comfortably seated in her office, and with the knowledge that I could trust her to keep my deepest and darkest fears secret, I could take the cork out and let off some of the pressure building up within me.

But it was at night as I glanced out my window that I felt safest. I still got to say goodnight to Mum.

8

Heavy metal

It was time to pack my bags and go. There was really only one thing capable of luring me out of my sickbed by the middle of 1996. The president of the Australian Olympic Committee, John Coates, had asked me if I was well enough to go to the Atlanta Games as a guest of the AOC. I didn't need to be asked twice. The only question was whether I could take my treatment with me.

Let's face it. There are not too many airlines in the world that appreciate passengers lugging on board a case full of toxic green-yellow chemicals. But after consulting with my doctors it was clear that I could pull this off. We tried to build the week-long trip around my treatment. But unfortunately, my blood levels were not what they should have been. This meant my infusion would have to be done in Atlanta. I rang Brian Sando, the Australian team doctor and an old mate of mine, and he said he was up to the task.

So it was agreed. The AOC's wonderful offer also included an airfare and accommodation for a carer. Barb was hardly going to turn down such an opportunity, either. Even if she had to hang around old miseryguts Boyle for the entire week.

The trip in late July gave me something to look forward to and an opportunity to stop feeling sorry for myself. And I was chuffed by the fact that the AOC had even thought to invite me. "She has done a lot for us and we just thought it would be nice," Coates told the Australian press who had gathered in Atlanta to prepare for the Olympics. "We think she is one special person."

I slept a lot on the flight to Los Angeles. Then we caught a connecting flight to Atlanta. I had my drugs with me, along with a letter from my doctor authorising me to carry them in my backpack. Once on board the connecting flight, we stashed the backpack in the overhead luggage compartment and settled into seats for the last few hours of our journey.

We were on the runway when Barb and I heard a voice that chilled us. "Excuse me," called out a man in the seat behind us. One of the flight stewards walked over to him. "There's something dripping on me," he told her.

Barb and I looked at one another and panicked. We could just picture the scene taking place behind us. The guy was sitting there harmlessly and disgusting globs of fluorescent green chemical were raining down on him. This was a disaster, and not just for the hapless passenger behind us. My entire chemotherapy course would be thrown into confusion. We might even have to return to Australia immediately.

But the hostess didn't seem concerned. After the plane took off, Barb stood up and took out the backpack. One of our water bottles was dripping. We broke into hysterical laughter, as much in relief as at the humour of the situation.

We were collected by an AOC official at the airport and taken to our hotel. I was keen to get there as quickly as possible. We had missed the opening ceremony, and while I would have loved to have seen Muhammad Ali light the cauldron, I had really come to see Cathy Freeman run. But now there was someone else I wanted to visit. Just before leaving Australia I had been told something that I couldn't quite believe — Dawn Fraser had suffered a heart attack in Atlanta and had been rushed to hospital.

There is usually someone in your life you come to regard as invincible, a superhuman figure who is not subject to the usual problems suffered by the rest of us mere mortals. As a child it is usually your parents. For me, it had been Dawn. We had been good mates since the early 1970s. I first met her when we were lounging around the pool at the Olympic athletes village in Mexico City in 1968. I was a fresh-faced teenager suffering from a severe dose of homesickness and Dawn was already a larger than life heroic figure, her reputation cemented as one of the greatest athletes ever produced by Australia.

Dawn was rough and tough, an amazingly blunt woman who always said what was on her mind. That was all right by me. By the early 1970s I had been earmarked by some officials and journalists as the next great Australian female ratbag, a natural successor to Dawn's title. I've always hated being categorised and stereotyped. Yet it was easy to understand why so many saw me that way. Dawn had created plenty of trouble in her time. She liked a beer, too. But I never saw myself as Dawn's equal. Her feats in the pool at three Games were the stuff not just of Australian sporting legend, but of the Olympic movement, too. I was a silver medallist who had never won gold.

I visited Dawn the morning after our arrival, courtesy of a personal driver that Billy Payne, the chairman of the Atlanta Organising Committee, had organised for her for as long as she needed. Dawn was hooked up to machines and an array of tubes, but it was clear her recovery was well under way. I asked her what had brought on the heart attack.

She wasn't sure, but the past few months of her life had been hectic, she said. Zac, her adored German shepherd, had only recently died and she was sure that had played a part. I understood what she meant. My dogs had been an integral part of my life for as long as I could remember, too.

That afternoon, Brian Sando gave me my chemotherapy infusion, and as I'd suspected, he struggled to find a vein. It took him a while, and by the end of it my arm was black and blue. This was my second infusion and by then my veins were brittle and many of my veins had collapsed. But I was fortunate Brian was there — I trusted him and he did not let me down.

The next few days involved me sleeping as much as possible. We were staying at the Days Inn hotel. Across the road was the Fox Theatre, where Foster's had installed a hospitality lounge. The AOC's offices just happened to be there, too. I watched a lot of the Games on television while lying on a couch in the Foster's lounge. The scene must have been remarkable and I'm sure few believed it. Raelene Boyle could be found in the hospitality tent of a major brewing company, and not once did a beer pass her lips.

I felt too sick most of the time. I had one glass of champagne, but the chemotherapy, as usual, had thrown my tastebuds into a state of total confusion. It felt like I was drinking razor blades. Once again I couldn't get that metal taste out of my mouth.

But it was still terrific to be there and feel a part of it. The likes of Greg Norman regularly sauntered through the lounge, and I caught up with many of my old friends, including Jim Barry, who had been general manager of the Australian team at the Brisbane Commonwealth Games, and for whom I had a huge amount of respect. A few days later I also caught up with Poland's Irena Szewinska, who had just beaten me with a new world-record time in the 200-metres final in Mexico in 1968. Four years later she won a bronze behind me and Renate Stecher. Irena had heard about my condition — it was remarkable how word moved through the international Olympic network — and we chatted and relived some great times.

But it was Cathy Freeman I was waiting to see. I had trained her for a short time when she had first moved to Melbourne from Brisbane in the early 1990s, and ever since I had kept a close eye on her development. I knew she was an incredibly gifted athlete, but there had been times when I questioned her commitment. Cathy was such a nice, pleasant kid that I wondered if she really had the fire in the belly to make it on the international stage. I told her one day that my prediction was that she would never make an Olympic final.

Of course, she proved me wrong. Murph and I caught a cab to see her run in the semi-finals. But once we arrived at the stadium I took one look at the enormously long queues and shook my head. The homemade bomb set off in Centennial Park which had killed four bystanders had forced security arrangements to tighten even more, and it was getting more and more difficult to move around. A light drizzle had begun to fall and the hot, humid conditions had grown even clammier. "I can't do this," I told Barb. So we went back and watched on television as Cathy progressed to the finals.

The next day in the Foster's lounge I told the company's chief executive, Ted Kunkel, that I doubted whether I would get to the stadium to see Cathy run. An hour spent standing in a line and then having to undergo security checks was just too daunting to contemplate. "Nonsense," said Ted. "Why don't you come with us?"

I don't know how he did it, but I learned a valuable lesson. Executives of world-famous brewing companies wield a lot of power. Ted simply ushered us in to the VIP area of the main Olympic stadium, where I could watch several events in comfort, as well as Cathy's big run against the gifted Frenchwoman Marie-José Pérec.

It was a great race. In many ways I regard it as probably a better race, in the old-fashioned sense of it being a true sporting contest, than Cathy's incredible gold-medal winning performance in Sydney four years later. It was a classic contest between two fine athletes, either of whom could have won it. When Cathy lifted with 150 metres to go, and then challenged again 50 metres later, I was shouting and caught up in an incredible surge of emotion. It was one of the most exciting races I had ever seen.

She didn't quite get there, but it was a performance that stamped Cathy as one of the finest international competitors Australia had produced. In my opinion, there is a big difference between an outstanding athlete and an outstanding competitor. There has been a long list of brilliant runners over the years, both from Australia and overseas, who have set dazzling times in their national titles and at other events. But come the big day — and as far as I'm concerned the Olympics remain the ultimate test, ranking higher than the world championships — they just cannot produce their best. But Cathy, to my surprise and others as well, revealed a depth of talent and character that gained the victory many of us believed might elude her.

I saw Cathy that night and wished her well and wondered to myself who looked worse. She was exhausted and I knew that feeling. There was simply no energy left in her body and it was an effort for her to move around and smile and chat with the hordes of well-wishers. I understood the pressure she had been living with for months; the build-up to an Olympic event is incredible. And the media coverage was far more intense than it had been during my career. Sydney was four years away but already Cathy was being hyped as one of our best chances for gold on the track in 2000. Her Aboriginality, of course, was already an underlying issue. There was no escaping it, and by draping herself in the Aboriginal flag at other events she had made a statement of her own. For the media, she would be a story for the next four years. But it's funny how athletes and former runners like myself never really understood the colour issue, at least on a political level. I saw Cathy as a 400-metre runner, and what interested me most was her style and ability to perform under pressure.

This is not to say that athletes are colourblind when it comes to matters of race. Athletics these days is so dominated by black athletes — the sprints by those with origins in West Africa and the distance events by Kenyan athletes — that it is difficult not to suspect that they have some inherent physical advantage when it comes to moving quickly. But the scientific evidence is poor. Scientists tell us there is no such thing as race, that when it comes to genetics all humanity is virtually identical no matter what part of the world you live in. But physiologically there is no doubt that some black athletes are built for speed. Just look at some of the women with their long tapered legs and pronounced bums. Some researchers into this area say this is purely coincidence, and that the dominance of the black athlete in modern sport has more to do with sociology and what they call a self-perpetuating myth. It goes like this. The belief that black athletes are athletically superior to white athletes is just that — a myth. But after a while both black and white athletes come to believe it. Fewer white athletes bother competing in the sports where black athletes excel — middle-distance running, sprinting and basketball — and because of that, black dominance is underlined yet again.

I have no idea who is right. To tell you the truth, I don't really care. Skin colour never even crossed my mind when I was competing. My opponents were all the same to me. They all had to be beaten.

Amid the noise and celebratory atmosphere in those hours after Cathy's race, I gave her a cuddle, admired the medal and told her to cherish the moment. They were few and far between.

THE WEEK in Atlanta passed quickly, but I must admit I was glad to be going home. The heat, the crowds and the constant noise had got the better of me and for the only time in my life I found it hard to be infected by the Olympic spirit.

I was also sick of putting on a brave face and slapping on a smile for everyone. It was certainly nice that so many people I knew — and some I didn't — cared enough to approach me, ask how I was and extend their best wishes. You know what it's like when you don't feel well. All I could fantasise about was climbing back into bed.

The day we left I asked Dawn if she would mind if her driver could take Barb and me to the airport. By then Dawn was up and about again — her stamina never ceased to amaze. All I was thinking about was getting to the airport, getting on board the flight, and then not waking up until we arrived in Melbourne.

Dawn said no. She couldn't spare her driver. She wasn't sure what she planned to do that day, and whether she would need the driver.

If I hadn't been feeling so sick I might have said something to her. But by then all I could mutter was a quiet farewell. I was annoyed, but I knew it would do me no good to get involved in an argument. Barb and I managed to find a taxi, bundled our gear into it, and told the driver to get us to the airport.

There was a bitter taste in my mouth, mingling with the flavour of cold, hard metal.

AT FIRST I didn't recognise Dawn's voice when I picked up the phone early on a Wednesday morning in late August, just a few weeks after returning home from Atlanta. Dawn was crying. I'd never heard her cry before. It was something you never imagined her doing, she was just too tough to weep. But she was sobbing, and that stunned me almost as much as the news she delivered.

"What's the matter?" I asked.

"Whit's dead," she said.

It took a few seconds for the realisation to hit me. Bev Whitfield, a great mate of ours, had been found dead of a suspected heart attack in the bedroom of her Wollongong home the night before. She was only forty-two, just a couple of years younger than me. It didn't seem possible.

I'd had some crazy times with Bev. We had holidayed together many times, and I had held Whit personally responsible for some of the largest hangovers I suffered in my life. She had been a surprise gold medallist in the 200-metres breaststroke at the 1972 Munich Olympics, as well as taking home a bronze in the 100-metres breaststroke, and we had quickly formed a rapport that had lasted a quarter of a century. She used to drive us all insane with her incessant phone calls. The woman was addicted to the telephone; I suspect she had one wedged against her ear whenever she wasn't asleep. Your phone would ring and it would be Whit on the other end.

"G'day," she'd always begin. "What's happening?"

Then, before you had a chance to reply, she would be regaling you with all sorts of wonderful gossip she had picked up in her previous calls. It was that constant gossiping that had led to a bit of a falling-out between the two of us earlier in the year. I'd begun to suspect that it was Whit's love of a story that had led to news of my breast cancer being leaked to the media. I rang everywhere looking for her, ready to give her one of the greatest serves I had dished out to anyone. But I couldn't find her, although plenty of friends certainly passed on the message that I suspected her of opening her mouth, perhaps inadvertently, once too often. Not long after, a large group of former Olympians gathered in Sydney for a photo shoot for *Who* magazine. Whit and I exchanged withering glances across the room and never spoke. But it was quickly forgotten. I could never stay mad at Whit for long. She'd called me just days after I had come home from Atlanta, and I didn't even raise the subject with her. We just resumed the friendship as if nothing had happened.

Whit loved the Olympic movement. She had grown up in a tough environment and her mother had died when she was young. But you rarely heard her complain. She was, in every sense of the phrase, larger than life. She had never lost her passion for swimming, and every swimmer could count on her for advice or just plain friendship.

Her successes in Munich had come at a wonderful time for Australia's female swimmers. Shane Gould and Gail Neall also triumphed in Munich, but the horrific massacre of eleven Israeli athletes meant Gail's and Whit's victories never really received the recognition they deserved. Whit was hardly a household name, unlike many other swimmers, and while this never seemed to bother her I felt sorry that someone who had achieved such remarkable things was not as lauded as she should have been.

In her last few years she had let herself go a bit — her weight had ballooned and she'd started smoking. Yet she always seemed unstoppable. She had worked with juvenile offenders at a detention centre not far from her home, and was constantly making visits to schools to display her medals and spread the word about the Olympic movement. I often thought that some of those cold-hearted bureaucrats responsible for running the Olympics had no idea they had a free publicity machine working overtime for them back in Australia.

Whit always believed that a locked door was simply an invitation to come up with a way of getting inside. She usually stayed at my place in order to attend the annual Sports Hall of Fame dinner. She would never tell me how long she intended to stay — long-term planning was never part of Whit's character. One year the Australian cricket captain Allan Border was inducted into the Hall. We'd had the usual riotous evening and post-dinner party, and

Allan had organised tickets for a group of us to watch the Australians play in a limited-overs international at the Melbourne Cricket Ground the next day.

The tickets gave us an excellent view of the match. But the seats were not in the members' enclosure, that exclusive sanctuary in the MCG where everyone who is important, or thinks they are, gets to rub shoulders with others of their kind. Whit believed our group — by this stage it numbered almost a dozen — deserved to be in the members'. She went up to the man on the gate and asked him, "If I showed you my Olympic gold medal and let you touch it, would you let me and my friends in?"

Whit usually carried that gold medal around in her purse — it was her proudest possession. The gate attendant was obviously a sports fan and needed no further prompting. A quick touch of the medal and the gate magically opened for us. We ended up having a great day inside the pavilion. But our presence was duly noted. Not long after, Whit received a stern letter from the secretary of the Melbourne Cricket Club — the custodians of the MCG — rebuking her for sneaking into an area she didn't deserve to be in. Petty? Of course. But that was a sports official for you.

In the end it was that large, warm heart of Whit's that eventually betrayed her.

I flew to Sydney for the funeral. Dawn decided she would make the drive from Sydney to Wollongong. But which road to take? Dawn saw a policeman on a motorcycle and pulled up next to him.

"Which way to Wollongong?" she asked.

"Follow me if you can keep up," replied the cop.

There are enormous benefits when it comes to travelling with Dawn Fraser. Before we knew it, we had a police escort all the way to the funeral chapel — a police motorbike at the front, and another at the rear. I'm sure Whit would have appreciated it. Now that was arriving in style.

BY NOW, 1996 had become marked with gravestones and I was really struggling on two levels. Emotionally I was a mess and physically the chemotherapy was starting to wreak havoc on my body. There was a small positive — the hair had fallen off my legs so I didn't have to bother shaving the damn things. But my depression, mixed with the effects of my treatment, had become a potent brew. I began bleeding from my nose and just about every other conceivable place. My skin was thinning and my mouth was filled with ulcers. I had to place a glass of salt water near every tap in the house. Every time I passed one, I'd rinse my mouth with it. Some days I became quite agitated. Like everyone who goes through intensive therapy, there were moments of such frustration that I wanted to stop the treatment right there and then.

The anxiety would reach its peak every Monday morning when I had to go to the clinic to receive my infusion. (I consumed the drugs in tablet form for the rest of the week.) My heart rate would begin to quicken and it felt like ice-cold water was running through my veins. My problems weren't helped by the fact that my struggles to provide a vein in my arm for my infusions were worsening. Where were the damn things? When I wasn't anxious and uptight, walking through the house unable to concentrate on anything, I was sleeping. I didn't know it at the time but the chemotherapy had triggered the onset of premature menopause. I was having hot flushes and my body ached all the time. When Edgar "Dunc" Gray, a gold-medal winning cyclist at the 1932 Los Angeles Games, died at the age of ninety, just ten days after Whit's death, all I could do was shrug.

His funeral was held at the same chapel as Whit's, at Kembla Grange near Wollongong. Dunc had actually been there for Whit's funeral. Once again, I was among a large gathering of former Olympians who gathered to say farewell. Perhaps because of his age there was not the sense of overwhelming tragedy that had been present when Whit had died. One of the speakers in the chapel brought a smile to everyone's face when she told them: "I guess one of Dunc's favourite stories is what he should have done with the flagstaff when Adolf Hitler passed close to him in the marshalling area in 1936 ..."

But while I found this seemingly constant parade of funerals wearing, it was also a comfort to me to be among the Olympic fraternity. It's a difficult thing to explain, but there is a deep bond that runs through all those who have represented Australia at the Games. The Olympics represent the peak of athletic competition, and anyone who is fortunate enough to make the team knows the sacrifices and pain it has taken to get there.

Yes, I have grown increasingly disillusioned with the Olympic movement over the years — the hype, the commercialisation and particularly the bribery scandals and drug taking have disgusted me. But deep down that innate conservatism I have has always drawn me back to the Games. Despite my rebellious and questioning nature, I have an in-built respect for institutions and authority figures. And I still cling to those old-fashioned Olympic ideals of fairness and co-operation, no matter how sullied or tainted they have become. It sounds corny in this age of cynicism. But if you don't have a set of standards to live up to — a list of rules or guidelines to help you through life — then it's a simple thing to lose your way.

All I knew back in 1996, however, was that no-one could show me where it said in the rules that I deserved to go through what I was enduring. Self-pity. It's one of those emotions and phases you inevitably encounter when you are battling cancer and things are not going right. As you may have guessed, there were times when I viewed myself as being at the centre of the universe. I managed to see everything in terms of my own condition. Other people dying was a possible omen that there was a grave marked for me, too, somewhere out there. Other people falling sick, or having a tough time, was an excuse for me to measure my condition against theirs.

My job in the Gardens had ended. Redundancies were handed out and the park would be the responsibility of a group of people who couldn't possibly have the same devotion I had shown over the past six years. But by then I hardly cared.

It was time to leave. The Melbourne winter had laid me low again with a severe chest infection and my chemotherapy was stopped for a month. This meant that instead of finishing the course at the end of August, it would take another month.

But somehow, as I prepared to move to Queensland, I persevered. Team Boyle kept up its regular watch over me. And every time I had the strength to wander down to the Prahran market, I was carried along by the warmth and support of so many people.

One day late in September I sat at the kitchen table and stared at the bottle of chemotherapy tablets. They were the last I would have to take. I looked at them for more than an hour. What was the point of taking them? Surely these last few would make no difference. The therapy had blasted its way through my body for the past seven months, and if it had failed then surely these last couple of pills would not save me.

It was a critical moment. In a way I was thumbing my nose at the whole year. I wanted it to be over, the whole bloody thing.

It was a feeling I had experienced throughout my athletic career. Whenever I became frustrated or disillusioned, a showdown always took place. It had always been the way. And almost every time it had helped me to go on to win.

I reached over and swallowed the tablets. It was time to look to the future. Radiation treatment awaited me, a six-week intensive course where a large machine would zap my left breast with x-rays to destroy any remaining cancer cells. But that would be a cakewalk compared with the chemotherapy.

The worst was surely over. I now had an opportunity to rebuild both my body and my mind. And that was something I knew I was good at doing.

I'd been practising it all my life.

CHRISTMAS 1996 finally arrived. It had been a horrific year and toward the end of it I had impatiently counted down the days until it was over.

The family gathered once again in Melbourne. It wasn't quite the same. Mum was no longer with us, but it was just as crowded. I felt surrounded by the ghosts of the past. So many people had died and gone missing from my life. I even wondered at times if I had lost a large part of myself. My spirit had been sorely tested this past year. I was still searching for my old sense of humour; I didn't know if I had lost it for good.

But there were also positives and I tried to concentrate on them. If anything, Mum's death and my cancer had brought me so much closer to my brothers. I finally understood, better than at any other time of my life, the importance of family and friends. Team Boyle had stuck closely with me throughout the year and I was still there. I had beaten chemotherapy. I had beaten the radiation therapy.

I was even starting to think I had beaten cancer, and that I could tame that awful black dog.

This Christmas was going to be one of the best of my life. I was determined that we would stage a memorable Boyle party and have a great time.

And then the itching began. I had a pain across my back. I couldn't stop scratching. The doctor told me I had shingles.

Shingles. Was there anything else this year could squeeze in to torment me? Shingles is a virus of the nerve pathways that can be triggered by stress. And I had certainly had my share during the year. What was probably the last straw had come at the start of

December. The Hall of Fame was going through a turbulent period, split by internal controversy and bickering. Dawn was due to chair the annual general meeting, but had fallen ill, leaving the job to me. The meeting was a debacle — a long, drawn-out excuse for some people to express a lot of bitterness and resentment that had built up over the years. One of them was Shirley de la Hunty, formerly Shirley Strickland, who had been my coach during my ill-fated trip to the Montreal Olympics. I felt like Shirley used the meeting as an opportunity to hit back at me. Shirley had been targeted as being partly to blame for my failure in Montreal, and our relationship had deteriorated over the years to the point we could barely look at one another.

I had never looked forward to hosting the meeting in the first place. But with Shirley and others criticising me and the rest of the Hall of Fame committee for some of its alleged problems, the meeting was one of the most excruciatingly painful encounters of my life.

And so I spent Christmas and New Year nursing huge watery blisters across my body, moving between my bed and a bath filled with lotion.

I cursed. I swore. I cried out. And then at some stage I laughed. If blisters were the worst thing that could happen to me now, I was in good shape. When you've been running all your life, you know how to live with them.

PART II

THE FAST LANE

9

The Coburg castle

Enough of the recent past, at least for now. For obvious reasons, I find it painful to dwell there for too long. So let's travel back a little further. Let me show you my earlier years. My journey through them was just as eventful.

The Boyle history is woven into the cold, misty country of Scotland and the Irish north-west. My family can trace some of its origins back to the areas around Glasgow, where the de Boyvilles, Anglo-Norman knights who arrived in Scotland after the Norman conquest of England in 1066, set up camp in a string of castles. But there are strong arguments that I must have at least a little Irish blood in me.

In Ireland, the name Boyle is thought to have come from the old word "Baigell", meaning "having profitable pledges". Having spent the past few years badgering people into giving money to support breast cancer research, I can at least now claim that I have been living up to my name.

It seems the Irish Boyles didn't mind a family fight, either. Back in the sixteenth century the clan staged a great battle for the chieftainship and the fight continued down the generations, resulting in the deaths of hundreds. Having been involved in a significant internal Boyle dispute of my own, let me tell you that forgiveness is not one of our strongest traits. Clearly, though, some of us learned to run very fast and survive. Perhaps because of this, the name Boyle soon ventured beyond the Scottish and Irish borders. Eventually the clan spread throughout the New World, including America and, later, Australia.

And so it was that in the 1950s, one tiny thread of the Boyle tribe settled into its own castle in Sutherland Street, Coburg, a working-class suburb in northern Melbourne.

Well, castle is perhaps not the right word.

After a time I came to see it more as a dungeon from which to escape. Even after all these years I still find it difficult to drive down that street and pass that small weatherboard home without feeling distinctly uncomfortable. I don't really understand why. For most of my childhood it was a place of great love and warmth. Perhaps it was the manner in which I finally left it — amid screams and accusations and hurt pride — that saw me vow to move on, to get on with my life and not look back. The past. You leave it all behind, but it always stays with you.

It's funny how, as children, we see the world as being larger than it really is. Perhaps because we are always looking up, straining to see what the world looks like to our parents, we imagine it as being bigger and stranger than it really is.

Ever gone back to the family home years after leaving it? Strange, isn't it, how everything seems to have miraculously shrunk. That shed in the backyard — funny how it looks so ramshackle and claustrophobic these days. Back when you were a kid it used to house the lawn mower, a pile of old newspapers, a rusting old bike missing its chain ... and a horde of goblins and ghouls who, at night, scratched and screamed in an attempt to escape and scare the hell out of you.

The kitchen — it was always the centre of the home. But look at it now — how was it possible to squeeze all those people in there and still have room to reach over and turn the radio volume up when the news came on? And what about that bedroom? It was always a place to escape to. Now it seems so small. How could you hide in there?

The world began shrinking a lot earlier in my childhood than it did for many other kids. I was born at Vaucluse hospital in Melbourne on 24 June 1951. Ron, my elder brother, was already four years old. And when I came into the world, Rick, who would eventually share a bedroom with me, was still four years away.

One of my earliest memories is studiously scraping away at the peeling weatherboards of our home. I had grand plans. I would scrape those pathetic white flakes away, somehow save enough money for a large pot of paint and then give it a bright makeover. It pained me that our house was the worst-kept in the street. Dad was one of those men who seemed determined never to be kept prisoner in his own castle. For him, life was not to be wasted with Sunday afternoon rituals of lawn mowing, painting or gardening. There was too much to do, too many other interesting things going on with which to occupy his time.

Fortunately for us kids, we were among them.

My father's name on his birth certificate was Gilbert MacDonald Boyle, but no-one ever called him that. He despised the name, and when he was in the company of other adults I only ever heard them refer to him as "Mac". He was a gentle man and it is only now that I can imagine some of the difficulties he must have faced, coping with a wife who was cursed with bouts of severe depression. Back then, being treated for a mental condition was hardly a topic for discussion over a cup of coffee with the neighbours. With three energetic kids, I'm sure he had his work cut out.

My father was an endlessly curious man. A former professional runner whose career had been interrupted by the war years, he loved to study the mechanics of sprinting. He would break down the movement of various body parts before reconstructing them so they all flowed together, rather like a musician writing separate pieces of music before melding them together into a symphony. An engineer, he spent almost his entire working career with the Melbourne City Council. But it was hardly his passion. I can remember catching the tram into the city one day and walking into his office in that wonderful town hall on the corner of Collins and Swanston Streets. Expecting him to be hard at work, I caught him napping.

Work was a means to an end for Dad. He was always home in time for tea, and the dinner table was a place where discussions about current events were encouraged. Dad was happy for all of us to have our own opinions. The last thing he seemed to want was a flock of sheep living beneath his roof. He wanted us to question why things were the way they were, and to buttress our beliefs with strong and logical arguments. Just because I was a girl did not mean I was treated differently to my brothers — my opinions were given the same weight and respect as theirs. Remember, this was the 1950s and 1960s, a decade before the feminist and equal rights revolution. But in the Boyle household I was fortunate to know equality long before others. It's probably one of the reasons I've never shied away from speaking up about issues that affect me.

To me our home always seemed to be filled with clocks. There was just one problem — none of the clocks worked. (And people wonder why my timing was never quite right during my athletic career.) Dad's endless curiosity — *How does that work, how do all those small, individual parts come together to work as a whole?* — always led him to pull them apart. My brothers say there were not that many of them. But I remember their innards being strewn everywhere, giving the impression that we had let one of our rooms to an unemployed Swiss watchmaker. Dad never seemed to have the inclination — or the time — to put them back together.

It was the same with his cars. Dad seemed to have an amazing ability to match his cars with the exterior decor of our home. His cars were ugly-looking things that I hated seeing parked in the street. The seat covers would be torn, while the rest of the vehicle would be in an equal state of disrepair. I used to jump in the back and try to repair those torn seats, just like I used to dream of repainting the house. No-one else in the family seemed to notice or mind these things. Sometimes I would vacuum the house, just to satisfy my urge to try to make our home presentable.

One of my overwhelming memories of childhood is the stains. My parents were not drinkers; I think a bottle of beer would have lasted a year in our place. Instead, Mum and Dad had another powerful vice — they coated the inside of our home with a strong, fetid nicotine yellow that seemed to eat its way into the walls and everything else in our house. The smoke clung to the furniture, to our clothes, our hair. When Mum and Dad kissed me goodnight there was smoke on their breath, and it was there again first thing in the morning. There was always a cigarette burning somewhere in the house, and an empty ashtray was about as common as a copy of *Home Beautiful*. Mind you, I'm sure it was nothing unusual for its time. Back then there were entire Australian suburbs permanently shrouded in smoke. But I'm sure it is one reason we three kids tended to play outside.

We were always outside. One of my favourite haunts was the dairy just half a block down our street. Out the back they used to keep a team of Clydesdale horses and early each morning you could hear them clip-clopping past as the milko left a bottle at our doorstep. I was forbidden to go to the dairy on my own; Mum warned me repeatedly that it was a dangerous area for a young girl. Her warnings, however, were not enough to frighten me away. I loved those horses. In our neighbourhood, where bitumen and concrete reigned supreme, big animals were unusual and I found myself drawn to them. I would sneak out the front door, run down the street, and with just a passing glance over my shoulder to make certain Mum wasn't watching, I would wander across to the dairy and then down the back to pat them. I loved the way their big, languid eyes stared right through me. And I marvelled at how gentle, yet strong, they were. After spending as long as I dared with them, I would scoot back home sheepishly, pretending that I had just gone for a stroll down the street. But I'm sure that through the ever-present curtain of smoke that hung through our house, Mum could detect the unique perfume that only horse dung and straw can manufacture.

To her great disappointment and despite her best efforts (she loved to curl my blond hair, which I found to be a revolting experience), Mum could not entice me into playing the stereotypical role of a little girl. She bought me dolls and frilly dresses. I instead gravitated toward cricket bats and belting up the neighbourhood boys. I hate the expression "tomboy" these days — it's become a pejorative word over the years, yet another way for people to categorise you — but hanging out with my brothers was clearly my preferred way of passing time. The only doll I ever showed any interest in was a black one in overalls called Marvin. I still have Marvin and he remains in pristine condition — thanks no doubt to the fact there was too much going on outside our front door for me to remain inside for any length of time and cause him injury. I wasn't keen on wearing dresses, either. I was sent home from the Church of Christ kindergarten one afternoon and told not to come back until I was in a dress. I was only four, and my mother sided with the kindergarten teacher, but I made my stand and won.

My reasoning was simple. If I wore a dress I couldn't go on the monkey bars because the boys would see my undies. I was back at kindy the next day. In pants. And the teacher said nothing.

Still, as I grew older Mum was always there hemming and sewing something together for me at the last minute. It always had to be at the last minute, because I was notorious for being slow in making up my mind about what to wear.

Puberty arrived late for me, and I barely noticed. I was outside playing with the neighbourhood boys when I discovered my first period had arrived. I can remember knowing what it was. I had no fear or panic. But I was frustrated. It was a damn nuisance to have to interrupt the game we were playing. I went inside and told Mum. Within minutes I was back outside joining the fray.

Some of the most seriously contested cricket matches staged in the western world took place outside our house in Sutherland Street. Boxes, crates and rubbish bins served as wickets, and because cars were not as common back then it was rare for one of our Test matches to be interrupted by traffic. In winter, football matches took over, even though our family was one of the few in the neighbourhood not to be infected by that peculiar Victorian disease.

Sutherland Street also became my first training venue for sprinting. Whenever I was in a fight with the neighbourhood boys I was always the first to reach the front door of our home, leaving my frustrated pursuer well behind. I always thought my natural speed might come in handy one day. Just down the street from us was the large bluestone Pentridge Prison, a notorious jail that housed some of Australia's most dangerous criminals. The possibility of a jailbreak was often joked about. I figured I could outrun even the swiftest criminal.

But while I disobeyed orders occasionally by venturing into the dairy to pat the horses, I always knew there were forbidden areas. Dad was a typical white, Anglo-Saxon male of his era, distrustful of many things foreign. At the top of his list was the local Maltese population. We were told not to mix with them — those "wogs" were not to be trusted and the same went for their kids. And so we kept our distance.

MUM AND Dad met during the war when both were working at the Sale air force base. Dad was a flight engineer who hailed from a comfortable middle-class family. His father had been a teacher and my memories of my grandfather are of a learned gentleman, a dignified elder in the country town of Bendigo where he became grand master of the Freemasons' Lodge. When I was little I used to holiday in Bendigo and, as the only granddaughter, enjoyed being fussed over. But on occasion I would announce to Grandpa that I wanted to go home. He would nod patiently, help me into his large, powerful Plymouth and begin the long drive to Melbourne. By the time we reached the small town of Kyneton I would change my mind. He would sigh knowingly, turn the Plymouth around and head back home. I'm sure he suspected the reason for the trip. I knew a small girl who lived in Kyneton who was lucky enough to have a horse. We often saw her in the park there when we broke our journey to Bendigo for a drink and toilet stop. I would press my face up against the window of our car and watch her until she disappeared from view. Horses — in fact, any animal — were my obsession then. Not much has changed, since.

My mother, who caught Dad's eye while she was working as a parachute packer, had grown up in a far more humble environment. Her family were from Perth, where they lived in a little timber house. My mother's father worked in the dispatch area of a large department store, and while they often went without the luxuries of life, it was always a warm and safe home. Later on when I moved to Perth, my grandmother would act as my de facto mother.

Mum and Dad were close. Their marriage, perhaps unusually for the era, was very much a partnership. Dad was never one to hang around in the pub after work, gulping down beers in what became known at the time as the six o'clock swill. He was always home and sharing the responsibility for raising us kids. When Mum wasn't well, it was Dad who took over the running of the household.

They were not openly affectionate, and they did have their arguments. Yet it is only now that I can begin to fathom the undercurrents that swirled through their relationship. Mum's depression and her health problems — endometriosis, the curse of the female Boyles, was always present — must have severely tested the marriage from time to time. Yet my father rarely seemed to complain.

He was my hero, after all, and to me he could do no wrong. On Saturday nights I would take our two small cocker spaniels for a walk around the corner to the local milk bar, buy the evening paper for the sports results and pick up the family block of chocolate Dad would treat us to. In fact, Mac was such a softie that when one of our dogs died he spent hours driving around the countryside in an attempt to find the right tree under which to bury it. The only time Dad let me down was when I entered hospital to have my tonsils removed. For some reason he never came to visit. He was busy at work, I was told. I was crushed.

But his standing reached new heights one afternoon in the late 1950s. I came home from school, probably puffing slightly because I used to run and skip most of the way, at the same time picking flowers from neighbourhood gardens to give to Mum. In the lounge room was a strange man, bent over a large box sitting in the corner. Our first television was being installed and I remember growing extremely impatient with the repairman as he fiddled with the aerial trying to restore the flickering image of Roy Rogers.

And that was pretty much what life was like in Sutherland Street — probably no different from thousands of other similar homes around the country at the same time. Australia was a fairly sedate place in the 1950s. One of the few significant differences in our house, apart from the peeling weatherboards, was that my father had noticed something special about his only daughter. She could run fast. Mac believed I had been blessed with a gift. He would do his best to ensure it wasn't wasted.

DAD WAS a tinkerer and a lot of his tinkering took place inside a small bicycle shop he ran part-time down the road. He liked bikes, and there was never any discussion in our house. As soon as you were old enough to reach the pedals, you joined the local pedal club. It was held on Sundays at a nearby oval and I quickly learned to love riding. By the mid 1960s I would become the Victorian women's sprinting champion. Ron, who spent months in hospital as a child suffering from a rare form of encephalitis, would go on to even better things, winning a berth to represent Australia at the 1976 Montreal Olympics.

I copped a bit of teasing at school about my bike riding, and like a lot of kids I hated being the target of derision. It probably gave me just one more reason to dislike the place. Let me be perfectly clear about this, I was not a good student. From primary school through to my years at Coburg High School, I found it a chore to be inside the classroom. I had few goals or ambitions outside athletics back then. I was a bit of a loner and never really understood the logic of learning about English history. To me, it was enough to know that plenty of wars had been staged in the past. But I often wondered why our teachers didn't tell us more about Australian history. I wasn't good at relating to things that I felt had no connection to my life. I can recall my French teacher, Mrs Cosic, saying to me as she threw me out of class one day for not paying attention: "Raelene, one day you will regret not concentrating in these classes." By then I had developed a smart-alec reaction to everything. "Who cares?" I replied. "I'm never going to France."

The ladder I would have to climb — or descend — in life seemed pretty obvious. Girls left school and became secretaries. Was there any argument? Most of us were drilled in the techniques of typing and shorthand during those interminable hours in the classroom and that's how most of us thought. We would then marry, have a couple of kids, and by the time we hit our mid to late twenties, we would probably be out of the workforce and continuing the same cycle performed by our mothers.

That it never turned out that way was hardly through any strong desire of mine to avoid such a fate. My running career simply happened. Even as a teenager coming back from her first Olympic Games with a medal, I never seriously thought that it would carry on until I was in my thirties. It was just something that I loved doing. No-one told me you could make a career out of your passion.

It is hard to describe the feeling I used to get from running quickly, and there are times even now when I would give anything to experience it again. There was nothing complicated about it. Through my parents I had inherited a genetic gift to be able to run fast. And for many years it gave me far greater enjoyment and pleasure than anything else on earth. To move quickly across the ground, and to be the best at it, gave me the sort of high that other people rarely get to experience in everyday life. Some athletes talk about "finding the zone" or "being in the zone", and believe me, such a zone is a very real place. Time slows for the participant, even though it appears to carry on as normal to the spectator. A 22-second race across 200 metres can feel like an hour in normal time to the competitor. Your body is moving quickly, but you are concentrating so much on the task at hand that everything else — from the crowd noise to all those little things that keep whirring through our brains and occupying our attention — is simply erased. The great cliché in sporting movies is the slow-motion scene (think *Chariots of Fire*). There goes the hero, lunging for the line. It seems to take forever, particularly for the audience. Yet film makers are close to reality with such scenes.

I have heard of a similar feeling experienced by soldiers who are engaged in battle. When that first bullet whizzes past they suddenly become so focused, their senses so attuned to the danger at hand and to the task of protecting their lives and those of others, that anything else becomes superfluous. A half-hour battle seems to last a day. When it is over, all the hormones and adrenaline that kicked in to heighten the senses evaporate. Exhaustion sets in. It was how Cathy Freeman looked to me in the hours after her race in Atlanta. I understood the feeling. So many people these days seem to rely on artificial stimulants and drugs. I was more fortunate. My highs came naturally.

Perhaps that's why I've never been a very good spectator. I don't have the patience to sit in the stand and watch others. I don't even watch that much sport on television, to be honest. A lot of other athletes I know are the same. Naturally, when I perform commentary work for television I do my homework, study videos of overseas events and observe the competitors as closely as possible. But watching sport all day is my idea of cruelty.

My poor attention span as a spectator goes way back to when I was five years old. In the lead up to the 1956 Olympics in Melbourne, Dad took me along to a pre-Games meeting at Royal Park. Some of the greatest athletes in the country were competing, including Betty Cuthbert, who would go on to become Australia's greatest sprinter. She was famously dubbed the "Golden Girl" when she won three gold medals in Melbourne. And while I barely had a hero in the traditional sense when I was growing up — I guess Dad came closest — Betty was to become one of the athletes and women I most admired as I grew older. To have enjoyed such a warm friendship with her over the years is something I cherish, along with memories of a certain night many years later when I had the opportunity to push her wheelchair into the spotlight — that was one of the proudest moments of my life. But unfortunately at that Royal Park competition in 1956 I was too young to notice or admire the athleticism of the contestants.

Running was fun to me; it was not until I reached my late twenties that I started taking it seriously. There were many people who thought that had I applied myself more I might have enjoyed greater success. There have been times when I have agreed with them. But let's face it. I was a runner. I loved the sport, I loved to run quickly and there was a time in my life when to win a gold medal was my greatest ambition.

There's nothing wrong with that at all. But as time passes you come to see it for what it was — a phase in your life that helped shape and change you. In my darker moments I sometimes wonder if it was all worth it. Were all those years of training, all those days and nights spent putting up with the pain of injuries and, even worse, trying to endure the heartache and frustration of never quite achieving what I set out to do just a waste of time?

It seems so long ago, now. But you never really forget. Those years were worth it. They were wonderful times. To be sixteen years old and named to represent your country at the Olympic Games was the greatest thing in the world.

10

The world at my feet

THE CROWD WAS BAYING FOR BLOOD. IT WAS A HOT AFTERNOON — had Mexico City ever known anything else? — and as the temperature rose so, too, did the blood lust of the spectators. Now I knew what it must have been like in medieval times when life was cheap and those who could wield a sword were revered and worshipped. This was a crowd that had paid for the privilege of witnessing a death. At times they had grown impatient and a chorus of whistling and heckling — the Mexican form of booing and jeering — began sweeping through the stands of the Plaza Monumental. I sat quietly amid the noise and tried without success to block out the sounds, the sights and the smells. I was already in the throes of suffering a severe dose of culture shock. Now, watching blood mingling with sand, I simply felt like throwing up.

I hadn't long turned seventeen and I was one of the youngest members of Australia's Olympic team at the 1968 Mexico

Olympics. We had arrived six weeks before the Games began in an effort to acclimatise to the high altitude of Mexico City, and our team managers had decided that it was in our interests to take in some of the culture of the locals. So that meant we all had to attend an afternoon of bullfighting.

It hadn't sounded so bad to begin with. No doubt many of us had been brainwashed by the outstandingly effective public relations the "sport" had received over the years; it was almost a rite of passage for an aspiring Western writer to visit a bullfight in one of the Latin countries and then turn it into a romantic contest between man and savage beast. I came from Coburg High School, however, and my idea of romance was best found in a Mills & Boon novel. This wasn't art, it wasn't even noble. It was pure savagery, nothing more than a grotesque ritual that belonged back in ancient Crete and Rome where it began.

Of course, they disguised it well: the bugles announcing the arrival procession of the combatants; the matadors and *banderilleros* dressed in their satin finery with gold embroidery, stockinged feet and tightly fitting trousers. There was the anticipation with the opening of the *toril* door and the sudden appearance of the bull, little more than a genetically engineered specimen bred purposefully for aggression and a short, brutal life. But on this day, the bulls evened the score a little.

When the *toril* door opened the matador normally assumed a position directly in front of it, for the bull would usually come charging out and then lunge to the right or the left. But this time, as we watched in horror, the bull kept going straight ahead. The bullfighter had no chance as he was in the more daring position on his knees, playing to the crowd. The Bull leaned forward instinctively and speared one of its horns into the luckless matador. He was thrown high, then flopped to the earth like a rag doll. The bull was lured away as a group of *banderilleros* — the matador's assistants who first tire the animal before it is finally put out of its misery — grabbed the matador and hauled him away to safety. It was no use, however. He had lost too much blood and he died just a few hours later.

If I had not been feeling my normal self when we arrived in Mexico, then by the time I climbed aboard the team bus to return to the Olympic village I was desperate to go home. The Games hadn't even begun and I wanted out. I missed my mum and dad. I missed my brothers. My home in Coburg had suddenly become a mansion in my mind compared with some of the squalid shacks I had seen. I started to think that Dad might have been right all along. "You don't need to go to Mexico," he'd said. "You're too young. Why not wait for four years?"

I'd talked him into letting me go. Now, stunned by the poverty around me and the sheer difference in cultures, I had decided it was time for me to get out of there and go home.

I was almost an accidental tourist, anyway. My athletic career was hardly the all-consuming obsession it was for many others. While I loved running — there were times when I even liked training — it had always been just a pastime. Dad had always looked upon sport that way. Yes, you took it seriously when you participated, you did your best, and if you had been blessed with a genetic gift like I had you certainly did not waste it. But Dad was hardly the stereotypical overbearing father who stood on the sidelines urging me on to greater fame and fortune. Everything was always put in perspective. Before leaving for Mexico he had sat me down and given me what amounted to his view of life — I was not to accept anything for free. Nothing in life came without a hidden price tag. I was an amateur and there was something noble about being one, even in an age when the first hints of professionalism were beginning to surface. In Mexico one day the distance runner Ron Clarke tried to get me interested in wearing adidas gear, but daddy's girl stood her ground. He might as well have offered me a glass of green water from a fetid pond in one of the slums on the outskirts of the city. Dad's word was the only one I trusted.

Before I left for Mexico, Dad had learned that I would be running on the first synthetic track ever laid for an Olympic Games. Somehow he managed to obtain a two-inch piece of the same material that I would be running on in Mexico City. From that tiny segment of track he was able to put his engineering skills to the test, designing a pair of spikes for me that were groundbreaking. Commercial spiked running shoes of the time would have simply become stuck in the synthetic track, but Dad invented a rounded bottom for each spike that had the opposite effect — they rebounded off the surface. Dad was well ahead of his time. If he had patented the design back then he could have made a fortune, particularly given the boom in sports footwear over the past thirty years.

My rise into the ranks of international athletics had happened quickly and caught me by surprise as much as everyone else. I had been dominating events in my junior years and it had become pretty clear that Mac and Irene Boyle had done more than make a little sweet music between themselves in the last months of 1950. Their genes had mingled to produce a natural runner. These days the scientists would say that I was born with fast-twitch fibres. These gave me a terrific burst of power over short distances and by the time I hit my teenage years I was regularly beating women with far greater experience. But Dad was not one to take this gift and flog it for all it was worth. He wanted me to remain a junior as long I could. "What's the point of going up and competing against adults so soon?" he would say. "You've got the rest of your life to do that. Enjoy this while it lasts."

That was Dad. Deep down I don't really think he was looking forward to watching me grow up and become a woman. At the national titles in Adelaide in 1968 I was sixteen and competed as a junior; in those days senior and junior events were intermingled and staged as one giant competition. A great many senior officials, however, were against the idea. They thought it was time I graduated to senior ranks and came up against some real competition. So we struck a compromise that no-one seemed happy with. I would compete at both levels. I ran the 100-metres final as a junior and won it easily. Just a few minutes later I was required for the final of the women's 200 metres. By then my legs felt like lead weights and the track suddenly took on the characteristics of quicksand. But I still managed to finish fourth. I had already compiled several qualifying times for the Olympics and had beaten Commonwealth gold medallist Pam Kilborn over 100 metres at Royal Park in January. At the age of sixteen I became the youngest athlete in the Australian track and field Olympic team ever.

But Dad wasn't sure if I should go. There were a few nights spent sitting around the kitchen table debating the merits of the trip. There was no question that Mum and Dad could be there to see me, they simply didn't have enough money to make the journey. Eventually, Dad came around to the idea. But he was dead against any change in my training methods. Up until the time I boarded the plane for Mexico I had done nothing more than three 45-minute sessions a week over a three-month period. I was, in fact, the laughing stock of the Australian team. No-one could really believe that someone had made the team — an Olympic team for God's sake! — with next to no training.

After school I would catch a tram down Sydney Road in Brunswick. It would rattle its way down one of the loudest and most congested streets in Melbourne. By then new stores were beginning to appear. These shops had strange languages painted on their windows and out of their doorways swirled exotic odours that were unrecognisable to a teenage Australian nose that had only ever known the nightly fare of chops and three veg. A few further stops down and I would get off and amble over to Royal Park where Dad would be waiting on the side of the cinder track, having knocked off work in a hurry to get to his most important date of the day.

They were never overly strenuous sessions. I would jog two laps, then do two 100-metre sprints, two 200-metre sprints and two 300-metre efforts. And that was it. We would go home in the darkness of the Melbourne winter and head straight for the kitchen and try to swallow a plateful of hardened peas and dried-out meat — in those days Mum left our meals on the plate above a simmering pot of water. At least it kept the meal warm.

Some of my earlier training had been performed on a grass oval near our house, and the switch to a harder cinder surface saw me quickly develop shin splints. Even given that, my training regime was remarkably low-key. "You can either run or you can't," I told a reporter who came around to interview me one morning. "I haven't done any training ... Occasionally I take the dogs for a run, but officials say I'm too young to do much because my muscles aren't properly formed." Already I was laying the groundwork for what was to come. Because I was a nervous and shy teenage girl, I tended to overcompensate by sometimes sounding a bit too arrogant and confident. It was a trait I was to keep throughout my career. Over the years many of my team-mates and opponents came to see me as an abrupt and, I guess, selfish athlete. Not many of them understood that it was my method of coping with my insecurities. After all, I hadn't long turned seventeen when our flight took off for the long journey to Mexico. I had never been overseas before and I was still an incredibly naive teenager. There was a social revolution going on around me — boys my age were rebelling by growing their hair long, girls I knew spent all Monday at school discussing the dances they had attended at the local town hall and how far they had gone with their boyfriends — and I had barely noticed it. The papers described me in the quaint terminology of the time as "a vivacious blond schoolgirl". I don't know about the vivacious bit now, but they had the schoolgirl bit right.

I was innocent in every sense of the word. Part of me was thrilled by the prospect of going to Mexico, even though I had little idea just how big and important the Olympic Games were. But another side of me was terrified. For one thing, I soon discovered I would require several needles to protect me against myriad illnesses the team doctors believed we might fall prey to. But even more, I suspected that a journey like that would change me and the safe little world in which I lived.

How right I was.

BACK THEN almost the entire team travelled together, something that never happens now because many athletes are already in the northern hemisphere competing and preparing in their summer season. It was a long plane journey and I spent quite a few hours sleeping on the floor in the aisle between seats in order to get comfortable — that could never happen these days. As the time of departure neared I had begun having second thoughts, particularly when I was confronted with the list of injections I would need. It's fair to say that needles are not among my favourite objects. Even the smallest ones tend to look extremely large when they come near me. Sitting in the doctor's surgery one afternoon waiting to receive my shots I noticed a series of dirty marks all at one height running along one wall. Surely, I thought, the marks had been left by people struggling to escape while the doctor was giving them their injections.

I also had to endure an entire day's series of tests and examinations, the worst of which was a "sex test" to confirm that, yes, every female in the Australian team was in fact a female. Our fingers were pricked to obtain a blood sample, then the insides of our mouths were swabbed for a specimen of saliva. But after that came the "visual test".

"Drop your pants, love," was the request we encountered, an Australian phrase being echoed at the time in drive-in cinemas around the country. It was a humiliating experience for anyone, let alone a shy kid from Coburg. I was in a group with two swimmers, Sue McKenzie and Sue Eddy. For some reason Sue Eddy, who was only fourteen, had disappeared when it came time for the final unveiling, and McKenzie and I were dispatched to find her. "Sorry Sue," we told her when we located her. "You've failed the sex test."

The look on her face suggested our joke had backfired. It didn't take long for her to burst out laughing as well, however.

Mexico had seemed like a great adventure. But at one stage it seemed none of us would get there. In the weeks leading up to the Games, Mexican students protested in the streets of their biggest city, criticising their government for spending millions of dollars on the Olympics when so many of their nation's people struggled in appalling poverty. Just ten days before the opening ceremony, the demonstrations ended tragically when more than 300 protestors were killed and another 1000 injured when troops opened fire on them. The curse of the modern Olympics had arrived. Months earlier, fifty nations had threatened to pull out of the Games if the International Olympic Committee reinstated South Africa to the Olympic fold. The IOC ended up backing down and decided that South Africa would remain out of the Games until the system of apartheid was renounced.

But politics was hardly at the forefront of a seventeen-year-old's mind. Not long after arriving in Mexico I discovered a ranch behind the athletes village that housed Andalusian horses. I naturally spent as much time as I could down there, watching them go through their paces. And the Mexicans were certainly friendly.

They had lined the streets on our journey from the airport to the village, waving and cheering our arrival. There seemed to be musicians and dancers with castanets around every corner. But the bullfights, the squalor of the slums and the sheer strangeness of being in another part of the world soon had me knocking on the door of Julius "Judy" Patching, the general manager of the Australian team. Patching was a workmate of Dad's at the Melbourne City Council and I probably felt confident he would understand my dilemma. Mac's girl had been to the Olympics. I had spent a fortnight in Mexico, I explained. I had learned a great deal. And now I would like to go home, thank you very much.

I'm sure I was the first athlete in Australian history to want to get out of participating in the Games. I was sharing a room with another seventeen-year-old girl, Maureen Caird, and while we got along well, we had little in common. Maureen was a hell of a lot wiser in the ways of the world. She would go on to win a surprise gold medal in the 80-metres hurdles — a surprise not only because she wasn't the favourite, but because of all the partying and socialising she did in the lead-up to her race. All I wanted to do was stay in our room and look at the view outside the window. I was paranoid about going out; we had been warned that drinking the local water might lead to a severe dose of Montezuma's Revenge. We were only to drink the bottled water provided for us in our rooms, but even then several of the team came down with severe bouts of diarrhoea.

Patching gave me a sympathetic hearing, probably because he was completely dumbfounded as to why an athlete would want to leave the Games before they had really begun. He passed me on to the team's surgeon, Howard Toyne, who sat me down, listened to my fears and put up with my tears, and then told me I should give it a few more days.

As it turned out I was in for a greater shock than the cultural one

I had first experienced. The team's athletics coach, Ray Weinberg, decreed we would all train twice a day in an effort to better acclimatise to the altitude. I thought it was an enormous workload, but it soon paled into insignificance compared with the duties Weinberg had to shoulder when the athletics sectional manager, Jim Howlin, suddenly died of a stroke. Howlin's body was kept in Mexico, and returned to Australia at the end of the Games. Weinberg, meanwhile, took on his responsibilities.

As Howard Toyne had probably suspected, the combination of intense training (for me, at least) and a busy schedule soon saw my homesickness become manageable. And once the Games actually began, I had something to focus on. That ability to eliminate all other distractions and concentrate on the job at hand would become my strength over the years.

SOME CALL it the vomitorium, others have even less complimentary names for it. Underneath the stadium there is a room where the competitors in a race gather before being led on to the track for their event. No matter what the weather is like outside, the atmosphere in this room is always the same — thick with tension, nervousness and even fear. By the time you reach this room your coach or manager has already said good luck and left you. Suddenly, you are on your own. The last few minutes tend to be quiet. You can hear the muffled applause and sighs of the crowd outside, while inside you begin the task of concentrating on your event.

Some athletes use this time to try to intimidate their opponents. I've seen it done, from a constant stare to physical intimidation by brushing against a competitor, or standing toe to toe. I could rarely be bothered with that sort of thing, and, as I grew older and more experienced, if my opponents over the years ever tried it then I'm afraid I was concentrating too hard on what I had to do to really notice.

Mexico was my first real taste of international competition. There was little pressure or even expectation on my shoulders. I was, after all, the youngest member of the track team. I had come from nowhere and clearly had done little training. I was not in Mexico because people expected me to win a medal. Instead, it was an opportunity to "blood" me. I could learn what an Olympics was all about and the experience would put me in good stead for the years to come.

The heats of the 100 metres came first and I was stunned when I entered the arena. The sheer noise was incredible. The stadium probably only contained 40 000 people, but the Mexicans are notoriously passionate and strongly and loudly let you know just how they feel. But even then, as I squatted on the blocks for my first heat, I managed to put the noise to one side and quickly settled into my stride.

It was a surprise that I even managed to win my way through to the final. Two Americans — Wyomia Tyus and Barbara Ferrell — were clear favourites. Tyus was one of those brilliant sprinters with a wonderful action who had already won gold in the event in 1964 in Tokyo. But clearly my sudden rise to prominence was worrying her. As we stood in our lanes — I was in lane two, with Tyus next to me in three — she stepped right in front of me and began doing what, to me, was a bizarre hip-swivelling dance. It went on for some time and I couldn't work out if she was warming up, or trying to dislodge something that was caught in her pants. Had I been a little older and wiser I'm sure I would have caught on. Tyus was simply trying to distract me. You become a little territorial about your lane when you are running, but in 1968 I had no idea that part of the game involved intimidation. Completely guileless, I took my position on the blocks and waited for the starter's orders.

The 100 metres is a desperate lunge for the finish line. You start down low on the blocks and then gradually, over a distance of about 25 metres, begin to straighten up. But the main thing is not to think about what you are doing; instinct should take over from analysis. Whenever I squatted on the blocks and placed my fingertips behind the white starting line, I attempted to clear my mind of every extraneous thought. Nothing was to distract me. When the starter called "SET!" and your bum hit the air in what is not one of the most natural positions in the world, your mind was a clean slate. You waited for the starter's gun and tried to anticipate it. But you couldn't afford to think about it, or the sprint ahead. Analysis is disastrous in a short race. Years of training should have programmed your body to take over.

That's why I don't recall much about that 100-metres final, except my final lunge at the line. I could tell Tyus had won it, but I wasn't sure if I had managed to finish third. There had been no time for me to do the famous Boyle head-swivel and look over my shoulder. That was a trait that perplexed many coaches and officials over the years, but I had started doing it at a young age and had never seen any need to stop it. It didn't matter to Dad, either. But it used to infuriate a lot of people. They thought it was either a sign of arrogance or a significant flaw in my technique. I never really cared. It had hardly cost me a race and I liked to know where I stood in the field.

As I tried to regain my breath a race official grabbed me and told me I had won the bronze. I was elated. I was escorted almost immediately from the track and into a waiting area below the stand. I had just equalled the old world record of 11.1 seconds, and Tyus had shaved a tenth of a second off it. Barbara Ferrell had won silver with the same time as me, while on the outside Poland's Irena Szewinska, the world-record holder in the 200 metres, had stormed home in the same time as well. The viewing judges had decided I had just beaten Szewinska home.

For the next twenty minutes I couldn't stop trembling as I waited for the medal ceremony. I had actually won a medal in my first event at an Olympic Games! People were congratulating me. And then I noticed something. Tyus, Ferrell and Irena Szewinska were being lined up for the medal ceremony. I asked a Mexican official nearby what was going on. An examination of the photo finish had shown that Szewinska had narrowly edged me out of a medal place, he said. I was shocked and demanded to know why I hadn't been told this earlier. He shrugged and muttered something about it not being his responsibility. Now there was a phrase I would encounter over the years. It didn't take me long to work out that while they came from countries all over the world, athletics officials all belonged to the same species. Deep down, I figured, they resented athletes. Power, truly, was their aphrodisiac. Even at the end of my career my view had hardly softened. I had seen too many amateurish and sloppy athletics officials embark on power trips designed to exert authority over athletes and make themselves feel a little better.

Outside a torrential downpour was taking place. These were frequent during the Games. At times the athletes village was flooded and we had problems finding a way to get to the food halls. But I was also making a fair contribution to the rising water levels. My tear ducts must be among the most overworked parts of my body. Ray Weinberg gave me a consoling hug. But by the time I went to sleep that night wishing I could see my family — Dad, surely, would have fixed things up and put that little Mexican official back in his place — my disappointment had turned to anger. There was no way now that I would go home without a medal.

THE HEATS of the 200 metres — my favourite event — began the next day, and with my added motivation I suddenly felt older and a lot wiser. I worked my way through to the final by winning my semi-final and beating Tyus and Szewinska. Now, I was no longer thinking about a minor placing. I was there to win gold.

In the first half of the final it looked like I was a chance to do just that. I had gone into the 200 with a simple tactic: blast out of the blocks, burn off the opposition and then hang on until the line. By the time we came out of the curve and straightened up, I knew I had the Americans beaten. But Szewinska was simply too powerful, mowing me down and going on to win in a new world record time. Once again, I equalled the previous world record to win silver, and another Australian, Jenny Lamy, finished third to capture the bronze.

Now there was no dispute. I was a clear silver medallist. That night I put a call through to home, ever mindful of the cost. Dad had given me $400 to take with me to the Games — quite a sum back in those days — and because I had grown up learning to be careful with money, I had barely spent any of it. My only disappointment was that at the other end of the crackling line Dad already knew the result. I hadn't quite realised that my race would be broadcast live on radio back home, evidence yet again as to how naive I was when it came to understanding the importance of the Olympics.

It had taken me 22.7 seconds to run the 200-metres final, a minute amount of time in the span of a person's lifetime. Yet those 22 seconds would have a profound effect on my life. It was too early for Dad to tell over that static-filled line, but I was already changing. His little girl was growing up. I was still homesick. I was still a true innocent abroad. But my experiences in Mexico had triggered a strain of independence within me that previously I had not experienced. And there were all those incredible images I retained. I had been witness to one of the most remarkable Olympics in modern history. These Games had seen the Black Power movement reach its height when the two Americans, Tommie Smith and John Carlos, controversially raised their arms and saluted their flag with fists clenched in black gloves. I was also there on the night the American Bob Beamon recorded the greatest leap in history when he soared 29 feet, 2½ inches [8.90 metres] to shatter the world long jump record. The rarified air of Mexico City might have had a huge impact on runners — Australia's Ron Clarke collapsed and almost died at the end of the 10 000 metres and needed 60 litres of oxygen just to regain consciousness. But it certainly helped the jumpers. In the triple jump, the world record was broken nine times before the event was won by Russia's Viktor Saneev.

By the time I arrived home everything had changed. People recognised me everywhere I went. Kids at school who had thought I was weird and a bit of a loner now hovered near me. The house in Sutherland Street seemed smaller and more claustrophobic than ever. But most of all, Dad's word was no longer law. I had undergone a psychological growth spurt while I was away. I had been forced to look after myself. When I cried myself to sleep some nights there had been no-one else to tell me it would all get better in the morning. So I had grown up and discovered that I could think for myself, and do things for myself.

The signs were clear. A great split in the Boyle clan was looming.

11

Running away

DID I MENTION THAT I'VE NEVER BEEN THAT GOOD WHEN IT COMES TO history? Perhaps it has something to do with the fact that so much of my early running career was spent surrounded by fossils. Of course back then they were known by a different name: the Victorian Women's Amateur Athletics Association. If ever there was an organisation filled with old, dust-encrusted ways it was the VWAAA. Their views about how things should be done were straight from another time and place. I had been back barely a year from Mexico when I had my first significant clash with them. I was reprimanded one December afternoon in 1969 for not "extending" myself in a 400-metre race. I had finished second last, but I had easily beaten my opponent who came from University High School, the club Coburg was competing against.

It was a "points" contests in which my club (Coburg) won points if I defeated my opponent in the race. It didn't matter where I finished in the field, and it didn't bother me, either. I was a member of a club, I was abiding by the rules, I was nursing sore tendons in my heel and ankle and I intensely disliked running the 400-metres event, anyway. As a sprinter, I found its two bends taxing, and my training so far had not prepared me for the stamina that was required over the distance. Had it not been for the fact that I was representing my club and they needed the points I would never have run it.

But none of this mattered, of course. I was rebuked after the race by a VWAAA official for running slowly and looking over my shoulder a couple of times to see where my opponent was. Suddenly, the whole business became big news. Dad leaped to my defence, telling the press: "Raelene is going to stick to the rules. The officials will have to back up or keep quiet. As for looking over her shoulder in a race, Raelene has always been a devil for doing this, but she means no harm. She sincerely doesn't want to break the hearts of the kids behind her, and deliberately tries not to win most of her races by a street."

It was true, too. I could easily win all the races I entered, but I always held back. My shyness meant that I hated being the centre of attention, and I detested people who simply showed off against weaker opposition. "I have no ambition to thrash people," I told one interviewer. "If I ran flat out all the time the girls behind me might want to give up. I wouldn't like that. Often I felt like giving up when I was being thrashed earlier in my career. I have no desire to humiliate people."

My biggest problem was that I had little competition, and the cost of going to the United States or England for a season was simply prohibitive. Fortunately, the one thing that saved me was the press. A controversial story was always a good story to them and I seemed to have the ability to create a stir. Judy Joy Davies, a former Olympian, was one who supported me. Writing in the *Sun*, Davies suggested: "Well-meaning women athletic officials would be wise to realise that Raelene is one of the greatest sprinters in the world ... the great American athlete Jesse Owens, who won three gold medals at the 1936 Berlin Olympic Games, saw Raelene competing in the Mexico City Games. He said: 'I have not seen a girl so beautifully balanced.'"

But such defences seemed to make things worse. I was only eighteen but already those officials had decided I was rebellious and difficult to handle. A couple of weeks later there was another incident, this time when I was threatened by the male-dominated Victorian Amateur Athletics Association. At a meeting at Olympic Park I was warned I would be disqualified if I grabbed the finishing tape with my hands as I crossed the line. There was no such rule, of course. But clearly these "well-meaning" male athletics officials had decided to bring me back to size a little. I explained that the reason I used my hands at the finishing line was because they were using the wrong sort of wool — sometimes it failed to break as I crossed the line and I was left with burn marks on my throat and across my upper arms. As if to prove my point, one of the girls competing in the next race had to be treated for throat burn after finishing in first place. So when it came time for my next event I made sure to defiantly grab the tape with both hands. I looked around. There was no protest. That was how it usually went. Few of them had the heart to follow through on their threats, but they still managed to waste everyone's time with their pedantic interfering.

I knew that many of these officials were volunteers with the sport's interests at heart. And don't get me wrong. I might have waged wars with several of them over the years, but there were just as many athletics officials I admired and deeply respected. Quite a few of them ended up becoming tremendous friends and I still catch up with several of them for a drink and a trip down memory lane.

But sadly, there were always some officials who allowed power to go to their heads. They ruled with an iron fist. They were inflexible. And they loved to squash and bring back to earth anyone who had enjoyed success.

IT'S AMAZING when I look back on those times how seriously some people took athletics, including me. I hardly lived and breathed the sport, but after Mexico it became pretty clear that running was my destiny for the next few years. I would say goodbye to Coburg High with my Leaving Certificate not long after, and apart from a few odd jobs — I worked part-time in a florist's store, cleaning up and watering the plants — I was virtually a full-time athlete in a sport that was still not professional. My training had naturally expanded and I was experimenting with new techniques and methods.

My private life was also far different to the one I had left behind when I went to Mexico. I was still living at home, but I was far more social and outgoing. There was no shortage of invitations to attend a wide variety of functions, and I was at an age when there was no way I wanted to attend them with Dad as my date.

One of my training partners at Royal Park was Robert King. We had struck up a shy friendship at first but by the end of 1970 we had been going out for eighteen months. Robert was a handsome blond guy with a moustache (facial hair was very fashionable back then). He was studying geology at university and I was always out at dances or on dates with him. It worried Dad. I don't know if he saw Robert as competition but he was certainly not happy that I was spending a lot of time with him. I didn't understand then that every father finds it difficult to let go of his daughter. Dad and I had started arguing a little — I was questioning his views on many things and also, having depended on and trusted his advice for so long, I wanted to stamp my own imprint on the world. It was as though it all came tumbling out at once. Those things that anchor every relationship between child and parents — trust, authority and independence — were at odds with one another.

Still, Mum and Dad remained my fiercest supporters. And in the middle of 1970 I was prepared to give up even the opportunity of a gold medal for them.

Grandpa Wilkinson — Mum's father — had died in Perth and Mum had gone across for the funeral. But while she was there she fell sick with a virulent case of meningitis. She was rushed to hospital and at one stage it seemed she was close to death. This all happened in the lead-up to the Commonwealth Games in Edinburgh, Scotland. The Commonwealth Games were still a big deal back then as some of the best athletes in the world represented countries in the old British Empire. The standards at the Games were far higher than they are these days, too often seeming little more than a competition between Australia and Canada.

I was favourite to win gold in both the 100 metres and 200 metres, but with Mum desperately sick I had no intention of travelling to the other side of the world. Dad, however, put his foot down. "You're going and that's it," he told me. "Your mother would kill me if I didn't make you go."

Fortunately Mum began turning the corner, although it would take her months to fully recover. I went off to Edinburgh and did what was expected. I won both events, and then anchored the 4x100 metre relay team to another gold.

With Mum on the mend and my confidence high I enjoyed the Games immensely. I joined in the pranks that were constantly being staged in the Games village, and when it was over joined a couple of team members on a quick two-day trip to Amsterdam to take in the sights. I had been offered the opportunity to race in Ireland and Trinidad after Edinburgh, but I was tired and, to be honest, the notion of seeing a European city was far more enticing.

But I might have been better off competing. I thought I was a young woman wise to the ways of the world, a mature girl who had long shrugged off her suburban mentality and shyness. But when we arrived in Amsterdam I was in shock. The Free Love movement was beginning to take off around the world and Amsterdam had quickly taken to it. A stroll through the red-light district left me confused and almost sickened — the sex was so blatant and so coarsely on offer that it seemed little more than a rank meat market. Two years had passed since the Mexico Olympics and I was an innocent abroad no longer. But those forty-eight hours in Amsterdam gave me another severe dose of culture shock. I couldn't wait to get home. Once again Sutherland Street and our family life seemed the most normal thing in the world.

IN APRIL 1971, that normal world of mine began to fall apart. Once again, athletics officials played a significant part in it by providing the spark that would eventually lead to me traumatically leaving home and ending my relationship with my father.

A month before, I had gone to Sydney for the Australian women's track and field championships. There, waiting for me, was Mrs Jean Gell. Think of a stern schoolmistress in a Hollywood movie with her hair in a too-tight bun that has squeezed all the humour and mischief out of her. That's how I saw Mrs Gell. To me she became the embodiment of every haughty athletics official I had the misfortune of meeting during my career. Jean was what you might call a member of the old school — stuck somewhere in the late 1800s to be exact. She was not the sort of woman who should have been appointed to manage a group of young women who were beginning to make decisions about their lives in one of the most turbulent periods of the century. I had hardly been politicised by the various movements going on at the time; women's liberation was beginning to flourish and while I admired the cause, I wasn't out in the streets burning my bra. I knew little about the anti-Vietnam movement and, when it came down to it, my inherent conservatism and belief in authority figures (except those in athletics) would have seen me support the decisions of the government of the day. Painful as it now sounds, I was not what you would call a deep thinker back then. I was a runner. I competed in races. The rest of my life was reserved for having a good time.

There were several incidents that rankled Jean. I popped out to have a haircut one day without permission. But the thing that seemed to annoy her most was my fashion sense. I had a pair of flared jeans with frayed ends that were among my proudest possessions. Around the hotel, I liked wearing them without any shoes — now that was the height of fashion. So Jean reported me (along with four others for various other misdemeanours) to the VWAAA for a series of heinous crimes. By then I had decided there was nothing I could do to placate the woman so I might as well have it out with her. When I discovered that she was encouraging team members to attend a meeting in the hotel at which adidas would be plugging their latest styles of shoes, I told her that she was breaking the amateur rules and was placing the amateur status of some of the girls under threat. By then I was wearing Puma shoes and I found it an affront that a particular brand of footwear should be shoved so blatantly under people's noses. I certainly wasn't going to be singing the praises of adidas, but I thought that if such a meeting was held, all the shoe representatives should be present.

My troubles didn't end there. At Easter I had been invited to the Victorian country town of Horsham to compete in the Wimmera championships. It wasn't high on my list of priorities at the time but I decided I should honour the invitation and go.

A group of my athletic friends came with me. Straightaway I was at odds with the organisers, declining their invitation to stay at a local hotel. My friends had pitched a tent at the local caravan park and I was hardly interested in listening to them describe me as a snob for the rest of the weekend. So I elected to stay with them. Then I arrived at the Horsham football ground to discover it was little more than a cow paddock. I won my races but my times were closer to those you might find recorded at an over-70s event. There was no way I was going to risk injury at such a venue. Looming on the horizon was the possibility of racing in America in a few months during the northern summer, and because of a neverending series of Achilles injuries I was always conscious of my fitness.

While my times were ordinary, what really riled the Horsham organisers was the 400-metres race. Three of us agreed before the event that we would skip the first 100 metres, jog the back straight, then run backwards over the third 100-metre segment before sprinting home. There were quite a few in the crowd who found the sight of this hilarious, including all my friends. But the Horsham people were not amused. Smart-arse city girl, they thought. Well, they would show me. They sent in a report to the VWAAA as well.

And so I was summoned to a hearing that you would have thought was a war crimes trial. It was a big media event for the time. The back page of one of the Melbourne newspapers splashed with the news about Horsham and Sydney: "MORE CHARGES ... she went barefoot, she looked untidy..." Reporters were loitering out the front of our home and the phone never seemed to stop ringing. I hated it. I loathed the intrusions into my privacy, but it also drove me crazy that my life was basically put on hold while I had to answer frivolous charges that hurt my reputation.

Each girl was summoned into a room and grilled separately. We all ended up leaving in tears, my eyes were ringed red as I walked out with Mum. She was ropeable as well. In the end we received nothing more than raps on the knuckles — reprimands and, in my case, a three-month suspension that meant nothing at that time of the year. But it did cost me the opportunity of going to the US for a series of races. And it also left hanging over me the prospect that another "conviction" could lead to a lifetime ban. It was absurd.

LOVE IN A TIME OF WAR: My mum, Irene Joy Wilkinson, was a parachute packer in WWII when she caught the eye of the bloke on the right.

MY DAD: Gilbert MacDonald Boyle turned me into an athlete. But we fell out in the years before he died. Mum blamed me for his death.

GREEN THUMB: I took on the responsibility of caring for the garden in Coburg at an early age. Well, who else was going to do it?

CHRISTMAS MIRACLE: Ron, Rick and the old bloke with the beard marvel at Mum's victory in making me wear a dress.

CROSS MY HEART: The class of '57 at Bell Street Public School. Mum used to mark us in photographs so Grandma in Perth could recognise us.

THE WHEEL THING: We took cycling seriously in the Boyle house (Ron, middle, became an Olympic cyclist).

STEPPING OUT: Dad was passionate about running technique. Here I'm working it with pro runner Steve Ward at Coburg football ground.

WINNERS ARE GRINNERS: Xmas, 1967, and a 16-year-old has just beaten Olympic medallist Pam Kilborn over 100 metres at Chelsea in Victoria.

THE SPEED SISTERHOOD: Jenny Lamy and I helped usher in a new era for Australian female sprinters.

MEXICAN FACE-OFF, 1968: The 200-metres Olympic medallists. (LEFT TO RIGHT) Jenny Lamy (bronze), me (silver) and Poland's Irena Szewinska (gold).

SCHOOL DAZE: Now there's a first — I'm smiling in the classroom. Mexico memories took a long time to fade.

ON YOUR MARK: Preparing for competition at Royal Park's grass track. I'm sure running on grass extended my career.

THE MINI ME: Smiling as I model the Pacific Conference Games uniform in 1969.

YOU LOOKIN' AT ME? Dad said athletics should be fun. But some days training was very serious.

THE FAST LANE: One of our relay teams preparing for an overseas meet. (LEFT TO RIGHT) Jenny Lamy, Marion Hoffman, Pam Kilborn and me.

TALES OF THE TAPE:

TOP RIGHT: Trying to break the world 100 yards in 1970.

TOP LEFT: The official photo showing places in the 100-metres final at the 1970 Commonwealth Games in Edinburgh. I won gold.

BELOW LEFT: Alice Ammun, silver; Me, gold; Marion Hoffman, bronze.

BELOW RIGHT: My habit of "handling" the finishing tape resulted in many confrontations with officialdom. So what else is new?

ANSWERING THE CALL: Melbourne television personality Mike Williamson and me during a telethon to raise funds for the 1972 Australian Munich Olympics team.

PRE-GAMES FEAST: Beaumaris school children wish me well for Munich.

POWER AND GLORY: Renate Stecher (FAR LEFT) crosses the line in the 100 metres final in Munich to win gold, despite my desperate lunge (FAR RIGHT).

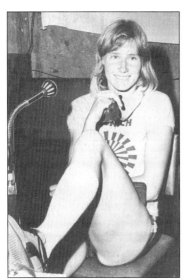

SECOND BEST: I'd gone to Munich with high hopes of winning gold. But Stecher's strength left me with silver in both the 100-metre and 200-metre finals.

MORE AWARDS: I've just won the Caltex Sports Star of the Year Award for 1972. Little do I know that I've just won my last Olympic medal.

The whole event was surreal and it would have been hilarious had it not been for the fact that these officials were deadly serious. They would bring Raelene Boyle back to size. And they would let me know just who was the boss.

It was at this time that Dad thought it would be best for me if I moved out for a few days and effectively went into hiding. I could continue training without people asking me questions and whispering behind my back. And that was how I moved in with Aunty Dot, and how the bonds between Dad and me were finally broken.

DOT WALKE was called Aunty Dot by everyone. She was an athletics coach and former state hurdles champion who lived in Hampton, a bayside Melbourne suburb, with her husband and three daughters. The plan was for me to move there for a few days, allow the storm to blow over and then go back home.

But the moment I walked in the door at Aunty Dot's I felt like I was truly home. The house was clean and comfortable and its front and back yards were neat and tidy. There was no paint flaking from old weatherboards, no clock innards spread all over the place. The house was not far from the beach and it sat in a quiet, leafy suburb that hardly resembled the concrete and bitumen jungle of Coburg. Dot and her husband, Jack, had a pleasant home that rarely had the odour of tobacco wafting through it. And I was more comfortable with Dot than my own parents; I could have discussions with her that I could not have dreamed of having with Mum and Dad.

She also started coaching me. While there was not that much difference between her methods and Dad's, that change also helped cement the notion that I wanted to stay there in Hampton.

The calls began a week or two later. Dad would be on the phone wanting to know when I was coming home. Soon, I would say. Just a few more days.

But the weeks soon became a month. I didn't want to go. Dot's three daughters felt like sisters to me and at a stage in my life when I desperately wanted to show the world that I was an independent woman who could think for herself, moving back to Coburg filled me with dread. I would pop back home from time to time (by now I had my driving licence and had bought a small car to get myself around), but my stays were never pleasant. Dad, I'm sure, came to see Aunty Dot as a rival, not only for my affections but also as a coach. Mum, too, must have been feeling a little inadequate when she compared herself to Dot, who was such a dynamic and well-organised person. I never saw it that way — Mum's problems were all too evident by then and the fact that she still struggled through each day with her depression was testament itself to her courage.

But Mum and Dad began to believe that Dot was putting the idea in my head to stay with her. I'm sure they also came to think of me as a snob who felt it was beneath her to move back to her old suburb. It wasn't that, although I will always choose grass over concrete any day. It was just that the dynamics had all changed. I wanted to leave the nest.

So let's cut to the climax. The scene: the Boyle kitchen in Sutherland Street, Coburg, the site of so many debates over the years. Dad has started talking to me, squatting on his chair the way he always has. My father has never sat on a chair in his life — he always puts his foot down first on the seat and then lowers the rest of himself. It's similar to the way Indians and many Asians squat whenever a chair is not available. The rest of us have never really thought that much about it. It's just one of Dad's little idiosyncrasies and we've grown up with it.

He's lecturing me about why my home is in Coburg. The volume begins to increase. I'm starting to pace around the kitchen. Dad yells at me and then he's on his feet, pointing an accusing finger at me. This goes on for some minutes. Mum is up in the front room, weeping and trying to block out the noise. Now it's become a screaming match.

Dad can tell he's getting nowhere with me. So he pulls out his biggest weapon.

"Make a choice," he says. "Stay here or go there. But if you go there, take everything with you. You won't belong here anymore. We'll have nothing to do with you. Understand that?"

Given my stubbornness and my refusal to surrender my position — I can't see why I cannot share my time between the two households — I make my choice.

It is early evening. I grab as many things as I can squeeze into my little car, and hit the road for Hampton. There's no time for goodbyes, no sense that this is going to be forever. I'm a mess by the time I arrive, but Aunty Dot already knows what has happened. Dad has called her, presumably to tell her she is the reason his family has suffered such a devastating split.

The battle is finally over. But a simmering cold war will continue until my father's death.

12

Bloodied rings

In February 1972, Richard Nixon went to China in one of the most historic diplomatic and political journeys in modern history. With an American president on Chinese soil for the first time it seemed anything was possible. If West could finally meet East, then perhaps it was possible that all Cold Wars could finally come to an end.

But there was one set of hostilities where détente would not be possible. In those late summer days of early 1972, the battle between Mac Boyle and his twenty-year-old daughter was as intense as ever. We were like two guards from opposing nations patrolling the last border post. We saw each other at inter-club meets on Saturdays. But we could not acknowledge one another's presence. Too much history had passed between us for even the slightest nod.

There had been the odd conversation on the phone since my dramatic departure from Sutherland Street, but, sadly, they had always ended the same way. We were two stubborn creatures and neither would give ground. When Dad rang one afternoon and launched into one of his now regular tirades, telling me I would be removed from his will if I did not return, it had no effect on me. I lived simply, I didn't care much for money and inheritance had never been an issue with me. Besides, I would hardly have anticipated a windfall anyway. All his threats did was raise the temperature of hostilities and increase my determination not to yield. It had taken me a long time to assert my independence, probably longer than most young people. But now it was as though I had to make up for it and I was determined to prove I could stand on my own through sheer bloody-mindedness.

Some people have said to me since: "Surely, you still loved your dad. How could such an apparently small thing get so out of hand?" I have no answer for that. I wish I could go back in time and repair the damage that it inflicted on both of us. Yes, it was rash and I was far too obstinate. But by my early twenties I was also determined to make decisions for myself. As an athlete you become cocooned in many respects from the world around you. There are physiotherapists on hand to treat every muscle twinge or spasm, doctors to examine and heal the tears and strains and coaches to keep your mind focused. You become so focused on the job at hand that everything else assumes less importance. It's a world separated from reality. Standing up to Dad was my way of waving the flag of independence.

Because athletes were almost all part-time back then, practice was usually a late afternoon affair. The ritual became so ingrained in me, and so embedded in the inner workings of my body clock, that 5pm always signalled training time, no matter where I was in the world. Without Dad around, the ritual continued with Aunty Dot.

On Saturdays at inter-club meets I would arrive at the track with my bag and gear, see Dad preparing some of the athletes he was

Raelene

training and walk the other way. He would do the same. I'm sure most people weren't even aware of the enmity that existed between us. Dad had long been a familiar figure around the tracks in Melbourne. Tall and fairly thin, he had dark greying hair and always wore a long-sleeved white shirt to inter-club fixtures with the collar turned up. Under the fierce Australian sun his fair complexion was always prone to burning.

Mum was dragged into this dispute, too, and it was clear where she stood. She supported Dad and she never quite understood why I had to be so stubborn. I was my father's daughter, after all. Why couldn't I do what I was told? Mum was being the dutiful and loyal partner, I guess, and I couldn't really blame her for taking Dad's side. But because she had little sympathy for my position, I felt betrayed and began growing apart from her, too.

The numbers, actually, were running pretty strongly against me. Ron, too, felt that I had done the wrong thing and as time passed he and I became estranged. He couldn't understand just how stubborn I was and why I wanted to force an issue that had the potential to split the family.

In the end it was Rick who remained close to me in those days, and even he had strong reservations about my stance. But by then I had taken the decision not to bother trying to win people over to my argument. I had said my piece, everyone knew where I stood and that, as far as I was concerned, was that. Despite his concerns, Rick would come down with Tess, who was then his girlfriend, and visit me at Hampton. Sometimes we would go to the beach or the movies and it was always good to see him. I caught up with news on the home front, and I guess I allowed him to take news back with him that I was well and getting on with the only thing that commanded my attention. The Olympics in Munich were looming and I wanted to be in the best shape possible.

It was four years after Mexico and I fancied myself as a worldly-wise young woman. I had been around the world a couple of times and I was much stronger, physically and mentally. Deep down I regarded myself as an excellent chance to win gold. I had the ability to train "fast" rather than "hard", which meant I tended to practise with shorter bursts of high quality work, rather than masses of slogging track work.

I must have also been an extreme optimist. Back then I thought hard training and being blessed with a genetic gift to run quickly were all I would need to be successful.

THE BODY of an average adolescent girl produces about half a milligram of the hormone testosterone each day. But in the four years since the Mexico Olympics, doctors and coaches in East Germany had begun to master the complexities of using chemicals to boost the performance of their athletes. By 1972 many of the young girls in their charge were being given up to 35 milligrams of testosterone every day. Some were swimmers, others were runners. The males weren't left out of it, either. To have been blessed with any sporting gift in East Germany at the time meant that you became part of one of the most depraved and cynical exercises of the twentieth century. An entire nation had embarked on a bid to achieve international respectability by cheating in sport.

I knew drugs were rife in athletics. There had been plenty of speculation in Mexico about who was and wasn't using substances to improve their performances, but at the time I had no understanding of the problem, and probably didn't even realise the importance of what my fellow athletes were talking about. But by the time we arrived in Munich for the 1972 Games I had been around long enough to know that some athletes had done more than just invest in one of those $9.99 Charles Atlas improve-your-strength programs advertised on the back pages of comics.

I had travelled a little and seen a lot. It was common for runners and swimmers to sit around a hotel lobby or in a room and openly discuss what form of "medication" they were taking. "Are you using those blue pills?" someone would ask. Another would nod and mention how many they were ingesting a day. Someone else would offer a view that "red" tablets were better. These conversations usually took place among international athletes, although I was in no doubt that some Australian competitors had also picked up on the trend and were determined not to be left behind.

Even then the thought of taking drugs to boost my performance left me feeling cold and empty. Dad's insistence that athletics should be pure, that competition should be as even as possible, sounds quaint now, a throwback to a vastly different era. Such a notion was even unfashionable by the start of the 1970s, but it was still ingrained in my psyche. A new era had arrived and with it came a new credo: win at all costs. But it was the East Germans who took ambition to absurd lengths.

We all had our suspicions. By the start of the 1970s East German athletes, and those from several other Iron Curtain countries, had begun dominating their sports. What amazed most of us was their physical appearance, particularly the women. Many of them boasted broad shoulders and incredibly muscular thighs and calves. Those muscles were popping up in all the right places to provide power and strength. What we couldn't quite see then were the disturbing side effects which many of them were already suffering.

It wasn't until 1991, in a military hospital located on the fringes of the former East Berlin, that investigators discovered a ten-volume archive of horrific detail that finally laid bare just how far the East Germans had been prepared to go to achieve international sporting glory. Every athlete's name, from the mid 1960s to the day when the Berlin Wall came tumbling down in

1989, was recorded and next to them were listed the amounts of steroids given to them over a period of time. These files, culled from the archives of the Stasi, the East German secret police, provided the basis of a series of trials at the end of the 1990s in which convictions were handed down against a number of former East German sports coaches and doctors.

I feel sick even now when I read about what many of those athletes were forced to endure, and still suffer. Take, as just one example, the experience of swimmer Christiane Knacke-Sommer. At the age of twelve she was taken from her small town and her family to East Berlin to begin training with the SC Dynamo swimming club, then regarded as one of the finest swimming teams in the world. Now we know why. After two years of intensive training she was put on a program of injections and pills that within weeks saw her arms and shoulders broaden rapidly. But then severe acne began breaking out on her face and shoulders and her pubic hair began to grow up and spread out over her stomach.

As her voice deepened, her sex drive also leapt alarmingly. This was not uncommon — testosterone is a male sex hormone that has a significant effect on the libido. There were times when those overseeing the drug taking feared for the sanity of the athletes. Their sex drives were, quite literally, so powerful they threatened to send them crazy. When it became too much the authorities would truck in a platoon of soldiers to have sex with the girls to try to keep them sated. I would imagine that the East German army had no problem when it came to recruiting in those days.

Knacke-Sommer went on to win a bronze medal in 1980 at the Moscow Olympics. Two fellow East German swimmers, Caren Metschuk and Andrea Pollock, won the gold and the silver. In the same event Australia's Lisa Curry finished fifth. Take out the drug-enhanced performances and Lisa should definitely have finished with a bronze or a silver.

Lisa was one of many athletes denied an Olympic medal because of the East German program. But the cost to those who benefited from the drugs was enormous.

In a court case in 1998 Knacke-Sommer told the judge that her coaches and trainers "destroyed my body and my mind". Asked by the prosecutor if she had taken the drugs voluntarily, she replied: "I was fifteen years old when the pills started ... the training motto at the pool was 'You eat the pills, or you die.' It was forbidden to refuse."

In the years since, an alarming number of athletes from the former East Germany have suffered mysterious tumours and cancers. Many of their children have been born with defects, including an abnormally high rate of club feet and blindness, which doctors have linked to excessive amounts of testosterone. Other athletes discovered they were sterile, and in recent years many have died, or are dying, from diseases like pancreatic cancer. To think that the political leaders of a nation believed that by doing this they could attain international acclaim — and in doing so tell the world why communism was better than democracy — is something I have difficulty coming to terms with. Later on, it would be one of the reasons my opinion of international sport began to sour. It's an issue I'll explore in the next chapters. But back in 1972, in those first few days in the athletes' village in Munich, I still believed that fairness would ultimately triumph.

I told you I was naive, didn't I?

MUNICH WAS a remarkably clean, almost sterile city when we arrived. Those traditional German traits of orderliness and organisation were fully apparent as soon as we unpacked our bags and began checking out the village. Every official diligently went about their task. I found myself rooming with Judy Pollock, a distant cousin of mine. A remarkable athlete, Judy had been a world record holder in the 400 and 800 metres during the 1960s, a bronze medallist behind Betty Cuthbert at the 1964 Olympics and a gold medallist at the 1966 Commonwealth Games. But pregnancy had forced her to miss the Mexico Olympics and, as it turned out, she would miss out on competing in Munich as well — she was carrying an injury that ultimately would prevent her from taking to the track. Judy finally made it to Montreal to cap off an extraordinary career, only to be run out in the heats.

One afternoon I found myself on a shuttle bus with the hurdler Maureen Caird, my old roommate from Mexico. The bus driver was clearly a volunteer from the German armed forces — on his shirt he carried the insignia of the German parachute platoon. Maureen was intrigued. The driver had hardly even acknowledged our presence on the bus. So she leaned over and pointed to his badge. "They say parachuting is better than sex," she said. There was no response from the driver. Maureen persevered. "They tell me there's nothing else like it on the planet. Beats sex any day, huh?" The driver kept ignoring us. Only later did we discover he did not speak English.

Compared with Mexico, Munich was like a five-star hotel and it did not take me long to settle in. The team had arrived three weeks before the Games to once again acclimatise to the northern summer, and several of us were invited to a warm-up competition in the Italian city of Viareggio. When an airline strike meant the cancellation of our flight, we were forced to journey by train and the entire three-day trip turned into a debacle.

The train was crowded, it was hot and dusty, and after arriving we discovered we had to make another trip, this time by bus, just to reach our hotel. The meeting itself was also a shambles. We had gone along expecting to face stiff competition — by the time you reach the Games you are usually peaking physically and psychologically and the smallest things can throw your concentration and leave you feeling upset. Our opposition in

Viareggio was little better than club standard. But I still managed to discover a new technique guaranteed to get me across the finishing line before everyone else. Just before the start of the 100 metres, I had drunk a lot of water. The journey to Viareggio had been dehydrating, and the northern heat certainly hadn't helped much, either. But just before I was due to crouch into the starting blocks my bladder began sending signals that unless I went to the toilet pretty soon, the event might well turn into a 100-metres contest in which all of us were forced to swim freestyle. I sprinted off and found the loos below the main grandstand. I should have known from the smell that it would not be a pretty sight. The toilets were simply holes in the ground, with foot marks next to them to indicate where you should squat. I took one look, sniffed in the accompanying odour, and decided my bladder could wait. Once out of the blocks, I'm sure I ran the fastest 100 metres of my life. Then I waited patiently, if a little uncomfortably, for the bus to take me back to our hotel.

The program dragged on until the early hours, so we were fairly tired the next morning. And then we had to undertake a similarly long return journey to Munich. After that experience I vowed I would not go far again and restricted my lead-up to remaining within the precincts of the Olympic city.

As the Games drew closer, tension mounted. For the first time in my life I began to be bothered by niggling injuries. I suffered a small tear of the calf muscle which did not interrupt my training program, but more seriously my Achilles tendons were beginning to flare up. First there would be a sharp pain, followed by a dull ache that left me limping and wondering if I had suffered serious internal damage. But they were just warnings, like the low rumble and short shocks the earth experiences just before a major earthquake. So it was never going to take much to push things to breaking point and, once again, that old Boyle ability to be in the thick of the action soon came to the fore.

At the training track I began to have several clashes with the chief starter, an authoritarian and overbearing gentleman named Franz Buthe-Pieper. He didn't like the way I assumed the "set" position just before he fired the starter's pistol. I had practised my starts thousands of times in the lead-up to Munich and I knew what was required. But good old Buthe-Pieper had clearly picked me out as a problem child. He criticised me several times, complaining I was not putting my bum in the air quickly enough. I retaliated. He was holding us in the set position for up to 2.7 seconds, a full second longer than we were used to in Australia. The thought crossed my mind that if he wanted a decent view of my bum, I would make sure he was given one. But modesty prevented me from performing that traditional Australian salute of flashing a bare backside at someone you are not particularly fond of.

Instead, I opened my mouth and let fly a few choice curses that over the years I had become quite well known for. "Do you bloody expect us to change everything now?" was one of my gentler queries. Unfortunately for me, Buthe-Pieper had a brilliant translator at his side who was able to inform him of every word I had uttered, along with the emphasis I had placed on each syllable. In the end, the entire farcical situation saw me placed on report to the international athletics association responsible for the running of the track and field program.

I was told I was suspended from the Olympic Games.

I should have laughed, I suppose. But they were serious. Yet, before I could really launch into a new tirade — if they thought what I had called Buthe-Pieper was out of order then wait until they saw what else I had in store for him — the suspension was quashed and I was free to return to the track. I decided then that my mouth was better off closed. In future, I would let my running do the talking for me. I was feeling aggressive and it was best to let that aggression loose on my opponents.

What I didn't know then was that one of my opponents was ready for me. And she had much more than natural aggression to help her.

I CAN'T remember the first time I saw the East German sprinter Renate Stecher. She had not been in Mexico and had burst onto the athletics scene in the early 1970s from nowhere along with the rest of her muscly compatriots. Word had reached me pretty quickly that this muscular-looking girl was blowing everyone away. Her times had been phenomenal but it was also her physical presence that made you catch your breath. From the waist down and from behind you could almost think you were looking at a man. She had big buttocks and big thighs and when I first saw her up close I have to admit I was intimidated. But there was something else I noticed, too. Stecher had a peculiar smell about her. Perhaps my sense of smell had been sharpened by my experience with the toilets in Viareggio, but there was something definitely different about her body odour. It was quite strong and musky and detectable whenever she walked past me — not quite the smell of a male with body odour, but not quite feminine, either. Looking back, perhaps it was the first time I caught a whiff of that expensive cologne, Eau de Testosterone.

Most athletes mingled with those from other countries. The training track was a mini United Nations, with track and field competitors all huddled and swapping jokes and gossip. And just like the UN, athletics has its own hierarchy. At the top, naturally, are the sprinters who will usually admit to you that they are the elite of running. Then, a little further back, are the 1500-metre runners and the marathon runners. Now, there's a truly strange collection of people. Let's face it, to race others over 42 kilometres is not a particularly sane thing to do. To me, it's behaviour bordering on the obsessive. Marathon runners live in another world. They eat different foods and have different thought processes. I'm sure that if they weren't running marathons you would find them walking down a city street wearing a propeller hat and talking to themselves. Of course, I love them for all their eccentricities. I just wouldn't want to be like them.

So there was nothing unusual about Munich except for one thing. Everyone mixed (believe me, in the athletes village there is always plenty of intimate mixing going on) except for the Eastern European countries and especially the East Germans. They were a team who never came near the rest of us. During training they kept to themselves. They were herded from venue to venue and kept under strict supervision the entire time. They didn't mix, socialise or acknowledge anyone from anywhere else. The only thing they didn't have was a kelpie nipping at their heels and keeping them close together. But then, they didn't need it. They had the watchful eye of their security people to keep them in their place.

I won through to the final of the 100 metres in very good form. In the vomitorium before the final, thirty minutes before we were due to go out, Stecher was glaring at me the way boxers do when they meet in the middle of the ring and are asked to touch gloves by the referee. I wasn't having anything to do with it. I didn't go much for deliberate intimidation. I'm sure there are many who would laugh at that sentence, particularly a great many of my Australian opponents over the years because I became quite well known for having an intimidating presence. But a lot of that was due to my bark and my well-known impatience for anything that distracted me. I wasn't into the sort of combat techniques that Stecher clearly was intent on using to disrupt my concentration. She was intimidating enough as it was.

It only took her 11.07 seconds to capture the gold medal. I finished second in 11.23, and I could sense the power of Stecher from my lane. But I wasn't unhappy. I felt I had run poorly in the final — my start had not felt right and throughout the race I never seemed to get my technique smoothly under control. Yet I had still won a silver medal, beaten only by an explosively powerful East German competitor. By that stage anyone who finished behind an East German was consoled by Australian team officials with a sympathetic hug and the words: "Don't worry. At least you were the first female across the line."

Stecher was fast and it seemed she could beat me at just about everything. After the race we were summoned to provide urine samples for the mandatory drug test. Stecher walked in and a few minutes later the authorities had a jar full of her highly prized urine. At least, we can only assume it was hers — by then many East German coaches were providing their own urine for drug tests on behalf of their athletes. I, meanwhile, was so dehydrated that I could not summon a single drop. I drank a swimming pool's worth of soft drink. Nothing. Bystanders turned taps on and off so that the sound of running water might entice that full-bladder feeling. Still nothing. The official assigned to watch me was clearly looking at a hefty overtime bill. Toilets were flushed. Competitors in other races came and went. I started to wonder if I still had a bladder.

Finally, a couple of pints of hearty German beer were produced. That did the trick. Within minutes I finally delivered the much coveted urine sample. With my second Olympic silver medal dangling from my neck, I headed back to the Olympic village convinced that Stecher was not invincible and that somehow I would find a way to beat her in my favourite event, the 200 metres.

But something far more overwhelming was about to take place. And it would steal the last drops of remaining innocence from me and everyone else connected to the Olympic movement.

IN THE early hours of 5 September, eight Palestinian terrorists managed to penetrate the security perimeter of the athletes village

ON THE ROCKS: Resting those niggling Achilles tendons in the cool waters of the beach at Hampton, not far from Aunty Dot's home.

LOOKING AHEAD: It's late 1973 and my life is in turmoil. Dad has just died and Mum blames me for his fatal heart attack at the age of 50.

GONE TO THE DOGS: Dad's death, an estrangement from Mum and the onset of injuries … thank God Waldi was there to lend a sympathetic ear.

DON'T LOOK NOW: American 400-metre medallist Wayne Collett and I share a joke on the athletic circuit. By the early 1970s I'd lost my fear of travel and was becoming a woman of the world.

HATS OFF: On an indoor tour of the USA in '74, several of us paid a quick return trip to Mexico. John Walker, New Zealand's world-record miler, attempts to improve trans-Tasman relationships.

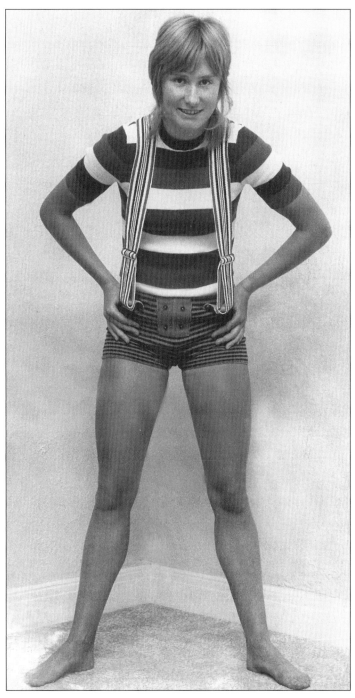

SUSPENDING BELIEF: Auditioning for a role in an Austin Powers movie? No, just back from London and showing off my new wardrobe.

STUDIO SHOT: Back in London in 1974 for a publicity shoot.

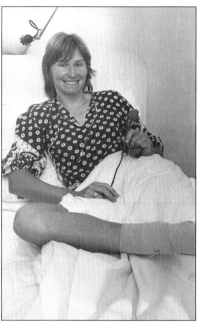

MY FRIEND, THE SCALPEL: A brave smile after my first Achilles operation.

STARTER'S ORDERS: In the lead-up to Montreal in 1976 I moved to Perth and trained under Shirley Strickland.

ROAD AHEAD: On my way to the Montreal stadium and hopefully a gold medal.

MTL-9 Montreal, July 28, AAP — High Drama at start of womens 200 metres semi-final as barefooted Australian champion Raelene Boyle leaves the track after being disqualified for two breaks. (AAP-PHOTO) djw/tp

DISQUALIFIED: That's me leaving the track after being disqualified from the 200-metre semi-final. Replays later showed I hadn't broken the first time.

INCONSOLABLE: Brother Ron and Shirley wait with me for the result of the protest.

May 26, 1980

The Australian Olympic Federation
141 Osborne Street
South Yarra
Vic   3140

Dear Sirs,

It is with regret that I formally advise my withdrawal from the Australian
1980 Olympic Team.

Competing at an Olympic Games means a total obligation that should overflow
with enthusiastic dedication.

Possibly the decision I am now making is as difficult as the A.O.F.'s decision of Friday. For those of you who know me, I'm sure you won't at first,
but after consideration, you will understand why I am taking this action.

My reasons for participating in my sport has always had at the top of the list
my love for it, followed by challenge and need to play out my ability to the
ultimate, giving it every chance.

In my life, after being a lucky young lady to be placed in the Mexico Team,
I have given up everything necessary to allow my sport all possible opportunities. My achievements are many, but never did I achieve my ultimate goal
- possibly I wasn't good enough, but nonetheless, I have always been in there
with a chance - even at this stage in my career, there is still the chance.

I have not enjoyed some phases of my Olympic career - but my desire to enjoy
it and better myself, have always survived, and in fact, many of the hurdles
have added to the challenge for Raelene Boyle, the athlete.

Unfortunately, of late a part of me has been slowly crushed and stamped into
the ground. I have been looking at the same shell in the mirror, but the
inside of that shell has emotionally been destroyed through the confusion.
I believe a certain number of my reasons for striving so hard and working
with the problems I have to make this team, have been crushed.

Please don't think that I am not backing your decision; I admire the A.O.F.'s
courage in doing as they have. I have never in the past, and I don't now
believe your interests, have been anywhere but with the sportspeople.

Finally, I would like to emphasise that the feelings I have indicated above,
are personal and have no political undertones attached, and that I wish those
athletes who have chosen to go to the Olpymics the best of luck.

Yours sincerely,

Raelene Boyle

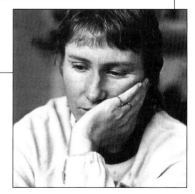

END OF A DREAM: My official letter
formally withdrawing from the
boycott-ravaged 1980 Moscow
Olympic team. My hopes of competing
at four Olympics were over.

PUPPY LOVE: Ty, the first of my Golden Retrievers. Dogs have been a constant in my life — more trusting and loyal than many humans.

GOLDEN GIRL: Jim Barry, General Manager of the 1982 Australian Commonwealth Games team, congratulates me after the 400-metres final.

A GOODBYE KISS: After all the pressures and expectations, my first instinct was to thank the public for their support.

VICTORY LAP: I always found the 400-metre event difficult, but this victory lap in Brisbane was the easiest lap of my life.

AT LAST: Retirement beckons and I finish not with a gold watch, but a gold medal.

LET'S SHAKE: My very last competitive event. We were just pipped by Canada in the 4x400-metre relay.

HEAD'S UP: I've been known to enjoy the odd beer, and this was one of several after the Brisbane victory.

by scaling a high wire fence. Unknown to the rest of us, they ambled through the women's quarters — right past our doors — disguised as coaches and athletes carrying bags. Then they burst into the level that was home to the Israeli team. In the ensuing drama, with bullets flying and screams piercing the darkness, an Israeli wrestling coach, Moshe Weinberg, was shot and killed. Another hostage, a weightlifter, would also die not long after when the terrorists refused to allow his wounds to be treated. The body of Weinberg was dumped outside as a warning to German authorities that the Palestinians were serious.

They threatened to kill a hostage every two hours unless their demand for the release of 200 Palestinian prisoners in Israel was met. As daylight arrived and the full extent of the carnage became known to the wider world, hundreds of police and army specialists descended on the athletes village.

I had no idea what was going on. In the previous two days I had competed in the qualifying heats of the 200 metres, remained competitive with Stecher and felt I was running at my best. But this day, a Tuesday, was a designated rest day and I was looking forward to doing as little as possible. Just before 9am I was told to get out of bed and get to the room of the manager of the Australian women's track and field team, Marlene Mathews-Willard, for a compulsory meeting. An Olympic bronze medallist herself, Marlene looked shaken. "There are terrorists in the village and some athletes have been killed," she said.

We were all shocked. I felt sick in the pit of my stomach. It was clear there was no danger to us, but the thought that a group of people could do something as profane and shocking as kill athletes for political objectives nauseated me. That was it, as far as I was concerned. The Games were over. As the negotiations dragged on during the day I caught a glimpse of one of the terrorists striding atop one of the nearby buildings. The sight of him revolted me. I was determined to get on the next possible plane and go home. This wasn't what sport was about and I no longer wanted to be a part of it.

After fifteen hours of the siege being broadcast around the world, the terrorists and their hostages were driven in an army bus to two waiting helicopters. They had agreed to fly to Cairo and negotiate with the Israeli government after rejecting a series of offers, including German politicians swapping places with the Israeli athletes. The helicopters flew their cargo to a nearby military airport as Munich police set up an ambush near the tarmac using trained marksmen. Once the helicopters landed, all hell broke loose. Floodlights lit up the tarmac and the marksmen began firing. The whole plan turned into a debacle. The terrorists in one of the helicopters turned their machine guns on their hostages, killing them all. In the accompanying chopper, one of the terrorists let off a grenade, killing everyone on board. Another shootout took place on the landing strip and in the end fifteen bodies lay scattered on the tarmac. All nine hostages were dead, five terrorists and a police officer. Three terrorists were captured.

There was no way, I thought, that the Games could continue. Along with the Israelis, the village of athletes had died, too. It had become a sad, sombre place. I wondered if I or anyone else would ever compete internationally again. If terrorists could do this at the Olympics, what hope was there for lower profile events such as world championships or even Commonwealth Games?

But the next day, at a ceremony to mourn the lives of the Israeli team members, the president of the International Olympic Committee, Avery Brundage, surprised me and just about everyone else. It was a solemn affair. As the Israeli team sat with eleven empty chairs representing their fallen comrades, Brundage uttered the words: "The Games must go on."

I disagreed. I wasn't even at the ceremony. For security purposes we were not allowed to join the 80 000 other people in the main stadium. We were forced to remain in our rooms and watch the event on television, crying each time the camera panned past the empty chairs in the Israeli section. By now I felt that Olympic idealism was dead. For the first time in the history of the movement, the Olympic flag was hanging at half mast and competition had been suspended. Everything my father had taught me about amateurism — all the hopes and standards he had instilled in me — had been exposed as nothing more than that — hopes and wishes. There was no place, it seemed, for a hopeless romantic in a sporting world as brutal and calculating as this one had turned out to be.

But in hindsight, Brundage's one simple but defiant statement may have saved the modern Olympic Games. He was an old man by then and the terrorist incident seemed to have bent and aged him even more. There were still many trials to come — the next three Olympics would be bedevilled by boycotts and political interference — but by refusing to bow to terrorism the IOC had vowed that it would try to remain above the dark deeds that people were capable of committing.

Nice idea. Pity the IOC has rarely since lived up to its promises.

ONE OF the bonuses of Munich was that Aunty Dot and one of her daughters, Janice, had flown over for the Games. Not only did I have someone to whom I was close to discuss training and technique with, but during the terrorism crisis she was also one of the key people to talk me into staying and continuing with my campaign. There was no doubt in Dot's mind that I, and the Games for that matter, had to go on. She had an enormous passion for athletics; in many ways she was like my father when it came to appreciating running for aesthetic reasons. And because she exuded such a convincing air of confidence — she was only 5'1" when wearing high heels but always seemed to stand much taller — I was always relaxed when she was around. During the hostage stand-off at the village I had managed to acquire an accreditation pass for Janice by telling the authorities I had lost mine and needed another. I simply slipped Dot an Australian tracksuit, and because of her self-confidence she could have walked into the most secure vault at Fort Knox without being questioned.

Aunty Dot arrived in my room at the height of the drama. The only problem was that once she was in there was no way of getting out — not even Dot was capable of achieving that in the midst of one of the greatest international crises of the century. So she bedded down in my room for the night.

I trusted Dot implicitly. In many ways she had replaced my father as the figure of authority in my life. She worked me much harder than Dad — she had insisted when I moved into her home that I get a job, which I had done — and our training program in the lead-up to Munich had been fierce and thorough, as it should have been because of my physical maturing. But it was more than just physical strength, stamina and speed that she had instilled in me. Dot had also made me believe in myself. Sprinters are strange creatures (although not as weird as marathon runners). Our personalities tend to be very selfish and arrogant. At our peak we are cocky and extravagant. We'll fluff our tail feathers in the face of the opposition. Just look at the line-up for a men's or women's 100-metres Olympic final. They parade, they strut, they pull faces and do all sorts of things to attract attention to themselves. Dot had helped nurture those qualities in me — and I call them qualities because they go with the territory. Without them you have no hope of succeeding. Dot had taken a shy little Coburg girl and helped transform her into a young woman with a sense of ambition and purpose. Of course, all my internal inadequacies were still there. But she taught me how to protect and cover them over by building a wall of toughness on the outside.

Dot knew Stecher would be a tough opponent in the final of the 200 metres. But she also had incredible faith in my ability. Once again I was able to rely on Team Boyle to help me through. Making up part of it were two members of the Boyle family, too. Up in the stands at Munich were Uncle Keith and Aunty Jean on my dad's side. Keith had decided after the 1968 Mexico Games, when no-one from my family had managed to make the trip, that he wanted to see his niece in action. And so he invested in a block of commercial land after Mexico. By 1972 he was able to sell it for a tidy profit that paid for his and Jean's journey to Europe. They did the same thing again in 1976 in Montreal. I'm sure it's one of the main reasons why it did not take me long to change my mind and decide to go on. If Brundage and the rest of the IOC could manage to stand so defiantly, then I figured that I at least should have the courage to take on Renate Stecher once again.

After the 100-metres final, a group of Australian reporters had huddled around me and asked me if I felt I could do better over the 200-metre distance. I shrugged and referred to Stecher. "Just say that I don't like looking at her back," I told them.

THE FINAL of the 200 metres was held two days after the massacre. The stadium was packed — it was as though the crowd, too, had decided to join with the IOC and show that it was possible to pick up the threads once more. I was nervous, the 200 metres was my speciality and I gave myself a strong chance of winning. Stecher had won her semi-final in convincing fashion two hours earlier, whereas I had finished second behind Ellen Stropahl, another East German. I had looked back over my shoulder quite a few times during the last 60 metres of the race just to check where the opposition were and gain some idea about how much energy I could conserve for the final. This, naturally, raised eyebrows in some sections of the Australian camp. Looking back over your shoulder in a race at international level was unprecedented. It was a lot like farting in church — the purists hated it. Not only did they regard it as a display of cockiness and arrogance but it was also believed that it could slow your momentum and alter your rhythm. I didn't know any better and there was little chance of me changing the habit of a lifetime.

Stecher set up a significant lead within a few strides of us exploding out of the blocks. But by the time we kicked out of the bend and into the straight I felt I could mow her down. Those last 100 metres remain a blur to this day, but I do remember how, with every stride, I seemed to be edging closer to her. She was in the lane next to me on my right and those final 40 metres were a desperate battle — Stecher charging toward the line, me surging and making up ground with every stride. I lunged at the line, but Stecher was just ahead of me, the East German equalling the world record of 22.40, with my time just a fraction behind at 22.45.

I was exhausted. When you have trained for an event for four years, the concentration levels are enormous and suddenly, in less than 23 seconds, it is all over. It felt as if all the emotion was draining out into a puddle at my feet. For a moment I thought I would collapse through lack of oxygen; I strained and heaved and my body seemed to have forgotten how to draw breath. I went over to congratulate Stecher, but she barely seemed to register my presence. Even at the end she was aloof, almost emotionless. I had heard a section of the crowd, presumably Australians, cheering and applauding. But I waved them off and tried to hush them. Another silver medal — my third — meant little to me in those moments after the race. Yes, it had taken a world record time to beat me, but I could not shake a sense of failure and bitter disappointment.

I wept on the medal dais. Stecher stood firm and erect while I buried my head in my hands and tried to stop myself from breaking into uncontrollable sobbing.

It would take me many years to put that defeat into perspective. It's a strange feeling to look back on that time through the prism of years of experience. That girl with tears in her eyes standing with a silver medal around her neck is a completely different person to the one who now bears the scars of so many deeper disappointments. Did I really take athletics that seriously? It seems incredible that finishing second in an Olympic event distressed me so much. If I could, I would love to reach back through time, put my arm around her shoulders and tell her not to worry about it. Look at you, I would say. You're twenty-one years old and you are the fastest non drug-taking athlete in the world. You are still Australia's only track and field medallist at these Olympics. In fact, you will be the country's only medallist on the track between 1968 and 1980. There's an often-repeated saying within the athletic community that to even make an Olympic team means you are an exceptional athlete. To go through to a final and win a medal means you are a freak of nature, lucky to have been born with a special gift in your genes to allow you to run fast. There are billions of others on the planet who would get nowhere near you. And besides, it's only a running race. It's not important.

I want to reach out and console that girl and tell her everything will be okay. I know how much she is hurting. I know how difficult she finds it pretending to be tough and hard when all she wants to do is give in to her inherent shyness and vanish from view.

But what I really want to tell her is that the disappointment of losing to Stecher will fade. Hell girl, you'd better get used to that feeling. There's a whole lot of deeper disappointments waiting for you down the line.

BY 1972 I had developed one method of coping with failure. In fact, by the time I arrived back in the village after the medal ceremony my plan of action was already firmly in place. A night on the town was required. Throughout Germany there were a great many cider bars and I arranged to meet up with the Australian rowers at one of them to drown our sorrows. They were in a similar mood to me. Medallists in Mexico, the eights had failed to make the finals in Munich and so we were determined to anaesthetise ourselves with as much of the local brew as possible.

I had a couple of "guardians" with me who were worried that, given my mood, things might get out of hand. And so I arrived at the bar with Marlene Mathews-Willard, our team manager, and Bob Hemery, section manager of the rowing squad, in tow. They were mere observers, however, as, over the next few hours, I proceeded to get myself quite drunk by keeping up with the drinking rate of the rowers. That was no mean feat and in the early hours of the morning I was gently carried back to the village and put to bed.

Apparently there were reports that night of a young blond woman cursing in the dark and waking many of the athletes. Unfortunately, I cannot confirm or deny them, as I have little memory of the entire evening. It certainly wasn't an episode of which I'm particularly proud. But at that time and place it was the only thing that helped obliterate the memory of what I considered to be a failure and help clear my head for my next commitments.

I still had two more events to complete before I went home. The most difficult was being part of the women's 4x400-metre relay team. I had always feared the 400-metre event. Having spent a lifetime training for shorter distances, my body found the one-lap race a gruelling and torturous affair. One of the great problems, as I would discover years later, is that a sprinter has an instinctive desire to burst out early and go hell for leather toward the finishing line. But the 400 requires far more strategy, including a high priority on pacing yourself. Go out too quickly in the first 200 and you'll discover what it feels like to run in a pool of jelly over the final 200. Lactic acid is an organic compound present in the blood and muscles. Under severe stress, such as a short burst of exercise, it builds up to the point where your legs feel like they have been stabbed by thousands of pins and needles. Whenever I ran the 400 I would find myself drowning in a sea of lactic acid. In the final of the 4x400 metres, which was held not long after I anchored our sixth-placed 4x100 team, I took off in my leg, and at the end of the back straight had mowed down several opponents. Somehow I managed to hang on and hand the baton over to Cheryl Peasley. We went on to finish a credible fifth as East Germany took another gold.

But moments after the race I was told by Ray Weinberg, who had clocked my race from the grandstand, that I had run an incredible 49.7 seconds. I'm sure I wasn't that fast; hand-held timing is not usually pin-point accurate. But my time may still have won me a gold medal in the individual 400-metres event. The winner of that race, East Germany's Monika Zehrt, clocked 51.08 seconds. However, that news did little to convince me that I should move up to the longer distance.

By then, all I wanted to do was go home. These Olympics had been momentous and extremely tiring for everyone, both physically and emotionally. They had seen extraordinary highs and lows. There had been performances of genuine brilliance. The pool, particularly, seemed to be home to a series of world record performances. The American Mark Spitz captured seven gold medals and Australia's Shane Gould, who had been born the day after the opening ceremony of the Melbourne Olympics in 1956, became the first woman to win three gold medals in world record time in individual events. She also took home a silver and a bronze and then, at the age of sixteen, she made the stunning decision to retire. No doubt the Americans, who had turned up in Munich hoping to psyche her out by wearing T-shirts declaring "All that glitters is not Gould", were happy about that decision. But they must have been the only ones. No-one has ever come close to repeating Gould's performances.

I wondered if I would ever get another opportunity to race for a gold medal. I was still young, but the Montreal Games were four years away and the sudden rise of athletes like Renate Stecher had convinced me that after two Olympics I might be lucky to make it to a third. And the Games had also lost a lot of their innocence over the preceding fortnight. The massacre had been bad enough, but its coldness had been compounded by the thousands of "spectators" who had crowded into the vicinity of the village when the hostage negotiations were under way. They were like those sick idiots who gather on street corners to stare at the carnage of a car accident. I was left with the same feeling in the pit of my stomach that I had experienced four years earlier at the bullfight in Mexico. Blood lust. And now the Olympic flag was forever stained with it.

THERE WAS one final journey to make before I headed home. The images from that trip continue to haunt me to this day.

For several minutes I stood silent and felt ashamed to be a human being. In the dust, in the bricks, in the air and every damn place you went I could smell the bones and vividly imagine the last, lingering screams of those sent to their deaths. But the most powerful thing was the silence.

The Australian team had come to Auschwitz, Nazi Germany's largest concentration camp of World War II and the place where the most horrific and unimaginable crimes had been inflicted on human beings. This was the culmination of Hitler's insane plan to exterminate the Jewish population. He almost did it, too — six million Jews would be slaughtered in the name of the Third Reich as part of his plan to create a superior Aryan race. Arriving in cold, dilapidated freight cars, the old, the weak and mothers with their children were culled from the main groups and killed. Some were sent to the *Badeanstalten*, or bathhouses, where they were gassed. Around the complex were the remains of *Leichenkeller*, or corpse cellars, and then came the ultimate horror — *Einascherungsofen* — the cremating ovens.

It was in Auschwitz that the camp's evil doctor, Josef Mengele, performed all sorts of hideous medical experiments. Up to 2.5 million Jews died inside this complex.

I cannot recall any other occasion on all my journeys overseas with Australian teams when such silence and respect reigned. As I glanced around at the ruins of Auschwitz, I finally gained some much-needed perspective.

This was, truly, a place that would forever remain haunted. Who was I to shed tears over a pathetic coloured medal?

13

The r e b e l y e a r s

IN LATE 1973 MY HEARTBROKEN MOTHER EFFECTIVELY ACCUSED ME OF murder. At the time I was adamant that I was innocent. But now I'm not so sure.

That year my parents moved into the new suburb of West Meadows in Melbourne's outer west. Dad had not been well over the previous twelve months. The doctors had diagnosed a heart condition and he was immediately put on medication. I was aware he was sick; Rick was still keeping me up to date with the news from the Boyle household. At one stage Dad made what amounted to a final peace offering between us. I would be welcomed back into the family if I moved into a bungalow he was prepared to build for me at the rear of Ron's new home.

From his point of view it was a major concession. But it was never going to interest me. Had I been in a better mood (I had just returned from a trip to Canada where my Achilles problems had

flared and I had no idea if I would ever run competitively again) I
might have found a way of gently knocking back his offer without
hurting his ego one more time. But I was a self-obsessed athlete
and every decision I made was framed by my stubbornness. And I
just couldn't see how moving into Ron's home would heal the
wounds that had opened up over the previous couple of years.
There was too much baggage now, too many memories of hurtful
things that had been said. I was enjoying my life, anyway. Aunty
Dot was still treating me as one of her daughters, I had a vibrant
social life, I was working with Puma and I could not imagine why I
would move back into a way of life I had already left.

That was the final time I spoke to my father. On Friday,
23 November, he went back to our old home in Sutherland Street to
complete some work he had been planning. Squatting on one foot
on one of his favourite chairs, he suffered a massive heart attack
and died on the spot. A neighbour across the road found his body.

I was at Aunty Dot's when Uncle Keith arrived. "Rae," he said.
"Your dad has died."

I didn't know what to feel, or even how to react. Here was a man
who had been the love of my life for my first nineteen years. Had
he told me the world was flat I would have believed him. I would
have walked off its edge had he asked me to. But the past few years
had forced me to shut him out of my life as best I could. I'd found
a closet in my mind, put all my fond memories of Dad in there, and
then locked the door. It would be years before I dared open it again
and when all those memories came tumbling out I was able to see
my father differently and in greater depth.

Mac was only fifty when he passed away. It was only when I
reached that age after my cancer scares that I realised just how
much he had missed in life. Fifty was too young. He should have
been looking forward to a couple of decades of relaxing and doing
what he and Mum wanted to do.

Mum took his death hard, and by the time I arrived at her home she had already decided I was to blame. I stepped inside quietly and gave Rick, who was distraught, a hug. Fortunately, Grandma was there and in her usual understanding and sympathetic mood. She threw a pair of welcoming arms around me. But I didn't stay for long. I was a stranger in the family home and Mum's coldness to me was clear. Even now, the residue from that time remains. Rick still believes that my behaviour and unwillingness to get along with Dad contributed to his heart attack, and while it is a difficult thing for me to accept, I can at least now understand his — and Mum's — point of view.

We said goodbye to Dad at a small funeral chapel in Sydney Road, the same strip of bitumen I used to travel down three times a week on the tram just a few years earlier on my way to training. I stood discreetly at the back of the chapel with Uncle Keith and Aunty Jean, and later I went out to the cemetery on my own for one final goodbye. By then I was emotionless. I didn't know how I should feel. So typically I shut my mind to it and decided to deal with it later.

Not long afterwards I went around to see Mum. It was a conciliatory gesture. With Dad gone I thought there was at least enough common ground between us for some form of reconciliation. But the discussion soon turned into an argument. I had broken Dad's heart by leaving and then refusing to come home, she told me. It was my fault that he was dead. It was the heaviest and most stressful argument I had ever endured. At first I tried to calm Mum down. But she was no longer interested in listening to me. Now it was time for her to get everything off her chest. All the frustration and anger she had felt during those years of quietly standing by Dad's side and supporting him came tumbling out. I ended up losing my temper, too, and we stood there and screamed at one another for a few minutes. Then I left, vowing once again never to return.

But all I was doing was running from the situation. Mum's lifelong battle with depression had not been helped by Dad's death. Deep down she was a lot like me. She was afraid to be on her own and so was I. She feared being lonely more than anything else. When everything falls quiet, you only have yourself to keep you company. Was that my mother's problem and, later, mine, too? Have I always been afraid of getting to know myself too well? I could look up at the mantelpiece and admire my trophies and medals. That was easy enough. The trophies told me the sort of person I was — a successful, highly motivated young woman. But they didn't tell me about the flaws — my stubbornness and selfishness were the traits I preferred not to see. It is only when everything falls quiet that you see yourself for what you truly are. And I always wanted to keep that silence at bay.

THOSE EARLY years between Munich and Montreal were pretty much the sort of years in the wilderness that many people in their early twenties experience. I wasn't too sure what I was going to do with the rest of my life. Losing to Stecher had certainly scarred me, and as a way of covering up a lot of the hurt I hardened a great deal on the outside. I became less trusting of other people and increasingly frustrated with the officials who ran my sport and had such a large say over how I ran my life.

It had begun not long after returning home from Munich. After every Olympics, or any other major event for that matter, I discovered that I had to prepare for a flat period in the months afterward. I guess it is similar to what many people endure after undergoing one of the high points of their lives. Once that feeling of exhilaration fades, a form of depression can follow. One of the classic examples of this was produced by T.E. Lawrence, the famous "Lawrence of Arabia". He made his reputation in the Middle East by dressing as an Arab, learning how to jump on the back of a camel from a great distance and enduring long days in the desert without food or water. He won the admiration of the local tribesmen and, through the sheer force of his personality — and a great deal of bribery — he was able to unite a group of warring tribes into a fighting force that helped beat the Germans and Turks in World War I. For Lawrence, these battles and deprivations were the high point of his life — his Olympics, if you like. His physical endurance in those times was above and beyond normal human limits and his leadership abilities also shone. Finally, he went home to England to live in his parents' house. His mother would watch him come downstairs for breakfast. He would sit at the table motionless for hours, sometimes until lunch, staring out the window, totally uninterested in life around him. Just before he died he wrote to a friend, saying: "You wonder what I am doing? Well, so do I, in truth. Days seem to dawn, suns to shine, evenings to follow and then I sleep. What I have done, what I am doing, what I am going to do, puzzle me and bewilder me. Have you ever been a leaf and fallen from your tree in autumn and been really puzzled about it? That's the feeling."

That was how I, and many other athletes, felt after returning from an Olympics. We were leaves and we had fallen from the only tree we knew. So we filled the void as best we could. For me, that meant staying away from hard training and filling my life with as many good times as possible.

I had only been back from Munich for three months when Victoria's women's athletics officials "recommended" that I run twice to qualify for the Victorian team at the Australian championships. It was the sort of petty directive that I had become accustomed to. I had done no training and even though I was lucky enough to have a body that could hit peak form in a short time, I was sick of running. I had been effectively training since well before the Mexico Games and in Australia the incentives to run quickly had begun to run out. There was little opposition for me and the opportunities to travel overseas to compete were limited, too.

But I stuck to orders and so it happened that I was beaten for the first time in years over 100 metres. Denise Robertson was an emerging sprinter from Queensland and she just managed to beat me across the line. If I was looking for a trigger to climb out of my slump, there it was. I pretended not to care too much about the result — "This is the deflation period after the Games," I explained to the press after the race — but deep down my competitive nature had been rekindled. Over the next few months I resumed training and began recording some of my best times.

But that defeat had triggered something else, too. One of those classic sporting rivalries had begun. At first, as Denise improved her times, it was friendly enough. But as the competition intensified between us things began to grow a lot less friendly. As is usual with these things, a lot of it came about because of simple misunderstandings blown out of proportion by careless remarks and a media that suddenly loved the idea of a battle royal being staged between two female athletes. This was something new for everyone. Remember, back then newspapers still described female athletes as "vivacious", "pretty" or even "dazzling" — as long as they were not from East Germany. To have two Australian girls caught up in an intense battle for track supremacy was almost too good to be true. At one stage Denise would be quoted as saying she "hated" me and I was hardly complimentary at times, either.

The bottom line was that we had two different personalities that under the circumstances of the time were simply not compatible. I laugh about it now — Denise lives quite close to my home and I often see her around town. We stop and have a chat and get along quite well. But back in the 1970s you would have thought we were sworn mortal enemies if you believed the papers. And I probably didn't help things. By my early twenties I had more than a healthy dose of suspicion about other people's motives, in large part fuelled by my neverending guerrilla war with officialdom. If I was aloof and wary of another woman vying to take my crown as the best female sprinter in the country, it paled in comparison to my loathing for athletic officials. Well, some of them, anyway.

It's at this point in those old black and white movies that the camera dissolves to a series of spinning newspaper headlines, their banners shrieking with indignation and horror. If you did that with my life, you would be left feeling dizzy and sick by the sheer number of them. So let's try just a couple.

February 26, 1973: RAELENE BOILS! Apart from the pun in the headline — I guess it was better than AUSTRALIA PICKS BOYLE, the obvious headline accompanying my selection into the national team — the article below it detailed yet another "controversial" incident. Once again my friends from the Victorian Amateur Athletics Association had taken the afternoon off from their regular jobs as nuclear physicists and brain surgeons to concentrate on the really important things in life. After I had won the Victorian 100-metre title for the third successive year, five male officials reprimanded me and threatened to have me disqualified from future races because I had once again committed the shocking act of breaking the finishing tape with my hands.

The following day I set a new national record for the 200 metres, running 22.8 seconds. I made sure to break the tape with my hands again, and then handed it to the nearest official. No-one complained.

February 7, 1974: I'M BEING CRUSHED. This one showed just how low I felt. I had only just come home from the Christchurch Commonwealth Games, where I had won three gold medals, matching my performance in Edinburgh four years previously. While over there I had been invited to race in Canada and the United States. But women's athletics officials had demanded that I produce a full itinerary of my trip and organise for the overseas promoters to pay for an Australian manager to accompany me everywhere. I was twenty-two years old and I was being told by my own country's athletic administrators that I could only go away to receive some valuable competition against the world's best if I went with a chaperone.

It was absurd. But by that stage I was so angry I could not even laugh at the ridiculous lengths to which some officials would go to get a free trip overseas, and to annoy me as well. So I went on Channel Nine's "A Current Affair" and gave them all a piece of my mind.

"If I could only change my nationality in two minutes," I lamented, "I'd be gone because I can't stand the pressures here any longer."

"I wouldn't like to tell you what I think of the people who run amateur athletics in Australia. I'm too upset. I feel very disillusioned. The body which is supposed to control everything I do is just crushing me. Most athletes from other countries at my standard are helped and sent to school. But I have nothing. I'm fed up. I just can't take it. It's so stupid to say I must be accompanied by a manageress. I'd have to look after the manageress. She wouldn't know what to do."

The press knew a good story when they heard one and they pounced. And they knew who I was talking about. Arthur Hodsdon was the secretary of the Australian Amateur Athletics Union and it was he who decreed that if I left without permission then I would be discredited with overseas associations and possibly banned. Newspaper journalists rang Hodsdon after my outburst. Clearly, he had not appreciated my comments. "I am not at all interested in what she said," he told reporters. "It was probably a lot of rubbish, anyway. I don't want to know anything about it."

This blow-up came after the infamous tracksuit episode in Christchurch, when I had come close to being banned from the Commonwealth Games and sent home because I refused to wear the adidas team tracksuit. By then I was an employee of Puma and they had been good to me, as far as the amateur rules allowed. They supplied me with running shoes, paid me a salary for the meagre work I gave them in return and generally gave me the sort of corporate support that was rare in Australian athletics at the time. I guess I was one of the first athletes of that era to make a stand. I certainly wasn't the last — by the time of the 1992 Barcelona Olympics, Michael Jordan, the most famous athlete in the world, had to cover his Nike logo with the American flag during a medal ceremony.

Eventually the controversy over my proposed US trip quietened and Hodsdon agreed that I could travel overseas as a private athlete and not an official representative of the AAAU. It was a worthwhile trip. I won and lost races, but it was the opportunity to compete against the world's best that most inspired me, and made me realise yet again that running was what I wanted to keep doing.

A few months later in 1974 I decided to move overseas full-time in a bid to further my career and begin the long haul toward the 1976 Montreal Olympics. I lived in a lot of places with a lot of different people involved with track and field. But I never seemed capable of settling. I was a homebody, and even though I was estranged from my own family, I missed Melbourne, my friends and the regularity of the life I had left. England was cold and wet, and travelling always seemed to require the preparations usually reserved for moving large land armies. I competed on the European circuit and my reputation was big enough by that stage for me to collect up to $250 in "expenses" for appearing at some of the meets.

I made friends and learned a great deal. But I never felt comfortable. My insecurities seemed to increase when away from home. I fretted. I grew bored quickly and began putting on weight. I wondered whether my best was already behind me. My times had hardly improved and I was afraid that I was now on that downhill slide. That really scared me because it meant the end of my running career might not be that far away. And that meant I would have to find another way of making a living. I had no idea what that might be.

Part of my problem, too, was that my Achilles tendons by now were almost shredded through overuse. Every time I ran I felt like screaming, and the pain lingered for days afterward, leaving me hobbling about like an old woman. After several months I decided it was time to go home. An English doctor examined my ankles one afternoon, shook his head and told me I could forget about running anymore. My career was over.

As it happened, Doc Toyne, the man who helped convince me to stay in Mexico City when I was attacked by a severe dose of homesickness, happened to catch up with me in London on his way home from a trip to Moscow. He took one look at my legs and told me to pack my bags and head home. He would operate on the tendons as soon as we were both back in Melbourne. He was confident he could do enough to keep me on the track for at least several more years.

I wasn't unhappy at leaving England. But this turn of events interrupted something I had been looking forward to doing for a long time — going back to school. I had won a scholarship to run for the University of California in Long Beach. The opportunity to race there against the best America had to offer was enticing, and so was the chance to study and make up for all my inattentiveness at high school. My insecurities about life after running were building and I was hoping the scholarship might lead me in other directions. But the trip home and subsequent operations meant I had to decline the scholarship.

I went home, greeted the surgeon's scalpel again and was soon up and about. Perhaps, I thought, I had turned the corner at last. But just as I began to believe it, disaster struck. I was diagnosed with glandular fever and the next twelve months were virtually wiped out as I spent most of that time recovering.

I knew that if I was going to come back one more time I would need a change of scenery. Perth beckoned. It was warm and sunny and never seemed to suffer the sort of debilitating winters that Melbourne could produce. My grandmother was also over there and she made it very clear she would love to have me join her. So I sat down with Aunty Dot and we decided that if I was going to realise my dream of an Olympic gold medal, then I would need to go to Perth. There was, we thought, only one person who could lift me to another level. Her name was Shirley Strickland. She knew what it was like — and what was required — to win an Olympic gold medal.

14

Breaking point

ARTHUR ASHE, THE BLACK AMERICAN TENNIS GREAT, ONCE DESCRIBED his life as "a succession of fortunate circumstances". He said that when he was young, long before he was struck down by the AIDS virus he had acquired through a blood transfusion. But I know what he meant. The present never allows too much time for analysis. It's only when you have moved on that you can afford to look back with any perspective and see those critical points in life that shaped and moulded you.

I have been fortunate to have met many people who have had a profound impact on me. And there is a common thread that links them together. All of them seem to have come along just when I needed someone to help lift me, to reignite me and remind me about who I was, and still am. Those who believe in fate — that our lives are played out according to an unseen plan, that we are all mere characters in the greatest show in the universe — will say that I was always destined to meet these people.

Unfortunately for them, I'd have to disagree. I think it was more to do with me. Deep down I think I always knew that I had to keep changing and reinventing myself. In order to do that, I would seek new faces to add to Team Boyle. Perhaps this need to always have others around me stems from a lack of faith in my own judgment and ability. Definitely some of it harks back to the self-doubts and lack of confidence that have always haunted me. Right from the start I had Dad to make decisions for me. I replaced him with Aunty Dot. And then, at the end of 1975, I went looking for another mentor. I found one in Shirley de la Hunty.

There were few more inspiring figures in women's athletics than Shirley. As Shirley Strickland, a three-time gold medallist, she became the first woman to successfully defend an Olympic title when she won gold in the 80-metres hurdles in Melbourne in 1956, four years after establishing her supremacy in the event in Helsinki. But it was more than just the gold medals and the brilliant international career that intrigued me. It was her toughness. Shirley de la Hunty was one of the hardest, most uncompromising women I had met. We had encountered each other on a couple of occasions at Olympics, where she had been given various managerial roles by the Australian Olympic Committee. She had always struck me then as distant, almost aloof, in her attitude and behaviour. I guess I was intimidated by her. She was a gold medallist and I had been to two Olympics and never crossed the line first. But she was also incredibly gifted intellectually. Shirley had trained as a nuclear physicist. She knew and understood how the world worked at a microscopic level the rest of us could barely comprehend. But it was in the larger world around us where I thought Shirley was at her best.

Toward the end of 1975 I had been having several long chats with Aunty Dot about my future. We both sensed that after my bout of glandular fever, which had left me listless and exhausted for most of the year, I was due for a change of scenery. There was no disguising the fact that I was drifting; there was a vague feeling at the back of my mind that the best of my career was already behind me. My Achilles operations had been successful, but I wondered whether I would ever run as fast again. Back then, I defined myself as an athlete. That was what I did. It was more than just a pastime; it had been an all-consuming passion since Mexico. Aunty Dot could sense that my passion was fading. I can't remember whether it was her or me who came up with the idea of approaching Shirley. But I can certainly recall picking up the telephone in Melbourne one day and calling Shirley at her Perth home.

Her voice was as officious as usual. I was as nervous as hell. "Shirley," I told her, "I'm thinking about moving to Perth. I need a big change in my life. Will you coach me?"

There was silence at the other end of the line. I could tell what was going through her mind. God almighty, how do I get out of this? Raelene Boyle! By then my reputation was well and truly cemented throughout the Australian athletic scene. I was a party girl who did what she wanted. I was famous for my stubbornness and my temper. Nothing bored or frustrated me more than repetitive work — at times it drove me to the point of tears. Mind-numbing sprint after sprint with no sense of achieving anything would sometimes see me storm off the track and straight into my car, hurling my bag and a few obscenities into the back seat. Then I would usually head for the beach, find a secluded spot and sit there waiting for the frustration to fade, to be replaced by an embarrassment about my behaviour.

I knew I was flat. But even worse, I was nursing a fear that had been nagging away at me for years. I thought I was soft. My character, I believed, was suspect under pressure. I always seemed to burst into tears when things went wrong and the really great runners never did things like that. I could not imagine Stecher ever shedding a tear, at least not back then. And Shirley? I was sure she was capable of running barefoot down a street littered with broken glass without even wincing. It often amazed me over the years how relaxed some of my opponents were just before a big race. I would look at them and wonder how they managed to seem so impassive and cold. Internally I was always a mess, my stomach churning while I wore out a path between the track and the toilet. I had learned to mask this tension with the same cold look worn by the others. But I could never help but feel that they were somehow better than me — tougher, harder and stronger.

If I was to rekindle my passion for running and have any chance of finally winning a gold medal, then I had to get out of Melbourne. There were too many distractions — too many parties to attend, too many good times to be had and too little discipline to keep me in check. The weather that winter had been cold and flu-friendly, and for someone who only ever felt comfortable in a T-shirt and shorts, wearing bulky clothes — well, okay, bulky tracksuits — was another little thing that assumed greater importance than it should have.

Gladys Wilkinson, my grandmother, had already made it clear she would more than welcome me into her home in Nedlands. Since Grandpa's death a few years earlier, she had lived alone, and while she was a tough old bugger, I'm sure the silence got to her as much as it did over the years to my mother, and to me.

But first I had to convince Shirley I was serious about a comeback, and I had little evidence to support my case. Denise Robertson had already beaten me in a couple of events at the start of the 1975–76 summer, and I knew the word was out that my career was floundering, and possibly coming to an end.

Shirley laid it on the line. I could come over, but I needed to be aware that she was the boss. We would do it her way or no way. It would be difficult. It would hurt — physically and mentally.

I felt renewed even by the time I hung up the phone. I had found myself a new member of Team Boyle. In the process, I had created another fortunate circumstance in my life.

GRANDMA WAS known simply as "Wilkie" to the kids in her street, and it seemed every single one of them stopped by her place for a piece of cake or a biscuit on their way home from school. She was the sort of grandmother that Hollywood script-writers might have invented. I never heard her say a bad thing about anyone. The kettle always seemed to be on the boil, she was a terrific cook, and even more importantly, she loved to care for me.

There was nothing Grandma would not do for her granddaughter. She was fully aware of the civil war that had split the Boyle clan back on the east coast, but not once had she passed judgment on me or questioned anyone's role or motives. She simply accepted me the way I was, and I discovered in her a human being whom I trusted and loved more than anyone else in my life at the time.

Grandma was proud of my achievements in international athletics and she fussed over me constantly. Naturally enough, I lapped it up. I have always been a tremendous sleeper. I can go to bed very early and still sleep in late. Once Shirley's training sessions began I found I needed more sleep than usual. Some of those sessions would last for six hours or more — tough, gruelling runs when every sinew seemed to cry out in pain. But within weeks I could tell I had made the right move. My old speed was coming back — it wasn't long before I had left Denise Robertson in my wake in several contests around the country — and my stamina was also improving.

In the mornings I would lie in bed for as long as I could. Sometimes the phone would ring and it was usually for me. I would get up, chat, and by the time I got back to bed, Grandma would have made it. This might happen three times during the morning. Each day she would wait until I struggled into the kitchen before asking me what I felt like eating. She was prepared to cook me anything at any time. Quite often my answer was simple: pumpkin. If there is one food that has sustained me throughout my life it is pumpkin. It's a vegetable I have never grown tired of, and Grandma would quickly put a little on the stove for me and serve it up piping hot.

What is it about grandmothers? They are unquestioningly loyal when it comes to their grandchildren. By the time I arrived in Perth I desperately needed to place my trust in someone like her. Grandma Wilkie was one of the few people in my life who never wanted anything from me. To her, the best days were the ones when we drank tea out on the front porch and talked about anything that came to mind. I respected her — not only because of her love for me, but also her toughness. Here was another person I admired who seemed more resilient and courageous than me. When I was young every couple of years Mum and Dad would take me and the boys to Perth to see Grandma and Grandpa for a holiday. When it came time to leave Grandpa's eyes would fill with tears and his throat would become choked. But Grandma was always the strong one — I don't think I had ever seen her cry. Back then, I thought that was a sign of strength.

There were always reminders, however, that Grandma was growing old. In 1976 she fell and broke her hip. They pinned it and inserted a plate, and amazingly she was up and about in five days. Her attitude was that if she didn't get up and start walking as quickly as possible, she never would. Tough? You have no idea. She had fallen a few years later and badly broken her left arm. Because her bones were riddled with osteoporosis, they were like shells washed up on a beach and left in the sun to dry for too long. They shattered easily and this time her left arm never quite healed. Quite often I would be talking to her and my eyes would be drawn to her upper left arm. The bones would have fallen out of alignment and I could actually see them sticking out at different angles.

"Grandma," I would say, "your bones are showing."

She would simply shrug, place her right hand over them, give them a shake, roll her shoulder and tug them back into place.

I sometimes felt as if my own bones were coming apart under Shirley's demanding training regime. Our day would usually start with a combination of track session, weight work, running in water, treadmill exercises or running up and down hills. I had always trained on flat ground and for a while I was perplexed when Shirley made me go up and down one hill after another. But there was method behind the apparent madness. Going up and down placed stresses on different leg muscles and that led to more explosiveness over short distances. At nights we would wrap up training with sessions solely devoted to speed. It was little wonder that on my rare days off Grandma would spend hours patiently waiting for me to get up.

But my confidence was soaring. By now I was beginning to believe that I could be the fastest woman in the world over 200 metres, drugs or no drugs. I tried to keep a lid on my own expectations, but it was difficult. As Montreal approached there seemed to be reminders everywhere that I was the hope of the Australian track and field team. A day barely seemed to pass when an article did not appear in the newspapers about my chances in the 100 metres and 200 metres. I thought I had an outside chance to win a medal in the 100, but probably not gold. The standard had leaped incredibly in the four years since Munich; the Eastern Bloc countries were still producing athlete after athlete of world class ability and at the same time Australia's fortunes had fallen away. Our track team was hardly a sparkling array of potential gold medallists. This had come about for a variety of reasons. Nations often go through a generational change which sees a gap before a new group of runners can fill the hole left by retirements. It was obvious that by 1976 Australia was experiencing a shortfall of talent. But we had also not kept up with the increasing professionalism and scientific approaches that many other countries were adopting. Athletics was no longer simply a matter of training three times a week, staying fit and eating steak before you ran. While the Eastern Bloc countries were clearly cheating with drugs, their vast teams of scientists and their studies relating to nutrition and fitness had revolutionised thinking about elite sport.

By the time Australia arrived home from Montreal with a paltry overall return of one silver and four bronze medals, questions would be asked both in parliament and around the country. Montreal would be our worst Olympic performance since Berlin in 1936, when we last failed to win gold. Those questions would ultimately lead to the establishment of the Australian Institute of Sport. But in the lead-up to Montreal I wasn't concerned about the fate of the team. There was only one athlete I was concerned about. Me.

"What am I going to get out of it except maybe self-satisfaction?" I said during an interview one day shortly before leaving for Montreal. "I guess that's a major thing in my life. I enjoy being self-satisfied. Part of it is an ego thing. You know you're almost the best in the world at something and you want to be THE best in the world.

"I love to know I'm running beautifully, with a certain amount of attraction to the eye. That's one way I can express myself. To move beautifully as well as running fast is a sort of perfection to me. That's what I get out of it. If I win that gold medal I will have justified the time I've put in over the past ten years. And unless I win that gold medal I don't really think I will have justified it."

In interview after interview I tried to play down my chances. "My chances are slim at Montreal and I realise it," I would say, time after time. But deep down I thought differently. Deep down I saw myself finally standing on the podium with a gold medal hanging around my neck.

MONTREAL, IT was hoped, would be an opportunity for the Olympic movement to come together and attempt to heal some of the scars left by the Israeli massacre in Munich. Like many aspects of the Olympics, it was a nice idea that would never achieve reality. Sixteen African nations would end up waiting until their teams were in Montreal before pulling their athletes out in protest against a New Zealand rugby tour of South Africa. Once again stupidity reigned. I understood the need to pressure South Africa, but I was tired of my sport being used as a political tool. Maybe I, just like the IOC, lived in a dreamland far removed from the realities of daily life. As it transpired, the Games would be the greatest financial disaster in the history of the Olympic movement. The City of Montreal would be effectively bankrupted by staging them. The budget trebled to almost one billion dollars, and the unfortunate citizens would be levied with high taxes to pay off the debt for the rest of the twentieth century. As well, plans for new sewers, subway extensions and parks had to be scrapped. Montreal would radically alter the way Olympics were conducted, and the next time they were held in the Western world, in Los Angeles in 1984, private enterprise would be the key.

Despite the red ink and the political turmoil, these Games would at least bring about the end of one long-running war. I finally managed to reconcile with my brother Ron. After years of barely talking following my dispute with Dad, Ron and I decided it was time to talk and see if we could share some common ground.

I had already begun talking with Mum again. I dropped in from time to time to check up on her and see how she was getting along, and we both began, tentatively at first, to learn how to speak civilly to one another once more. We were still some distance from bridging the gulf and becoming mother and daughter again. But Mum had decided to get on with her life and was looking forward to coming to Montreal to see me run, and perhaps finally win that elusive gold medal.

Ron and I caught up on the team flight. Ron had been named in the team as a track cyclist, and I was proud of what he had done. When we were growing up my athletic career had always come first — if funds were needed for a trip away, or special expensive shoes were required, I seemed to be first in line. Ron had always been a talented "bikie", but he had grown up, married, had a couple of kids and pursued his piloting career with the TAA airline. So to make it into an Australian Olympic team in his early thirties was a marvellous achievement.

The announcement had attracted a fair amount of publicity — we were the first brother–sister act to ever be named in an Australian Games squad — but it wasn't until we caught up on the flight that we managed to have a serious chat and settle some of our differences. Ron, as always, was the less stubborn of the two of us and without his gentle coaxing it might have been more difficult to lessen the gap between us. But within minutes I felt as though those years apart had been little more than the blink of an eye — we were laughing over old times, reminiscing about cricket matches in the street, Dad's eccentricities and how we'd sometimes gang up on Rick because he was the baby of the household and needed to be reminded where he stood in the scheme of things.

I was also happy about Ron because it finally felt to me, completely selfishly of course, that Team Boyle was complete once again. As it turned out, he would prove to be a tremendous shoulder to cry upon during the Games. He didn't progress very far in his event. But it was a huge achievement just to get there.

I HADN'T really expected the heat and humidity that we encountered immediately upon arriving in Montreal. To avoid the worst of it, we tried to train either early in the mornings or late in the evenings. But I settled in quickly. It seemed everything was coming together. My form was great, and my confidence received another huge injection when I was chosen to become the first woman to carry the Australian flag at an Olympic opening ceremony. "I knew there was a reason for all that weight training this year," I joked with everyone. But deep down I was incredibly excited.

"It's got to be an omen," I gushed to Shirley, who was now the manager of the Australian women's track team. "Just make it one," she told me with barely a hint of emotion in her voice. Shirley wasn't one to get carried away by pomp and circumstance.

That march was one of the proudest moments of my life. At the time I doubted whether I deserved the honour. My old insecurities were once again coming to the fore. I gripped the flagpole so hard for fear that I might drop it and embarrass myself in front of the huge crowd and the worldwide television audience that I was exhausted by the end of the ceremony.

But I was here to get a job done and I was determined not to let anything stand in my way. By the time the 100-metres heats came around I was at my peak. I'd won several lead-up races a week before the Games began, defeating a high-class field peppered with some of the best European and American runners. I won my opening heat, crossed the line second in the following heat and then moved into the semi-finals where the opposition suddenly became a lot tougher. All the old faces were there, along with some new ones. Once again, Renate Stecher finished ahead of me as I came in third, still good enough to make the final. But it was clear that Germans of all political persuasions were the ones to beat. Stecher, I always knew, would be a difficult foe. But there were also Annegret Richter and Inge Helten from West Germany. Richter looked close to unbeatable in her semi-final, recording a new world record of 11.01.

Still, I felt confident I might squeeze in somewhere to finish with perhaps a bronze. But my luck and confidence were beginning to change.

The final of the 100 metres was a debacle. There were three breaks, and each so unnerved the field that by the time we assumed the set position for the fourth time we were as highly strung as a pack of wild horses picking up the strong scent of a nearby predator. The first break was freakish — a momentary power blackout in Montreal for one brief fraction of a second caused the sensitive starting mechanism to think one of us had broken. We were a quarter of the way down the track, however, with me feeling as strong as a Mallee bull and in a good position to win a medal, when we were recalled. The second break belonged to me. Stuck in lane eight I noticed a camera flash going off just as I assumed the set position, and this triggered an instant reaction.

The third break was caused by Andrea Lynch. Now the stadium was completely silent. I have never known such tension at the start of a race as there was by the time we took to the blocks for the fourth attempt at a start. The gun went off and 11 seconds later we lunged at the line. I knew I'd just missed out. The gold went to Richter in 11.08, with Stecher second. Helten, the other West German, beat me home in 11.17. I finished in fourth place.

I wept. There was no chance of holding it back. After the frustration of the three false starts, and after my good form in the heat, it would have been nice to win a medal, but I was satisfied with finishing fourth. My main task was the 200 metres, and this was an indication that I was right on track. I waved away the journalists who gathered at the end of the track wanting a comment. I managed to give them a quote as I wandered off — the next time they saw me walking off this track after a final, I declared, perhaps not realising how arrogant I sounded, I would be a medallist. But I did not have the heart to stand there and analyse what had gone wrong at the starting line.

Another debacle awaited me. Despite finishing fourth and out of the medals, for some reason officials decided I would have to undergo a dope test. Naturally, the Boyle tank was empty yet again. Stuck in the medical centre, I found myself alongside West Australian Bethanie Nail and the British middle-distance champion Steve Ovett. They, too, were struggling to summon up the required amount of urine. I stared at the fridge filled with beers that normally I would have willingly helped empty. But I had my 200-metre heats the next day, and the last thing I wanted was to bloat up on beer and weigh myself down.

The torture once again dragged on for hours. Eventually I was accompanied back to the athletes village where, after a meal and lots more fluid, I finally delivered the precious little bottle of Vintage Boyle. By then it was too late to go back to my room in a separate area of the village because the night curfew was in place. A bed was found for me in the nearby headquarters and I spent a restless and exhausting night tossing and turning in my tracksuit, worrying about my preparation for the next day and going through one crisis after another in my mind.

I was a Boyle. I was a natural worrier. After the 100 metres I sensed something was going wrong. I had no idea, however, by how much.

THE HEATS of the 200 metres saw me return to a better frame of mind. I won my first quite easily, and in fact beat Richter home comfortably, which did a great deal to restore some of my confidence. By the time the second heat was over, only one other competitor — East Germany's Baerbel Eckert — had recorded a faster time. I now knew that if I performed as well during the semi-finals I would be exactly where I had planned to be — at the front of the pack and dominating everyone, physically and mentally.

But I woke on Wednesday feeling unsettled. The feeling seemed to invade every part of my body from my head through to my bones and my heart. Who knows why. I'd slept well. I hadn't woken much. Some days you can just wake up and know it's going to be a shocker. You might have trained yourself to a pinnacle of fitness. Your mind might be as sharp as it could be. You might have reached a high point emotionally and spiritually. But for some reason it all falls apart.

I felt rotten. I felt I could scream for no apparent reason. I've had a quarter of a century to dwell on this and the events that unfolded a few hours later, and I still haven't quite figured it out. Maybe it was me, a little voice often says. Maybe that flaw in my character that I had always suspected was there — that I wasn't really good enough to be at this level, that I was an imposter who couldn't possibly cope with the pressure — was the culprit.

Who knows. Feeling stressed, I arrived at the track to discover one of the girls I shared a room with had cleaned out my bag and left out one of my spiked warm-up shoes. Usually I began warming up running in a pair of flats, then switched to my warm-up spikes, before donning my racing spikes. It was really no big deal. It was not a thing that should have worried me. But little things always trigger something larger. Shirley tried to call the village to have my shoe delivered to the track but for some reason it couldn't be done. No doubt I should have checked my bag. But I'd had no reason to — I'd left everything in there from the heats and had no reason to go back into it.

The fuss upset me, but even then it was hardly enough to put me off the upcoming semi-final. But as Shirley and I walked toward the registration area, she turned to me and said something out of the ordinary.

"Whatever you do, don't break."

It was a funny thing for a coach to say. Breaking had never been an issue with me. That break in the 100 metres had been a rare incident in an almost blemish-free career. As I wandered off to the start of the semi-final Shirley's words played at the back of my mind. Breaking? I wasn't the sort of athlete who broke.

I was in lane one for the semi-final, not one of the great lanes in a 200-metre race. Lane four was always the preferred lane. There, by the time you reach the top of the straight and the staggered start reduces, you are usually the first to gain some idea of where you are placed in the field. In lane eight on the outside you feel like a rabbit, sent out ahead of the rest of the pack. In lane one you can feel as though you have the rest of the field to overhaul. But again, this was just a small thing. It should not have mattered.

I took the set position. The starter — a Canadian, Jack Fisher — had changed his position, moving from the rear of the field where he'd been for the heats, to the side. The gun went off and we were away cleanly. But then the gun went off again, recalling the field. I wandered back to the starting blocks, not even thinking the break had been called on me. But as we prepared to restart I noticed a yellow ball on my blocks, indicating I was being blamed for the break.

I didn't know what to think. How could I have broken? Fisher would claim later that he had seen my head and shoulders move. All the evidence since, including film and statements from others, proves that I did not break.

"Had it been a slight shake, that would have been one thing, but I'm convinced it was a head and shoulder lunge that definitely went forward," said Fisher later to Ron Carter, the experienced athletics reporter with the *Age*. "She is supposed to react to the gun, not anticipate it ... a movement of the head and shoulders is frequently the beginning of the start with many athletes. The rules state athletes must be perfectly still at the start."

I'm positive my head and shoulders did not move. But even if they had, Fisher was on shaky ground. A break took place many ways, but officially it was recognised by your hands leaving the ground. And my hands had certainly not left the track before the gun had fired. Years later I pored over Fisher's comments. They looked to me like a man who was trying to convince himself that he had done the right thing.

By the time we settled back into position my head was whirling. We were called into the set position and then, for some bizarre reason, I decided I had to raise the issue. Good old argumentative Boyle. I couldn't let it go. I couldn't just put it out of my mind and get on with the job and get stuck into Fisher later. I had to tackle Fisher and correct him, right there and then. But instead of raising my hand to indicate I needed to halt the race, I simply rolled out of the set position. Fisher called a second break on me. And that was it. I was out of the 200-metres semi-final. Out of the medal race. All those years of training — the months with Shirley under a hot Perth sun, the years of cold Melbourne winters … all of it had come to nothing.

Stunned, I walked across to the side of the track to let the race continue. The late Graeme Briggs, one of the Australian officials, came over to console me. "*C'est la vie,*" he lamented.

"Don't give me any fuckin' *c'est la vie,*" I told him harshly. "Get in there and bloody well protest. That's outrageous what he [Fisher] has done."

Mum was in the stand looking on and I was told later she would have killed Fisher had she been able to climb over the 72 000 spectators and get to him. I would have done it myself had I not started crying and shaking on the side of the track. I have never felt more alone than in those long minutes as the field lined up again and then took off. Stecher won the semi-final, and looked a chance to repeat her triumph in Munich.

My protest went nowhere, of course, because the rules state that once the field has been placed in his hands, the starter holds ultimate control. His authority is virtually unquestioned.

Ron had come over to the track to watch my race, and he was there quickly to try to console me, along with Shirley. But when it became clear the protest was going to fail, the last place I wanted to be was trackside with the eyes of everyone upon me. Ron took me back to his room in the village and gave me a large can of Foster's. I downed it quickly, and then we decided it was best to go back and watch the final.

It was hard to be an observer. I can't say I would have won it with 100 per cent certainty. Eckert won, with Richter and Stecher filling up the minor placings. But I was fairly sure that had I made it through to the final I would have taken it out. There was only one person, I decided at the time, who had cost me my last chance to win a gold medal. His name was Jack Fisher.

Later, I faced the reporters. There was no avoiding it, although all I felt like doing was crawling away and hiding in a large dark hole. "It's all so stupid," I said. "I've let everyone down. When the first break was called against me it didn't even register. I just didn't believe it was true. I should have been careful about the second start. But I wasn't. I felt I was in an unreal situation."

I had a relay to run the next day. "This time I trained so hard, I tried so hard and so many people helped me," I said. "I don't know whether I can go through all that again."

I almost didn't. Going back onto the track was the last thing I wanted to do and because of that attitude our 4x100-metre team almost didn't make the finals. I was slack — my mind was elsewhere and for one of the few times in my career I just ambled through an event. All of sudden I had to surge over the last 20 metres to get us through. Personally, it was an embarrassing performance. I felt as though I had let the team down, even though nothing was said to me. Eventually, we finished a creditable fifth in the final.

All I wanted to do was go home and hide. I was ambivalent about the future. I was twenty-five and by the time the Moscow Olympics arrived I would be twenty-nine and facing my fourth Games. There was no way I could be expected to keep pace over the short sprints, and the 400 metres was an event I hated with a passion.

My last chance at an Olympic gold medal had come and gone. The Games were over for me. So, too, was my relationship with Shirley.

DON'T BREAK.

Everything changed after that pre-race warning Shirley gave me. We went back to Australia and I decided it was time to relax, unwind and get rid of all the pressure that had been building up in me over the years. I went to Melbourne to say goodbye to Peter Crimmins, embarrassed myself by not even listening to what he was asking me, and then went back to Perth for that small operation to remove the harmless cysts from my right breast.

Running was the last thing on my mind. I had a catamaran which I liked to take out on the Swan River. I found a flat of my own to share with fellow sprinter and friend Bethanie Nail. I started thinking about life after running. And I partied a bit, too.

But Shirley thought differently. There was no point in dwelling on what had happened in Montreal, she told me. Now was the time to get back into serious training and break a world record or two to prove that I was the fastest woman in the world over 200 metres. But Shirley didn't seem to understand. World records weren't my thing. They didn't motivate me like the prospect of a gold medal. Records came and went — by the late 1970s and the rise of the sporting drug culture, those who kept world records only used pencil, because they spent more time erasing and updating the books than watching the events. A medal was forever. Shirley should have known that. She had won three of them.

Perhaps she was just trying to keep me motivated. Whatever the reason, a gulf developed between the two of us. We were two very different people. Circumstances had brought us together and I was grateful for the sense of purpose and discipline Shirley had instilled in me. But after Montreal it began falling apart. Shirley, I'm sure, thought I was reverting to my old self, happy to just coast along, have a good time and not put in the hours and commitment required to make it to and stay at the very top.

One day I was at Grandma's helping her in her garden before going to training when I was bitten by a redback spider. I went to hospital immediately — I knew how venomous the redback could be. They might have become a part of Australian folklore with their habit of appearing on outdoor dunny seats, but the moment one appeared on me there was hell to pay.

The doctors quickly jabbed me with antivenom. I asked one of the nurses to call Shirley to let her know where I was and that I was not in the best condition. I was scheduled to undergo time trials later that afternoon. But the message came back that Shirley was hardly impressed with my "excuse". She didn't believe I had been bitten by a redback.

A few weeks later she asked me to compete against two men in a time trial. I refused, telling her there was no way I was running against men. I'd already been humiliated in Montreal. I wasn't going to allow myself to be put in that position again. Once more all those little flaws in my personality came to the fore — the insecurities, the shyness, the unwillingness to put myself in a position where I could be embarrassed in front of others. So I confronted it the way I always did by being defiant and putting on a display of stubbornness.

From there our professional and personal relationship gradually ended. A curious situation developed. I would arrive for training, await orders and that was it. There was no discussion. I started turning up only sporadically and instead concentrated on doing other things in life.

Puma was still funding me, and until Montreal I had also received a lot of assistance from a sports fan in Cairns called Billy Long. He was quite wealthy and for some time he used to send me a "retainer" of about $100 a week, to assist me with my training and allow me to focus on running. It helped pay the rent and left me plenty of time to enjoy my life.

The next few years merged. I picked up a part-time job in a Perth florist shop. And there were events to run — I competed in the KB Games, a promotional series held in several cities, and earned good money for the time.

There were journeys overseas to compete in the burgeoning world athletics circuit, enduring near-penury while living in shared accommodation with other Australian athletes. I don't know what was worse — the fact that sometimes we barely had a brass razoo left on us, or the experience of having to put up with the smell of Ken Hall's running shoes. Hall, along with Rick Mitchell and Beth Nail, shared several places with me during a frustrating northern European summer in 1977 as we all tried to further our careers by competing against world-class opposition. But those shoes of his were a powerful argument against living with any middle-distance runner. Ken had been runner-up when the New Zealander John Walker set his stunning mile record of 3 minutes 49.4 seconds two years earlier. Little wonder Walker had looked like collapsing after setting that record. With the odour of Ken's shoes behind him, it was clear he smashed the world record trying to get away.

I engaged in my regular guerrilla warfare with officialdom, too. At a World Cup meet in Dusseldorf, Germany, the selectors decided to dump me from the 200 metres in favour of Denise Robertson. I was told I would only run in the 100 metres. So I sat it out. If they wanted to be petty, I figured, then so would I. Later, probably in retaliation for that display of stubbornness, I was left out of a 35-strong team for a Pacific Games meeting. And at the 1977 Australian championships in Sydney, where I won the 100 and 200-metre titles quite easily, I had another couple of run-ins with officialdom. These were the sort of trivial but annoying incidents that had marked my career. As I walked onto the track to warm up for the 100-metres final fifteen minutes before the event was scheduled to start, a male official tried to block my entry. He obviously didn't know the rules — athletes are always allowed entry to the arena a quarter of an hour before their event. So I ended up walking past him anyway. Memory fails me here, but I do have a vague recollection of referring to him as a silly old fart. If that memory is correct, I must have been in an extremely polite mood.

Then, after winning the 100 metres, I made my way toward the television crews waiting for my post-race comments. They were all kept in a fenced section at the end of the track. Lo and behold, a female official now stepped in front of me. "You can't go down there," she said. "You must report to the victory ceremony immediately." Did these people not understand how important it was that athletics received the best exposure possible? Crowd figures and public interest in track and field had fallen since the disaster of Montreal, and I believed it was in the best interests of the sport for it to gain as much publicity as possible.

I shrugged. Sometimes, it seemed, athletics was its own worst enemy.

The following year, the national trials for the 1978 Edmonton Commonwealth Games in Canada — where I would make an unprecedented attempt to win gold for the third consecutive time — were held in Brisbane. The Amateur Athletic Union of Australia decided not to make me one of the 47 athletes to be funded to the trials. It was a remarkable snub, even given my relationship with officialdom. Who knew how their minds operated? The story ran across the country, and while I was prepared to pay my own way, I was given a tremendous boost when Maggi Eckhardt, a model who at the time was married to the advertising guru John Singleton, angrily read about my dispute with the AAUA and sent me the airfare to get to Brisbane.

Once there I made the team. But it wasn't without the usual dramas. In the 100 metres officials placed me ahead of Denise Robertson. There was no photo or timing equipment. It was a debacle — there was no other way to describe it. Denise was justifiably furious — she thought she'd won the race by a foot or more. I had no idea who had won it. I knew it was close, but because Denise was not in the lane next to me, and because the race was simply a lunge at the line, I was concentrating heavily on my own effort. Peg McMahon quoted Denise in the *Age* as saying, "I hate her. That decision is wrong. I won by a foot. I didn't even have to bend into the finish. I'll clean her up by 10 metres in the 200 tomorrow, you'll see."

And now you can see why the press lapped up our rivalry. Neither of us was backward in coming forward. When I heard about Denise's criticism, particularly the part about hating me, I gave her a serve during a television interview. But her forecast was right. She soundly beat me in the 200, although I was relatively happy with my second placing given my poor conditioning and lead-up to the trials.

That "I hate her" phrase ended up becoming a long, drawn-out drama, with Denise denying she had ever said it. A few days later the *Age* published a letter from Denise which read, "I would like it made known that at no time did I ever use the following statement — 'I hate her' — while we are track rivals and both take our racing seriously, I have never felt or indicated personal animosity of this degree. I would not like to think that the sportsmanship which I have endeavoured to show over the years has been questioned or could be questioned ... any adverse feelings that I have are simply directed at the absence of photo finish equipment necessary for a meeting of such importance."

Life always provides a few unexpected twists along the way. As I've said, these days I only live a few minutes from Denise and we have seen each other socially on a few occasions. Without the backdrop of competition, we chat happily enough.

AS THE Edmonton Games approached, I asked Shirley to take me back on again, and while she agreed half-heartedly, there was never any warmth in our relationship. Besides, by then injuries were catching up with me. My Achilles tendons were playing havoc with my running and things weren't helped one day when, working out on a calf-raising machine in the West Australian Insititute of Sport's gymnasium, I lifted a far too heavy load and tore my right Achilles tendon.

Still, I felt there was no excuse for not winning the gold medal in the 100 metres at Edmonton. I had planned to give Maggi Eckhardt the medal as a reward for showing faith in me, but I was beaten across the line by Sonia Lannaman. I still maintain to this day that had I concentrated more on winning the race, instead of simply worrying about where Denise was and how I could beat her, the result might have been different.

Yet I could hardly complain, particularly after what happened in the heats of the 200 metres. My Achilles tendons finally surrendered to the inevitable. Like rubber bands stretched to breaking point, they snapped. The Games were over for me. I wondered just how much longer I could continue.

Coming home from Canada I stopped over in Melbourne and underwent my final ankle operation. The doctor was hardly impressed when he opened me up. "It was like a bit of chewed meat," was his graphic description. He doubted whether he could do much more. And from there, my career seemed all but over. The Moscow Olympics were hanging on the horizon, but I remained unsure whether I could last the journey through to 1980.

Part of me wanted to continue — after all, what else was there for me to do? Running was the only thing that made me feel confident and in control of my life. But clearly my body was ageing and beginning to betray me. If I was to somehow extend my career, then once again I would have to find a way of manufacturing another set of fortunate circumstances.

So I picked up the phone one day after returning to Perth and made another call that would change my life. I'd had a strong and influential man to guide my career when I was a young girl just starting out. Now it was time to convince another man to help me finish it in style.

15

Boycotting the Games

It was a cold Melbourne winter's night in 1980 when I sat down in front of the television set and decided, not for the first time in my life, to get drunk. It wasn't the best idea I'd ever had but I couldn't think of anything better. I was morose, feeling sorry for myself, and I knew the images on the television screen would do little to improve my mood. The opening ceremony of the Moscow Games had begun, and for the first time in four Olympics I wasn't there.

I had qualified for the Games — in both the 400 metres and 200 metres — several months before. But that was before the political turmoil that emerged following the Soviet Union's invasion of Afghanistan. The world was appalled by the move and once again the Olympic movement became little more than a glorified version of the United Nations.

I had trained hard for these Games, perhaps even harder than I had for Montreal. But the journey had been made easier by a short man with a quiet voice, an enormous intellect and, when it came to dealing with R.A. Boyle, the patience of a saint. Ron Dewhurst had made me believe in myself again. But not even his remarkable ability to keep me on an even keel had stopped me from making a decision that would end my Olympic career and any hope I had of finally achieving a gold medal.

Under intense pressure, both political and self-imposed, I had withdrawn from the Australian team to compete in Moscow. I was sick of my sport being prostituted by politicians trying to score diplomatic points. I was tired of the athletes always being the ones to bear the cost of the political jousting. Deep down, I suspect, I was also simply tired of fighting.

So there I was, sitting in the living room, watching the official end of my Olympic running career, and doing my best to get drunk. But I couldn't. I was only ever a good drinker when I was in a good mood. My flatmate at the time boasted an impressive wine collection of 38-dozen bottles, so there was enough ammunition to keep me supplied for the next year. But nothing seemed to work.

Instead, I cried. I wept like a baby. As the teams walked into the stadium I remembered what it was like to walk behind the flag (or, in my case in Montreal, carry it) and feel like you were floating on air. The Games always had that special magical feel about them. And now I realised I would never again experience it. I was twenty-nine years old and it was all over. It was not a nice feeling. That evening I felt as low as I'd ever felt during my career. Athletics, like all sports, is kind to you only when you are young. Then it turns on you. Isn't that always the way? Our entire society seems to be centred around youth and beauty, and sport has always been a heightened reflection of life. You become old in sport much faster than you do in real life. You wear out. You burn out, too. There is always someone younger and faster coming up behind you. I'd held off so many challenges over the past decade that I must have thought it could go on forever. But no-one is immune. Look at all the teenage tennis prodigies over the years who have flamed out spectacularly in their mid-twenties, washed up and already consigned to footnotes in the history books.

I was feeling all that. At twenty-nine I should have been hitting my straps in real life, fast approaching those years when you have enough experience behind you to feel confident about the decisions you make. But sport had distorted my view of life. Dad had instilled in me a romantic notion about the role of sport, and years of competing at international level had inevitably cut me off from the real world. I was feeling as though my best was already behind me. The future was an unknown country that I wasn't sure I wanted to visit.

The parade in Moscow continued. I forced myself to keep watching through the tears. How many nights had I spent down at Melbourne's Olympic Park, sometimes training in the darkness on my own, just to keep my dream going? Sometimes my legs ached so much I could barely lift them, but I always kept going because I knew the ultimate reward would be one more taste of that Olympic magic. I was a junkie, that was certain. Every four years I knew I could get a hit of adrenalin that nothing else on the planet could provide.

So I looked on at the spectacle of the Moscow opening ceremony. But after a while I could stand it no longer. I raced to the bathroom and was physically sick for what seemed like hours.

I HAD decided after the disappointment of Edmonton and my ongoing Achilles problems that if I was going to find a way to continue at international level and make the team for Moscow, I needed to reinvent myself as a 400-metre runner. It was a distance that filled me with dread — the few times I had attempted it had been enough to make it clear that I was not a natural over the distance. I was a born sprinter and I just couldn't help charging out of the blocks and going hell for leather.

So if I had to change my ways yet again, I would have to change my environment. And that meant leaving Perth and going back to Melbourne. The lure of the Swan River and the hours on my surfcat were too much of a distraction, as was the general Western Australian lifestyle. There's a reason so many people who travel west rarely return — the climate and the easygoing way of life in Western Australia become addictive pretty quickly. I knew that I'd miss my group of friends, and leaving Grandma almost broke my heart. But I was fast approaching a point when I would have to get myself a real job and a life in the real world. I found neither prospect particularly comforting.

The word within the athletic community was that Ron Dewhurst was a terrific coach. I'd met him a couple of times in previous years — he'd piggybacked me home on the campus of Washington State University after a big night out when I was suffering a badly torn Achilles tendon and was having difficulty walking in the lead-up to the Edmonton Commonwealth Games. He was a former steeplechaser whose greatest talent lay in his ability to get the best out of those around him. So I called him one day, asking if I could join his group in Melbourne when I returned.

He was pleasant enough on the phone, but I could tell he needed some time to think. By now I was pretty much seen as a spent force, a sprinter who was in danger of hanging on for too long. So I waited until he arrived in Perth for the 1979 national championships and then we sat down and talked. And talked. Ronny was a great talker, but even more he was a wonderful listener. He spent two days listening to me tell him what I wanted to do. He was clearly trying to discover just how much ambition I had left, and whether I had the commitment to become not only a 400-metre runner, but someone who could work with him without letting my ego run out of control.

I made it clear to him that I still had the fire to go on. But I also said I doubted whether I had much left in the tank. He would have to be sensible in the way he coached me; I didn't think my body was capable of coping with the sort of fitness regime Shirley had imposed on it a couple of years before. He must have liked what he heard. He agreed to take me on — with one stipulation. He would have to return to Melbourne and ensure the rest of his training group were prepared to include me as part of their team.

He flew home. And was told that a number of the team members rejected the idea. My reputation as an intimidating and sometimes disruptive presence, it seemed, had preceded me yet again. But Ronny overruled them. He believed I could become good enough to make the final of the 400-metres in Moscow, and after that, who knew ... a medal was not out of the question. I flew back to Melbourne to begin the long and gruelling metamorphosis into a 400-metre runner.

I UNDERWENT another Achilles operation in November, and once again I was fortunate that my fitness allowed me a quick recovery. Training with Ron Dewhurst had become a pleasurable experience — at least most of the time. I'd never really encountered a coach — in fact, a person — like him before in my life. That soft voice of his had a remarkable ability to calm me. It was a deceptive voice, it was so restrained, so controlled. What he said always seemed to make sense. He was also a master psychologist. One of the things Ronny has always said about me is that while I might have been a prickly and tempestuous person to deal with, he never had any doubts about my ability to get the job done. Under his direction I became a far more measured and confident person.

Ron was a year younger than me, and our decision to team up had certainly raised a few eyebrows within the athletics scene. Some asked why, as a triple Olympic medallist, I would throw my lot in with a relatively inexperienced coach. Others asked why, as an emerging talent on the coaching scene, Ron would be interested in taking on an old has-been like Raelene Boyle.

We both had our reasons. Ron had been a better than decent steeplechaser, but a knee injury at the age of eighteen had ended any ambitions of an Olympic career. By the age of twenty-two he had coached his first international-class athlete and had begun to develop his theories about how to manage athletes. With me, he believed his low profile might help me. He had observed my career closely and noted that I had tended to have a lot of high-profile people around me over the years. He didn't think that had necessarily been bad, but at this late stage of my running life Ron believed I needed as few distractions as possible.

One of his strongest wishes was to keep me away from people with negative thoughts. "It's irreplaceable time," he would say about sharing company with people who looked on the negative side of life. "You can never replace those minutes."

I qualified for the Moscow Games in March, winning the 400 metres by a street in tough windy conditions. It was the first time since the operation six months before that I had run without any ankle strapping or support, and I was relieved more than excited to have qualified. Running a 400 for me was like asking a naturally extroverted person to sit quietly at the back of a party and not dance or crack a joke. For one thing, Ron and I had worked on changing my running style. I was more upright and I felt less fluent. But it was a style that would enable me to get around the track and curb to some extent my natural tendency to sprint out of control. It was a difficult assignment. At one meet in Melbourne I took off like a rabbit out of the blocks. By the time I hit the front straight with just 100 metres to go, the track felt like quicksand and I came close to blacking out. Television camera crews were waiting for me at the finish line. Unfortunately, I couldn't even speak. After that, Ron walked up to me with a hint of a smile on his face. "Now, are we going to start doing it my way or what?" he asked.

And we did — at least most of the time. I even surprised myself by finishing runner-up in the 200 metres to Denise, my arch-rival, who by then had married the pole-vaulter Ray Boyd and taken his surname. I was the first track and field athlete in Australian history to have made four Olympic teams. But it was hard to get too excited. The US president, Jimmy Carter, was spoiling for a fight with the Russians, ever since their tanks had thundered into Afghanistan the previous year. His calls for an Olympic boycott unless the Soviets withdrew from their poverty-racked neighbour were gaining momentum, and I could see that another debacle was in store for the Olympic movement.

Over the next few months the controversy picked up heat. The Australian prime minister, Malcolm Fraser, had made it clear that he expected Australia to support the Americans and boycott Moscow. The arguments raged and the country was split. That debate was no more fierce than the one among the athletes. I honestly had no idea what was right or wrong. I knew some sort of message had to be sent to the Russians that their invasion of Afghanistan was wrong. But why was sport always the weapon? Perhaps it showed the potency and power of the Olympic movement.

Edwin Moses, the great American hurdler, seemed to sum up every athlete's despair that the Olympics had been flattened in the same manner that Russian weaponry was rearranging the Afghan countryside. "These are *our* games," he said defiantly. Few listened.

With just two months to go the Australian Olympic Federation seemed committed to defying the government and fielding a team in Moscow. Ronny and I discussed the issue daily. It was just about the only thing on our minds. I was growing increasingly angry because I felt so many people were looking to me to make a stand. I was the veteran of the team and the media was always quick to poke a microphone under my nose. I didn't blame them — I'd been good for a quote over the years and on a slow day I was always handy fodder to help develop a decent headline. All I knew was that my sport was once again being corrupted by a political situation.

One night at training the stress finally got to me. It was bitterly cold and my enthusiasm had waned along with the temperature. I told Ron I didn't think I could go on. The pressure was simply too much. Not only was the controversy on the front pages of the newspapers almost every morning, but the issue had plunged a dagger into the heart of Australian athletics, dividing colleagues and the Australian public.

I had even received death threats. We didn't take them seriously, and Ron certainly shielded me from the most vicious comments. But it had all reached breaking point. I felt exposed and extremely fragile. Ron tried to get me to refocus on the athletic challenges ahead, rather than the political debate. "Lift your game, RB," Ron said to me. "You've got to get your mind back on the job. Forget everything else. Just do what you're here to do."

With that, I stormed off. It was a rude and totally ungracious way to act. But my emotions had reached boiling point and I was already fairly sure that going to Moscow would be the wrong thing to do.

I grabbed my gear and took off. Ron came after me. I started for my car, stepping over a low fence that circled the outside of the track. Ron grabbed me in an effort to stop me and calm me down. I turned and whacked him in the ribs. I could hear the breath running out of him but I didn't bother stopping to see if he was all right.

I jumped into my car and sped home. That night, feeling ashamed and embarrassed, I lay awake for hours wondering if Ron was still lying in a crippled heap at the bottom of the fence, or if I had broken his ribs. But the Boyle stubbornness — and that fear of admitting being in the wrong because in my mind that meant defeat — remained. I didn't call him.

Instead, my phone rang the next day. "Are we still talking RB?" asked Ron. We were, I told him. But we needed to discuss something. I didn't think I would be going to Moscow.

Ron was silent. He'd known I was moving toward such a decision, but I don't think he honestly thought it would come to this. He and I had sacrificed so much just to get to this point that at first he could not quite understand what I was saying. I, in turn, felt dreadful. Ron had been an incredibly hard worker. In life he was one of those high achievers determined to stamp his mark on the world. Coming from a working-class family in Cheltenham where money was always scarce, he was in the process of building a career as an investment manager and stockbroker. Yet money and the accumulation of wealth had never come close to corrupting his moral code. As a coach he believed he had to make the same sort of sacrifices and give the same commitment that he expected from his athletes.

Remarkably, he had given up his job and sold his car to raise the funds for his air ticket to Moscow. That weighed heavily on me, although Ron was always quick to tell me it should not get in the way of any decision I made. But the turmoil surrounding whether or not to go to Moscow was proving too much.

A day had not gone by without Malcolm Fraser or some other politician making a plea for athletes to stay home and support the government's stance. My phone was constantly ringing with reporters and athletes wanting me to make a decision and to go public with it. For someone who simply wanted to run, the whole thing had become a nightmare. So I went through my reasons with Ron and made it clear it was final. He knew me well enough by then to know that I might spend a lot of time thinking about something, but once I'd made up my mind, that was it. I tried never to look back after making a decision. Such a policy had cost me a lot over the years. But it was the way things were.

I drafted a letter to the Australian Olympic Federation and the next day met Ron in a pub in the city. He'd had it typed up for me, and I delivered it that afternoon to the offices of the Australian Olympic Federation. Judy Patching, Dad's old work colleague and now the secretary-general of the AOF, came out and spoke to me, saying he understood my decision and how agonising it must have been. The AOF directors had voted 6–5 in favour of defying the federal government and going to Moscow, and I made it clear to Judy that my decision was not in support of the government, or in protest against the AOF's decision.

"Dear Sirs," said my letter, which was released a few hours later to the media. "It is with regret that I formally advise my withdrawal from the Australian 1980 Olympic team ... competing at an Olympic Games means a total obligation that should overflow with enthusiastic dedication.

"... [A]fter being a lucky young lady to be placed in the Mexico team, I have given up everything necessary to allow my sport all possible opportunities. My achievements are many, but never did I achieve my ultimate goal — possibly I wasn't good enough. But nonetheless I have always been in there with a chance — even at this stage of my career there is still a chance.

"I have not enjoyed some phases of my Olympic career — but my desire to enjoy it and better myself have always survived. And in fact many of the hurdles have added to the challenge for Raelene Boyle, the athlete.

"Unfortunately of late, a part of me has been slowly crushed and stamped into the ground. I have been looking at the same shell in the mirror, but the inside of that shell has emotionally been destroyed through the confusion ... I wish those athletes who have chosen to go to the Olympics the best of luck."

All hell broke loose the next day. My phone didn't stop ringing. There were media interviews to be conducted and friends to whom

I had to explain my decision. Some of the athletes who had elected to go expressed surprise and bewilderment; I'm sure some of them must have believed I had made a political choice to back Malcolm Fraser and the Liberal government of the day. Yes, it was true, I had been a Liberal supporter. But the entire Moscow imbroglio ended up leaving a bitter taste in my mouth for years to come. For years afterwards I would go into a voting booth and tear up my voting slip in protest over what I felt politicians and politics had done to me, my career and the sport I loved. Not even a cheque that arrived on Christmas Eve that year for $6000 from the federal government, meant as some form of compensation for withdrawing from Moscow, but which was inevitably seen as a pay-off in some quarters, would change my mind.

A few weeks before the Games began the influential American magazine *Track and Field* named me as the fourth best female sprinter of the 1970s, behind two East Germans — Stecher and Marita Koch — and Poland's Irena Szewinska. Many said it was a reminder of just how unlucky I had been in my career, coming up against such talented opponents (and, as it turned out in the case of the East Germans, such chemically enhanced athletes).

In the weeks after Moscow, where Australia managed to better its efforts in Montreal, capturing two gold, two silver and five bronze medals, I made one more decision.

There was no way I was bowing out of running in such circumstances. I'd tried too hard, and relied on far too many people over the years, to let it end this way. Ron Dewhurst had given up a promising career and been forced to travel on trains because of his belief in me. There was no way I wanted to be remembered for the circumstances surrounding Montreal and Moscow.

I would go on and give it one more shot. Surely, I thought, I could manufacture one more fortunate circumstance.

16

A golden goodbye

ONE OF THE MOST POWERFUL FIGURES IN WORLD ATHLETICS IN THE early 1980s walked with a limp.

Andy Norman was British and while the influence of the Poms had waned around the world over the years, Andy had set up his own version of the old empire. He could make or break an international athlete. He had been instrumental in running the grand prix European circuit, and as the first real signs of professionalism and commercial endorsements became apparent in track and field, he was perfectly placed to exploit the new era.

I had got to know Andy during a couple of my stints in England and we had become quite good friends. He had been responsible for organising many of my races during the European summer, and had ensured my meagre expenses and fees of the time were met.

But I hadn't seen him for a couple of years until I ran into him as

I crossed the training track just a few days before the start of the 1982 Brisbane Commonwealth Games.

The 400 metres would be my last hurrah, and Andy, along with millions of Australians, was very much aware that this was my final appearance. Ronny and I had already made that decision, long before my training campaign for Brisbane had begun. Ronny knew, without me even having to tell him, that my ankles had very little left in them. "Doc" Toyne had also shaken his head when he'd given me a physical examination one day. He didn't understand why I was still trying to keep running, he said. I would be lucky if my ankles held out for eight or nine more hard races. His considered opinion was that I had a 20 per cent chance of making the Games. Toyne had been around for a long time and I had always trusted his expertise when it came to diagnosing injuries. But those odds were better than nothing. In fact, they became a new motivational spur for me. I had a couple of T-shirts made up with the Roman numerals for 20 — XX — sewn across the left breast as my emblem for Brisbane.

But there was more to the retirement "deal" between Ron and me than the frailties of my body. There was nothing worse than watching an old athlete in any sport struggling on at the back of the pack, trying desperately to relive old glories and pretending they were immune to the ravages of time.

I'd seen a few like that in my time. I understood why they did it — it was always hard to let go of something that had been the passionate driving force behind your life. It was even harder when that force took you to the pinnacle of your sport. Let's be frank about this. Ego is a powerful thing. If you can harness its power it can help you achieve things you might never have believed were possible. But it also has a destructive side; it can blind you to your weaknesses and feed an illusion that you are indestructible.

I didn't want to end my career floundering at the rear of a 400-metre field, gasping for breath behind a pack of much younger and fitter athletes. And there was no way Ron Dewhurst, whose appreciation of the aesthetics of sport was similar to mine, and I guess my father's as well, was going to allow that to happen.

So Andy Norman limped over to me and after a little social chat said, "You know, you shouldn't win this race. But you will."

I shrugged my shoulders, feigned modesty, muttered thanks and tried to switch the subject. But Andy was having none of it.

"You will win this Raelene because you are tough," he said. "You're the toughest I've ever come across."

I didn't know about that — in fact, deep down, I strongly disagreed. But I understood what Andy was telling me. I wasn't as fast as a couple of the other girls. I wasn't as lithe anymore. My bones and muscles ached more often than they should, and running 400 metres still felt abnormal, as though I was using someone else's body and not my own. But Andy Norman was telling me I had the race won because I had psyched out the rest of the field.

This was the greatest compliment Andy ever paid me. He was a man who held his cards close to his chest when it came to international athletic negotiations. He knew a good bluffer when he saw one.

WE BEGAN preparing for Brisbane a few months after the Moscow debacle. The break had allowed my ankles to rest after two operations within a twelve-month period. Ronny, too, was clearly interested in nursing me through the next eighteen months.

We were both worried as to whether I had enough left, physically, to get to Brisbane and be competitive. We had a good friend at Falls Creek in Victoria's snowfields, Barry Jones, who owned a spectacular piece of real estate called Pretty Valley Lodge. In the summer he had few guests so Ron and I would go up for a week at a time and have a ball. We'd manage to squeeze in a few drinks and some nice dinners, but mostly it was hard, gruelling work. I would be summoned out of bed early each morning, something my body has never coped with very well. Then it was off to the aquaducts, up and down hills and mountains that stretched me to the limit and helped build up my endurance. In between, though, Ron and I would engage in long, and often deep, conversations on life and the meaning of everything.

It was one of the reasons I began to realise that Ron Dewhurst was a deceptively outstanding coach. He knew how to press my buttons, but he also understood that athletes needed to broaden their horizons and not just obsess about their form and what the ever-present stopwatch told them. Sometimes we would go on long walks and I would admire the plants and flowers that grew by the roadside. Ron would ask me questions about this plant or that; if he was feigning interest in one of my hobbies, he was doing a magnificent job. But Ron wasn't like that. He was fascinated by so many things. I was fortunate that he had decided that I would remain his biggest athletic project for the next eighteen months.

Back in Melbourne, I concentrated on my diet. I'd been lucky because I had always eaten vegetables and other healthy foods, and I'd always been careful not to over-eat before training. If I didn't manage to eat lunch before 1.30pm or so, then I would skip it completely. There was no point turning up at afternoon training and feeling nauseated for the entire session. But some did, and they never seemed to learn. There was one runner in our team who always seemed to eat a bag of chips on the way to training. He would endure one work-out, then before long you would see him crawling off into the surrounding bushes to help mulch the garden bed.

Eventually I had to have a word with him. Here I was trying to concentrate on my running. Every time I sprinted past him, I would have to put up with the distraction of him performing a decent impersonation of the lead singer of the Sex Pistols from within the nearby bushes.

I told him if he didn't have the [insert typical Raelene Boyle expletive here] discipline to [expletive] cope with our [expletive] training schedule, then perhaps he should [expletive] go elsewhere. His physical condition improved quickly after that pithy piece of advice.

See. I was getting good at this intimidation game. As the Commonwealth Games approached, I knew I couldn't put much trust in my ankles and legs, so sheer toughness would have to get me over the line.

ENDOMETRIOSIS, AS the millions of women around the world who have suffered from it will attest, is a crippling condition. It's a disorder of the female reproductive system which usually involves endometrial tissue growing in abnormal places in the body. I had suffered from it since puberty, and as I grew older, the pain associated with it intensified to the point that I was sometimes forced to spend days in bed. It usually struck in the lead-up to my monthly period. There had been times when I fainted because of the pain. Other days I simply curled up in bed in the foetal position for hours on end, or underwent violent vomiting bouts which sapped my strength for days. Over the years various doctors had examined me and tried to ease the symptoms, but little progress had been made. Eventually I would submit to a hysterectomy as a method of overcoming the condition. But as the Games drew close in 1982, my nightmare scenario was that I would again fall prey to my period just as the 400-metre final fell due in Brisbane. It would, perhaps, be the ultimate irony in a career dogged by bad luck and bad timing. So Ron and I decided it was time to do something about it.

The East Germans had long been tinkering with the menstrual cycles of their female athletes; as it turned out they had long been tinkering with their femininity as well. At one stage they aimed to have some of their athletes fall pregnant — those truckloads of East German soldiers must have been exhausted by then. Women usually receive a powerful boost in strength in the early stages of pregnancy as hormones surge through their body. The doctors would then terminate the pregnancy in its early stages. The moral corruptness of such a plan is almost beyond belief.

In Australia, altering menstrual cycles was not a widely discussed training method, even among the elite level of competitors. Like any woman, I knew there were times in my menstrual cycle when I felt at my strongest, and times when emotionally and physically I was at my lowest.

After a great deal of trial and error, I discovered that I was at my strongest and fittest soon after getting my period. In the days leading up to it I was often in pain. These attacks were usually accompanied by hot and cold sweats and a feeling of being bloated. It goes without saying that on those days, I was prone to irritation and a difficult person to deal with. I was also very injury-prone at those times and when my Achilles tendons tore or snapped it was always just a day or two away from my period.

By using the Pill, I was able to alter my menstrual cycle. By the time Ron and I headed to Brisbane in September to prepare for the Games, I no longer had any concern that my period would strike just as the starter's gun went off. By the time he pointed that gun in the air and a hush descended throughout the stadium, I would be in the second day of my period and at my strongest and fastest.

RON AND I decided that in the weeks leading up to the race, it was best that we eliminate as many distractions as possible. Looking back, it's clear that Ron understood my character weaknesses better than I did at the time. He has said since that when he decided to coach me, he believed I would need more help above the shoulders than below. One incident about a month before the Games proved

his point. I'd thrown my starting blocks at Ron after a huge
argument, and at that moment felt like walking out and ending my
comeback. My ankles were always on my mind, but it was my head
that, as usual, was my biggest obstacle. Ron had avoided the
starting blocks, however, as well as my verbal slings. From then on
he'd made it clear to me that he did not want any "negative" people
around me before the Games, and that included people who were
close to me as well as the media. To ensure I had the most positive
lead-up possible, Ron rented an apartment on the Gold Coast. I
could stay in the athletes village if I chose, but most nights I would
return to the apartment to talk strategy with Ron and my training
partner at the time, Mark Lancman.

"Lance" was a fine young sprinter, but it had taken a terrific
argument between Ron and me before I realised that he could help
me. Ron had asked me to run some time trials with him at training
one evening during the months leading up to the Moscow
Olympics and I had immediately refused. In fact, I came close to
telling Ron where to shove his coaching methods. Running against
a man, without doubt, would leave me limping along in second
place. People would be watching. They might laugh. They might
smirk and whisper about me among themselves. It took Ron's
finest motivational speech — typically performed in his quiet,
understated way — to bring me around to his way of thinking.
Since then, I had come to see the benefits of running with Lance.
He pushed me harder than any female athlete, and he was also a
pleasant man to be around. He is one of those genuinely funny
people who produce a neverending stream of chatter and jokes, a
frustrated stand-up comedian who, with me alongside him,
suddenly had the captive audience he had always wanted.

Only later did I discover that Lancman was also acting as Ron's
deputy on the track. Dewhurst would word Mark to keep me
buoyant and enthusiastic. "If Raelene says she's got a sore leg,"

DOG DAYS: My beautiful Ty helped me find my way through the difficult transition from athletics to "normal" life. I found the transformation awkward and was unsure what came next in life.

GARDENS OF DESIRE: By the late '80s I'd found a new direction — returning to my roots and becoming a gardener with a suburban council.

GOING FOR GOULD: Shane Gould and I share a few memories in the early '90s. It was good to talk to someone who had also ridden the rollercoaster of sporting fame.

HERE, KITTY: Two great friends — Fiona and Barb — were with me on the day I was told I had cancer. They were also with me during a wonderful vacation in South Africa when we met Cheeky the Cheetah.

'TWAS A JOLLY SEASON: Our last Christmas with Mum. Ron (TOP LEFT) was home for the first time in 15 years. With him are Tess and Rick.

ME AND MY MUM: Mum died in 1996. We had grown much closer in her later years but I never told her about my cancer diagnosis.

ANOTHER GOLDEN MOMENT: Ty's baby, Goldie. She continued the job of keeping me stable during my battle with cancer and depression. She died just after my 50th birthday.

MIXING POLITICS AND SPORT: Tokyo Olympian Judy Pollock, Prime Minister John Howard and me at a Hall of Fame dinner.

AMONG THE LEGENDS: At an Australian Sports Hall of Fame function. Wrestling great Dick Garrard chats while AFL great Ted Whitten looks on.

YOU LITTLE BEAUTY: It's 1.30 a.m. in Atlanta. I'm undergoing chemotherapy and Cathy Freeman has just made my day — and night — by winning silver in the 400 metres.

THE DRUG TRAIL: Judy and I were flown to old Stasi headquarters where we explored evidence of the East German sports drug empire.

THANKS, BROWNY: All smiles at my Testimonial in 1997 with supporter and former federal sports minister, John Brown.

FAULT-FREE: Wimbledon champion Evonne Cawley was one of many prominent sporting figures to attend my Testimonial.

DUET: Olivia Newton-John, fellow breast cancer survivor, gave an inspirational speech about confronting cancer.

SMILES ALL ROUND: Cathy Freeman, always smiling, always happy, always manages to lift me out of any bad mood.

WHAT A NIGHT! Judy and me at my Testimonial. It was a night of traditional moments and lots of laughter.

Ron would advise Mark, "tell her everything is okay and she'll be all right. Just keep her focused."

But I never really lost that wariness of being put in a position where I could be ridiculed.

Like a lot of people, I have always been careful about allowing myself to be placed in a position where I can be embarrassed or humiliated. Why? I pine to be loved and admired. I crave respect. It is a characteristic of my make-up that has always been with me, and has played such a large role in shaping my life. It was part of the reason I had moved out of our shabby Coburg family home so many years before and into the more comfortable middle-class surrounds of Aunty Dot's house.

One of my worst public experiences had taken place at the end of the Montreal Olympics when it was announced after the closing ceremony, following a suggestion by the prime minister at the time, Malcolm Fraser, that I be given the flag I had carried during the opening ceremony. A chorus of a traditional Australian song immediately filled the room.

"Hooray for Raelene," they sang, "Hooray at last, Hooray for Raelene, She's a horse's arse..." Instead of laughing it off, or putting on a brave face, I'd hurried from the room red-faced and with tears welling in my eyes. My sense of humour had long since deserted me by that stage; my disqualification from the 200 metres was still eating away at me. How dare my team-mates try to humiliate me, I'd thought. I'd rushed back to my room believing very few of my Australian team-mates had any respect for me. I eventually consoled myself by looking at many of them in a condescending fashion. As mental payback I decided, quite rightly as it turned out, that most of them were a bunch of hacks who were still a metre or two short of world standard. Several people have since said I over-reacted. Maybe. But I remain certain this incident was more than just typical, light-hearted Australian humour.

Clearly, I was still, and part of me will forever remain, that girl at the back of the classroom who stutters and turns red-faced whenever asked by the teacher to address the class.

Ron Dewhurst was one of the few people in the world who truly understood just how fragile my self-belief and confidence was, and so if it was important to him that I avoid negative thoughts and the people who generated them, I would do as he wished. He had already proven himself to me, not only through his unstinting loyalty throughout the Moscow Olympics controversy, but every day since. He knew my body did not have much left to give, and he had tailored my training program to suit. One example of this was his decision to try and lessen the wear on my Achilles tendons by getting me to run sprints in a straight line, rather than around bends, as I would in a race. He figured I knew enough about running bends by then, particularly given my 200-metre career. What was more important now was my longevity.

The media had naturally been taking a close interest in my progress. They had followed my career ever since the months leading up to the 1968 Olympics, and with me doing my best to avoid interviews, their angle now was the obvious one — would I be able to bow out on top?

Opinion seemed to be divided. England's Joslyn Hoyte-Smith was pretty well regarded as the favourite for the event. But a Welsh girl, Michelle Scutt, was also highly rated. Had this been an Olympic 400-metre event, it would have been no contest. Ever since Montreal, when my old rival Irena Szewinska had run the first sub 50-second 400 metres, world times had been getting faster. But with Brisbane hosting only Commonwealth countries, I was still considered an outside chance.

Andy Norman, however, knew the game was already up. Ever since then I've often thought he might make a decent fortune teller.

THE COMMONWEALTH Games began in Brisbane with the usual pomp and ceremony. There was a 60 000-strong crowd inside the Queen Elizabeth II stadium when I ran in carrying a baton containing a message from the Queen. It was a gusty afternoon, but no wind could possibly have wiped the grin from my face. It was one of the proudest moments of my career. The Duke of Edinburgh, Prince Philip, looked at me as I handed the baton to him and said I should have been wearing a tracksuit given the unseasonal cool weather. Perhaps he also knew something of my history, and feared I would come down with a bout of pneumonia to dash my hopes of a final Commonwealth gold medal.

But those days of awful luck were over. I was fit and there was nothing that was going to stop me. Over the next three days I trained lightly — one afternoon I ran two sets of 6x100 metres and Ron said we were done for the day. All we did were things related to high speed, and things that felt good. One training session was devoted to an evening at the movies. Ron was aiming at keeping me stress-free, and it was working. One of his techniques as a coach, if he thought one of his runners was performing well at training, was to cut the session short and say, "How did that feel? Great? Well let's stop right there. Remember how that felt. Don't forget the feeling."

The night before my first heat, the Australian team manager, Marg Mahony, asked me if there was anything she could do to help me. "Come and have breakfast with me tomorrow morning at 5.30," I told her. "Don't look at me, don't talk to me. Just sit there and be with me." I was staying overnight with the team in Brisbane and there was no way I wanted to be on my own in the dining room the next morning. Being alone was my greatest fear. But I knew I wouldn't be in the mood for small chat. Marg understood perfectly.

We had breakfast that morning. I ate. Marg said nothing. It was perfect. I comfortably finished the heat in second place, coasting past the line in the time of 52.71. Hoyte-Smith and Scutt both recorded faster heat times. A few hours later in our semi-final, Hoyte-Smith narrowly beat me in the time of 52.26, but I could sense that she seemed to be pushing herself toward the line, whereas I was happy to coast along just behind and get her full measure.

I felt confident, perhaps more so than at any other time in my career. I knew this was the last throw of the dice when it came to running, and I would never again have an opportunity like this. "Australians are very careful about what other people think," Ron would say. "They worry about what the neighbours think, about what they'll say about them. So they tend to be cautious. But when they suddenly get to their sixties they throw that caution to the wind. They go off and do a lot of things they've only thought about doing for years. You know why? Because they've suddenly realised that there might not be another chance. They might not make it to their seventies. This is their last big chance to do something they'll remember forever."

I was never great at school, but Ron Dewhurst had turned me into a half-decent student when it came to appending his wisdom. In running terms, I had hit my sixties and Brisbane was the place where I could throw caution to the wind. It didn't matter what happened afterward. And I didn't care what the hell the neighbours thought of me anymore.

THE NEXT afternoon, at 2.40pm, the starter pointed his gun in the air and the final individual athletic event of my international career began. At thirty-one I was the oldest athlete in the field and I was also carrying far more weight than any other competitor. I felt I was carrying the Australian population on my shoulders. The media interest in the race had reached quite remarkable proportions. It seemed every newspaper had carried articles asking if I could pull off a fairytale finish to my career. I'd felt the pressure building, of course. But Ron had been pushing the right buttons for so long that once the gun went off, I shrugged off the excess weight and allowed the routine of a lifetime of running to take over.

By the halfway mark I was trying to work out why I had not yet glimpsed Hoyte-Smith out of the corner of my eye. I was feeling strong and, as was my usual practice, I was talking to myself all the time. I often carried out conversations during races. The 100-metre sprint was only ever a short "hello, goodbye", but the 400 gave me plenty of time to think and strategise. I was always reminding myself to calm down, to conserve energy and not let my emotions clutter my mind and rob me of concentration.

With 150 metres to go — that critical point in a 400 when races can be won or lost — I began to sense that I had it won. As we came out of the last bend I looked back over my shoulder and saw that Hoyt-Smith on my inside was struggling and would not get close. Scutt, too, was nowhere near me.

For the first time I began to hear the crowd urging me on. With a stride or two to go before the finish I clenched a fist and pumped the air as I crossed the line. The relief was incredible. I have some idea how Cathy Freeman felt after her performance at the Sydney Olympics. My mouth was dry and my tongue, searching for moisture and finding none, kept sticking to the roof of my mouth.

A day or two before, Rick Mitchell, one of Australia's most outstanding male sprinters of the time, had suggested to me that if I won I should do a victory lap. I'd never been big on the idea — to me it looked like boasting and rubbing your opponents' noses in the dirt. But the crowd's applause was so strong — it was bedlam, basically — that I found myself swept around the track. People rushed up and hugged me, and all I could think about was finding a drink. As I looked around at the standing ovation I was receiving, I took it all in. It came close to being the highlight of my life.

But I retained a level head when, half an hour later in the large press conference that followed, a reporter tried to equate me with Betty Cuthbert. "There's no golden girl image with me," I told him. "That went with Betty Cuthbert. I haven't won an Olympic gold medal. I can't claim that because I have not lived up to the achievements of Betty or Marjorie Jackson."

My time of 51.26 was only slightly outside the Australian record I had set leading in to the Games. But I was adamant there was no going on. There was no point. To keep running and remain competitive by the time the Los Angeles Olympics rolled around in 1984 meant that I would have to lower my best time by almost three seconds — an impossible target, even had I been East German.

Eventually I headed back to the Gold Coast. That night about fifteen of us — just about Ron's entire training group from Melbourne — went out for dinner. I barely drank. I was exhausted and deflated; the adrenalin was seeping out of my body and the inevitable post-race letdown was taking place. A few weeks earlier the wine company McWilliam's had released a rare vintage to commemorate my retirement. The 1970 Mount Pleasant Old Paddock Hermitage was a nice drop. And now I fully appreciated its title. The old grey mare of Australian athletics had been finally put to the paddock. There would be no more individual racing (though in my final event I ran the last leg for the 4x400-metres relay, helping us to second place just behind the Canadian team).

But I couldn't sleep that night after winning the gold medal. The apartment looked like a carriage on a peak-hour train in Bangladesh. There were bodies everywhere. Perhaps it was the snoring that kept me awake, but more likely it was the realisation that it had all come to an end. All those years. The training. The operations. The early days when Dad and I were a team that I could never dream would be broken up. The highlights of Mexico and Munich, and the lowlights, too. It was all gone. I'd been a sprinter all my life, and time seemed to have passed so quickly.

Now I had to confront one of my worst fears — life after athletics.

At about 5am I tiptoed through the darkness of the apartment, stepping over and on the bodies that littered the floor, found Ron and woke him. "Come on," I said. "Let's go and talk."

We wandered down to the beach. It was cool and a soft breeze was still blowing. For an hour or two we strolled along the sand as the sun began to seep over the horizon, and talked. We discussed the race. We talked about the past few years and the sacrifices we had both made. As usual, I was more than happy to listen to Ron. He'd long since discovered that I was a difficult and abrasive person. But once I decided I could trust someone, that was it. They were a part of my life whether they wanted to be or not.

And Ron Dewhurst, despite the fact that a brilliant financial career awaited him, a career that would take him to the heights of business in New York and London, was now a permanent member of Team Boyle. Whenever I needed advice, whenever I felt low and just needed a friendly voice to listen to, I always knew I would be able to tap into Ron, no matter where in the world he and his family were living. The following year I would have my Brisbane gold medal framed, along with an Australia Post commemorative Commonwealth Games stamped cover, dated 4 October 1982, and give it to Ron for his thirty-first birthday.

It was the only appropriate gift of gratitude. Ron had managed to take my fragile and explosive personality and harness its best attributes for one final race. Along the way, he had also been there to give me advice about so many other aspects of my life.

But that morning, as we walked along the beach on the Gold Coast, there was one subject I did not feel like discussing.

The future.

At thirty-one years of age, I finally had to grow up and go out into the real world. The prospect of that filled me with dread and fear. I had no idea just how difficult at times that real world could be.

PART III

THE RACE OF MY LIFE

17

Take me as I am

MY PRIVATE LIFE IS SOMETHING I HAVE JEALOUSLY GUARDED OVER THE years. If it was a physical location you would find it in a remote area with "No Trespassing" signs littering the landscape. A little further down the road you would come across a huge fortress with almost unscaleable walls. Barbed wire would surround the perimeter. Scowling guards accompanied by vicious attack dogs would be on constant patrol. Somewhere deep inside this hidden and secure place would be me.

Of course the reality hardly resembles what I have just described. But some of my friends might suggest it comes close. To me, my home has long been a sanctuary, a place to hide from what has, at times, been a very public life. Don't get me wrong. It's not as if I'm a recluse. Far from it. From my athletic career through to my highly publicised battle with cancer, I have never shirked from publicly confronting some of the biggest issues in my life. Why so many people have shown such interest in me is something that perplexes me to this day. I was an athlete, that is all. I ran quickly. There are people out there — incredibly gifted and intelligent people — who will spend their lives in relative obscurity, yet devise and invent wonderful things to make other people's lives better.

But you won't hear about many of them. Sometimes I worry that we spend a little too much time feting our sporting greats and lose perspective about the really important things in life. So in a nation obsessed with sport, my opinions — the opinions of a female sprinter who never won an Olympic gold — have often been sought. Yes, people have written over the years that my long-running battles with officialdom ensured I would be held in high regard by a public that has traditionally been sceptical of authority figures. I'm not so sure. I'd like to think a little of it has to do with the fact that I kept going whenever I was close to being down and out, and that people respected me for always wanting to come back.

But I guess I'm the last person who should be analysing such things. All I know is that while my public image has helped me in so many areas — it has provided me with jobs and a steady income as well as allowing me to help raise awareness of public health issues such as breast and ovarian cancer — it has also been a burden. For someone who hates being the focus of attention, I've often felt that my private life is intruded upon. Over the years I have grown to be careful, trying my best to keep the public Raelene Boyle at a decent distance from the private one.

Answering machines have become the saviour of my life. People who manage to get through to me on my mobile phone are sometimes so astonished that I have answered a call that they are left speechless. I'm not secretive. I have never had a clandestine "other" life that I have hidden from my wide circle of friends and family. But I have always believed there must be a boundary, an ultimate line in the sand, behind which I can retreat and just be me.

Let me be frank. I'm wary about inviting people too far into my private sanctuary. I have always been at my most uncomfortable with strangers. It's that old trust thing yet again. Deep down I'm sure it's an inherent part of my make-up, a trait I was born with and one I am doomed to live with for the rest of my life. But part of it also has to do with my fear of rejection. To allow people to see the real me, to see all my flaws and deep-seated insecurities — the most complicated of my scars — may mean that they might judge me and not like what they find.

In the background, I can always hear the faint strains of "Hooray for Raelene, Hooray at last ..."

I ONCE wanted to have children. During my twenties I did my fair share of babysitting for friends, and at various times, like just about every woman, I entertained the idea of giving birth to my own child. I wondered what it would be like to conceive and then carry another human life in my womb. But circumstances were never right. My athletic career peaked during my premium child-bearing years, and my hysterectomy to end my endometriosis battles put an end to any ideas of having kids.

But there was another thing, too. I was never in a relationship that I felt was stable or long-term enough to justify having children. Welcome to one of the most complex contradictions in my life. I am a deep-seated conservative in so many areas. If it wasn't for some of the unconventional relationships in my life, you could easily mistake me for a passionate monarchist who would never even dream of voting for a left-wing party. Because, in part, that *is* me. I love the pageantry of the British royal family and all the tradition it stands for. (When I was awarded an MBE for services to sport in 1974, I was so nervous about receiving the award from the Queen — and so terrified, I'm sure, at the prospect of having to wear a glamorous frock for the occasion — that I knocked back the opportunity and instead received it in Australia.)

But how could anyone ultimately label me as a conservative? I have had passionate and intense relationships in my life with men and women. I have fallen in and out of love several times. So where does that leave me? It tells me once again just how dangerous it is to apply labels to people, to characterise and stereotype them.

I am what I am. At times I have been uncomfortable with that — even now I am thinking to myself: Will people dislike me for saying this? Am I about to be rejected? But that insecurity is gradually fading as I grow older. Yet it remains one of the reasons I dislike the terms "gay" and "straight". Those words carry far too much weight and far too many expectations in most people's minds. So don't even try to label me. Nothing fits. Some people might say I have never really come to terms with who or what I am. Good luck to them. I've always thought that people who think they really know themselves only understand the superficial exterior we all put on for the outside world. How can anyone really come to terms with who they are? Humans are so complex.

I like the institution of marriage. In 1977 I came close to becoming one of its fully paid-up members when a wonderful, red-haired hurdler from Western Australia proposed to me. John Sheridan and I had known each other for some time and we got along famously. We went to parties together, shared a similar sense of mischievous humour and had compatible views about what we wanted to achieve athletically.

Toward the end of the summer of 1977, I went to Hobart to watch the national men's championships and see how John fared. It was during the titles that he proposed to me. We got along pretty well, he suggested. Perhaps we should tie the knot. I'd fallen in love with John and it didn't take me long to say yes. Our decision was made public in April and we planned to marry later that year. But it wasn't long before it became clear to both of us that we'd made a pretty hasty decision. I was twenty-six and when I really thought about it, I wasn't exactly prepared for marriage at that time of my life. We were hardly ever together. John was establishing what would become a great career as a government valuer in Perth. In 1977 I seemed to spend more than half my time overseas trying to reignite my career after the Montreal debacle. He was off to the United States, having won a scholarship to run at a prominent university. By Christmas we had called the engagement off. Neither of us were really ready. But we have remained great friends ever since. Not long ago, my home phone rang. In a rare move, I answered it. It was John. I'd never heard him so excited. He'd just become a father after years of trying and thinking it would never happen. I was enormously happy for him. For a brief moment the old "what if..." crossed my mind.

At least that relationship had ended far more amicably than one of the most tumultuous in my life — my affair with the American athletics coach Brooks Johnson. We'd first met in 1971 when I was in the United States on a short tour to try and obtain some much-needed international competition a year before the Munich Olympics. Brooks had been a hurdler and he'd kept in touch with track and field by coaching a women's team in the Washington DC area. As they say in the classics, he swept me off my feet.

I had only just turned twenty and I hadn't long left home after my acrimonious split with Dad and the rest of the family. So I'm sure all those Freudian psychologists out there will say I was looking for a replacement father figure, a dominant male in my life with whom I would feel protected and loved. Perhaps. But I have a better theory. Brooks Johnson was the first man I had ever passionately fallen in love with. It was a genuine infatuation. He was elegant and classy. A history teacher, he was also well-read and knowledgeable. I should have known better, of course. His track record away from athletics was remarkable. He had already been married twice and he definitely had a reputation as a ladies' man. But I knew and cared little about that at the time. Instead, Brooks probably became the ultimate embodiment of the rebellious phase I was going through. Remember, I had been a late maturer, and it was only after I returned from the Mexico Games in 1968 that I first began asserting my independence. I had a lot of catching up to do. What better way was there for a naive girl from working-class Coburg to shock others, particularly in 1971, than by having an intense fling with a black American man thirteen years her senior?

But the affair was more than just a declaration of independence. I fell for Brooks Johnson in a big way. I spent a few days with him at his home and started thinking this was it. I was going to marry him. We would have kids. He could help me with my running. We would live happily ever after.

A problem soon arose. Brooks Johnson didn't want to live in Australia. He thought Australia was prejudiced against blacks back then, and he was probably right. Aboriginals, after all, had only won the right to vote a few years earlier. But the other problem was me. Old homebody Boyle had no intention of moving to the States, no matter how good it might have been for her running career. So we reached an impasse.

It did little to douse the passion and for a while, after I returned home, we stayed constantly in touch. But at some stage I grew suspicious. Brooks seemed to be curiously non-committal about our relationship. Perhaps, I began to think, he was interested more in pursuing me as a way of adding depth and publicity to his track club than he was in the personal side of things.

The relationship foundered. It reignited briefly a couple of years later in Canada for a few short days, but I never quite got over the feeling that I had been an interesting sidelight for Brooks and that he was never that serious about taking the relationship further.

Perhaps it was just a sign that I, too, was growing older and just a little wiser.

Other relationships came and went. Occasionally I went out with John "Sam" Newman, the high-profile Australian Rules footballer who has now become one of the most identifiable — and controversial — entertainment figures in the country. Sam and I would often meet with Hawthorn ruckman Don Scott for lunch on a Friday at the legendary Waiters Club in Melbourne. Both men were armed with a trove of hilarious stories and I loved to dwell over a bowl of pasta and listen to both of them. They are both intelligent men — Sam's rapid wit is well known. Unfortunately so, too, is his sarcasm. Yet he knows what it is like to be at the bottom of the heap. He's been broke because of his overly generous nature, but he's managed to reinvent himself to the point where he is now a wealthy man.

So they are a couple of the men who have been a romantic part of my life and I mention them because those relationships were publicly acknowledged at the time. I have also had relationships with women over the years. I don't need to justify myself here, or even explain how or why they came about. One of the lowest acts a person can commit is to kiss and tell — it's a gross act of disloyalty and one of the worst intrusions into someone's private life. Let me just say this. I am comfortable with who I am and I never intend to publicly discuss the intimate details of my private life. But before I hang out the "No Trespassing" sign again, I want to introduce a special person in my life who has had an enormously settling effect on me.

My partner, Judy.

THERE WERE not a lot of good things that happened to me in 1996. But as the end of that year drew closer and my chemotherapy course finally finished, allowing me to feel something like a normal human being again, I received a call out of the blue from an old friend I hadn't spoken to for quite a while.

I'd met Judy in the 1980s when I lived on the Sunshine Coast for a couple of years. After all the euphoria of the Brisbane Commonwealth Games, and after returning to work solidly with Nike for a couple of years to repay them for all the time they had given me to prepare for my 400-metre race, I felt burned-out and unsure where I was going in life. The move north helped me come to terms with my retirement from sport and made me realise that it was time to move on and find something else to fill the gap.

Judy was married then, had three young children and was helping to run an enormous caravan park. We became good friends; I always dropped by to see her and the kids. But when I returned to Melbourne and began studying horticulture in a move that would eventually lead me to a new life as a gardener, we lost touch.

Judy's marriage had broken up after I left the Sunshine Coast, and she had changed her life profoundly, moving in with another woman. You can only begin to imagine the pressures she encountered. The community in which she lived was scandalised. Judy was treated appallingly by many people. It was an ageing, conservative Queensland town and for months, if not years, she and her children endured gossip and finger-pointing from the usual hypocritical and self-righteous members of the community who had nothing better to do than pass judgment about someone they knew nothing about.

Judy had heard I'd had breast cancer, and was in Melbourne visiting her sister when she called. We caught up and our old friendship soon turned into something far more abiding and affectionate. I'd been speaking with my brothers about moving to Queensland with them. By Christmas I'd moved back up north — not in with them, but with Judy. Of course, this sparked another round of gossiping and rumour-mongering. But after a year of living so close to the edge of death, what other people thought no longer worried me that much. Over time people got to know us both and looked beyond labels and gossip. Now we are part of the community.

What was far more important was finding some tranquillity and stability in my life. Judy offered me that chance. Here was a woman who had already coped with several big crises in her life. What never ceased to amaze me was how she was so determined and at ease with herself. As I lurched toward the end of 1996 still struggling to understand what I had gone through, both physically and emotionally, Judy became a calm, stabilising presence in my life. She was an incredibly hard worker — I was a lazy sloth in comparison. She was not the sort of person to put up with the selfishness that had inevitably accompanied the surgery, chemotherapy and radiation therapy I had undergone during the year. We eventually become partners in a popular café. We bought a house and my big project for the year was overseeing a large and complicated series of renovations.

Judy also provided strong support during the lengthy six-week radiation treatment I endured. We would leave the coast by eight o'clock each morning in order to be in Brisbane by 9.30. Sometimes, because of public speaking duties or functions that required my presence elsewhere around the country, the doctors allowed me the unusual step of doubling up on the treatment. I would have to wait six hours between treatments, and fortunately we had friends who allowed me to take morning and afternoon naps at their place. At the end of each day we drove back to the coast. More than two hundred kilometres a day. Nine days a fortnight.

As 1997 rolled around — and I finally recovered from the shingles and what I hoped was my last medical crisis — I began the long, sometimes turbulent, haul back to health. My depression was still there. As anyone who has suffered from it knows, your good days can be very good. You exult in feeling well because you know just how quickly you can sink back into having a bad one.

Fortunately, though, Judy was capable of steering me in the direction of many projects. My favourite would be the house renovations. I'd always fancied myself as a bit of a handyperson — I'd done quite a bit of the work in my old home in Prahran, including constructing a wooden deck in the backyard. Now I had a perfect opportunity to oversee the complete remaking of our new home on the coast. I wasn't going to construct an impenetrable fortress. But I knew I'd finally found a sanctuary where the private me could feel comfortable and safe, and get on with the job of healing myself.

18

Testimonial

As I underwent my chemotherapy in 1996 I did my best to stay out of the public eye and make as few appearances as I could. Like everyone else who has endured the same thing, I found that even engaging in small talk could be an exhausting experience. Having never been that proficient when it comes to social chitchat — had I ever been a diplomat at the United Nations I can assure you that World War III, followed quickly by World War IV, would have broken out — I didn't miss such occasions. The Olympics in Atlanta had been a wonderful opportunity to renew a range of old acquaintances. But I'd been incredibly exhausted after returning home.

There was another reason for my reluctance to be seen in public. As those who know me well will attest, I am hardly a devotee of make-up. But as my chemotherapy course began nearing its end, even I had to admit that a touch of face paint would not go astray.

My skin had turned brittle; on bad days it felt as dry, and looked as transparent, as rice paper. I sometimes felt as though I was trapped inside a dry shell that stank and tasted of metal. Rather than be seen as a character out of a *Terminator* movie, I preferred to remain within a close circle of friends.

But in September that year an invitation arrived that I could hardly turn down. A group of businessmen in Sydney, led by the advertising legend John Singleton, were holding a testimonial luncheon for Betty Cuthbert and wondered if I would like to attend.

I didn't need much prompting. Betty was the female athlete I most admired; not only for the way she had run and dominated the sprint events of her era — the way she came out of retirement to win the 400 metres in record time at the 1964 Tokyo Olympics was just about her finest achievement — but also for the manner in which she had conducted herself during her debilitating battle with multiple sclerosis.

See-through skin or not, I was determined to be there and pay tribute to Betty. The luncheon was successful and helped raise a large amount of money for one of Australia's most loved athletes. The money was well-deserved, too. Here was a woman who had done much to enhance Australia's reputation as a sporting nation, but all those years of training and sacrifice had come without the big paydays modern athletes are used to. At the end of the luncheon — they had been held once a year for several years and featured such legendary sports figures as Dawn Fraser and Johnny Raper — it was the custom for Singleton to announce the beneficiary of the following year's testimonial. Just before the announcement was made, he leaned over to me and said, "Raelene, we'd love to have you as the recipient for next year's luncheon. Would you be interested?"

I told Singo that I thought there were people far more deserving of such an honour. Marjorie Jackson immediately sprang to mind.

But Singo was insistent. "I'm asking you, Raelene," he said. "I make the decisions around here."

At the time I didn't even think in terms of dollars and cents. To be asked to follow in Betty Cuthbert's footsteps was good enough for me. After all, I'd always felt I'd been following them throughout my career. I was just never good enough to match those golden footprints of hers.

THE RAELENE Boyle testimonial was held at the Regent Hotel in Sydney in September 1997, and I flew down from Queensland feeling nervous about being the centre of attention. Would they all stand up and start singing "Hooray for Raelene, Hooray at last ...?" I was also fearful that not many people would show up. After all, I'd never won a gold medal. I didn't want to see Singo or anyone else embarrassed by having a half-empty ballroom.

I need not have worried. The place was packed. Most of the seats had sold for $85 each, and many of the tables had been booked for months. The broadcaster Alan Jones gave an address that summed up my career and set the tone for the rest of the afternoon. Did you ever dream as a teenager of being a rock star, of being able to stand on a stage and acknowledge the plaudits and adulation of an adoring crowd? Well, I hadn't known that feeling very often — Brisbane was probably my last experience of it. And an athlete who said they didn't enjoy such an experience would be lying. So I was quite happy to sit for several hours and listen to everyone telling me how wonderful I was.

"She's been there, done that," Jones told the crowd. "Meeting royalty, shaking hands with prime ministers, mobbed by the fans, but paradoxically, vulnerable, isolated, disappointed, disillusioned — well, she's been there and done that, too.

"You think you have trouble with authority and authority figures? Success is always interfered with by obstacles placed along the way by many who've never had success. She's been there, done that.

"The Raelene Boyle that we salute today is very much an everywoman. And as such, she embodies the one truism in Australian sport and in Australian achievement, that invariably success is born of adversity.

"This woman became without doubt the greatest drug-free female sprinter in the world at her time, and one of the greatest of all time. Let there be no mistake about that. Wherever Miss Boyle ran, in the great stadia of the world, one thing was for certain. She was poetry in motion."

When Alan had finished his tribute I was sure that the Pope would be the next figure to take the stage to announce I had been nominated for sainthood.

Earlier, Olivia Newton-John had kicked off the luncheon. Probably one of the most famous breast cancer survivors in the world, Olivia offered a moving and confronting account of her own experience. I don't think I've ever heard a room as quiet as when she spoke. She drew parallels between our lives, too. She was diagnosed with breast cancer just as she was about to fly home from the United States to see her father, who was dying of cancer. My diagnosis, she pointed out, had arrived when my mother was dying of cancer. Olivia said she and I both hailed from the entertainment business — her career was in film and song, mine was on the track. She spoke movingly and from the heart about why she believed so many women contract breast cancer, and how the stress of being a mother, lover and worker sometimes proved too much.

Ever since it had become known that I intended putting up for sale my 100-metres silver medal from the 1972 Munich Olympics there had been a fair bit of eyebrow-raising going on. I'd been asked by many old friends and acquaintances, along with people I'd never met, if I was struggling financially.

While I'd never been wealthy, I assured them that I wasn't anywhere close to ending up on skid row. Of course I was selling it for the money (a portion of all proceeds of the auction went to Sporting Chance Cancer Foundation for cancer research) and having had no superannuation fund until long after my racing career ended, I always welcomed additional money. But few seemed to understand that the medal itself held no significance for me. The truth was I had been asked to supply some items for the auction and it was one of the few things I had left. I couldn't even recall where I had it stored until I found it, still in its box, tucked away in an upstairs cupboard. It wasn't like a wedding ring or some other object that many people feel symbolises something important in their life. It was a piece of metal that seemed to hold much more allure for others than for its owner. I've always owned something worth far more to me — my memories. As I've said, I'm not a trophy collector.

My first Olympic silver — the one I'd won as a surprise place-getter in Mexico — had been given as a gift to my godson, Marcus, the eldest child of Rick and his wife, Tess. The silver I'd received after finishing second to Stecher in the 200 metres at Munich had been given as a twenty-first birthday present to Aunty Dot's youngest daughter, Merrilyn, a great friend of mine.

I knew there was a chance that an overseas collector would try to purchase the medal and remove it from Australia, and I knew there might be an outcry over that. But I was prepared to take the chance.

"Life is a risk," I told one reporter. "That's the history of my life and I've got a future to think about now." I didn't think it would be worth very much, anyway.

As usual, I'd underestimated just how much interest there would be. Bidding at the auction for the medal began at $20 000 and soon grew quite fierce. For more than five minutes there was a constant babble as hands were raised or heads nodded to boost the price.

Eventually it was knocked down for $70 000 to a friend of mine, Melbourne-based trucking magnate Bill Gibbins, the owner of FCL Transport. He promptly announced he would take it home to show his sons, before donating it to the Olympic Museum at the Melbourne Cricket Ground. Bill also made it clear that I could make free use of it any time I wished. I thanked him. But the medal was his now. He'd certainly earned the right to call it his, and I was hardly going to argue. I'm not sure Bill even arrived at the lunch intending to bid for the medal. But he said his wife, Yolanda, raised money for breast cancer research in Melbourne, and he had been so moved by Olivia's speech that he wanted to make a contribution to the cause as well.

The medal was the highest priced item in the auction, but several others also fetched terrific prices. A plaque commemorating my participation in a world-record relay back in 1969 was bought by the stockbroker Rene Rivkin for $36 000, while my friend Nene King, the long-time editor of *Woman's Day*, paid $25 000 for the opportunity to join Kerri-Anne Kennerley as the one-off host of Channel Nine's "The Midday Show". Singleton, who'd done a lot of work ensuring there were bums on seats at the luncheon, coughed up $30 000 for my Olympic team blazer from Mexico, and the broadcaster and comedian Andrew Denton paid $6000 for the opportunity to be Lord Mayor of Sydney for a day.

It was a marvellous day. I was still a long way from fully recovered from the traumas of the previous year. My skin remained slightly transparent and was taking a long time to regain its former texture, and the blond hair I'd once been proud of had many streaks of grey. But to stand in front of so many people — friends I had not seen in years and strangers whom I had never met — was a tremendously humbling experience.

I was grateful, too. A few hours over lunch had solved one of the biggest issues that had been plaguing my life in recent years — my financial security. The testimonial ended up raising a remarkable $360 000. I'd never been wasteful with cash, and with a new house requiring extensive renovations I knew the money would be put to good use. I could keep my home in Prahran and rent it out. I would have one less thing to worry about when I woke at 3am and felt the weight of the world pressing down upon me.

"I feel one of the proudest and one of the most honoured Australians," I said, when the day finally came to an end. It had been a joyful, as well as an exhausting and nerve-racking, experience. Almost inevitably, one of the issues that had accompanied me throughout my running career flared at the end of the luncheon. A week before the testimonial, news had broken that new evidence had been uncovered in the files of the Stasi, the former East German secret police, that indicated Renate Stecher had been one of many athletes using steroids in the lead-up to the Munich Games.

I'd hardly been shocked at the revelations. By then, I'd accepted as fact that I had been beaten for gold by a drug cheat and had long come to terms with it. But the news that hard facts now supported my long-held suspicion had again ignited a sense of indignation within me. Asked by a couple of reporters at the luncheon about the claims, I reiterated my strong views about drug-taking and how it had become a curse on the entire international athletic movement.

But I also pointed out that my events had taken place twenty-five years earlier, and Renate Stecher and I had gone our separate ways and moved on with our lives.

Little did I realise that the two of us were about to be reunited. Within eight weeks I would finally be able to confront her with a question that had nagged me ever since we both stood on a podium listening to the polite applause of the Munich crowd back in 1972.

19

They told me to swim, not sing

THE JUDGE HAD AN INQUIRING MIND. IT WAS MAY 2000, AND CAROLE Beraktschjan, a former world swimming champion, had taken the stand in the last of a series of celebrated trials investigating the extent of East Germany's sports doping scandal.

Beraktschjan, who had dominated breast-stroke events in the mid 1970s, was one of the lucky ones. Subjected to her nation's doping regime from an early age, she had suffered no side effects. In fact, she had taken the bold step of declaring publicly that she was handing back all her medals and trophies, because they were "tainted, spoiled, rotten symbols of a toxic society". Now Beraktschjan had an opportunity to tell Judge Dirk Dickhaus and the rest of the world what had happened to her as a young girl.

Judge: Which drugs were given to you and in what form?

Beraktschjan: When I began, at age eleven, I got a few pills. As I got older, I was given more and more; up to thirty pills a day.

Judge: Did you know what they were?

Beraktschjan: At first they were in wrappers, but as I got older the colour changed and they had no markings or package.

Judge: What was the colour?

Beraktschjan: They were little blue ones.

Judge: Did you get injections?

Beraktschjan: Yes, in my buttocks. Dr Binus injected me, and he got angry when I asked to see the label. I gained lots of weight — 20 kilograms that year.

Judge: How did the doctors explain your very deep voice and your changes?

Beraktschjan: They told me to swim and not sing.

And so most of the East German athletes did as they were told. They swam. They ran. They lifted. They threw. They jumped. And almost always, they lived up to the Olympic motto of being stronger, faster and, given the dope running through their system, higher.

But finally, they began to sing. To the authorities.

It took the fall of the Berlin Wall and the collapse of communism to do it, but gradually the full, horrific story began to unfold. I'd like to be able to say it came as no surprise to learn about the extent of the East German doping program. But to be honest, I was just as shocked as everyone else. I'd known their athletes had been on something for many years. After all, I'd inhabited the same dressing-rooms as the East German girls and I'd often thought I had mistakenly stumbled onto the set of *Planet of the Apes,* there was so much body hair to be seen. But who could have imagined the extent of it — the thousands of young people who had been subjected to the world's largest and longest-running medical experiment on human beings? The appalling side effects and the generation of children to come who would be born malformed and mentally disabled? For more than three decades the old East Germany had sought to justify its political system by dominating world sport. Hundreds of doctors and coaches had been involved in the scam; some had been forced to go along with it, while many others had embraced it as a way of proving their loyalty to the state.

The East German program also forced athletes from other nations into a neverending game of catch-up. By the 1980s drugs were rife — everywhere. I remember how, at the 1982 Commonwealth Games in Brisbane, many of the athletes who trained under the Canadian coach Charlie Francis seemed to be much more powerful and confident than the rest of their Canadian team-mates. Charlie wasn't a big name then — it would take the Seoul Olympics six years later and the disgrace of his most famous runner, Ben Johnson, to earn him a special place in athletic infamy. Johnson, so juiced up on steroids by the time he trounced the field in the 100-metre final that his eyes were tinged a dirty nicotine yellow, had his gold medal stripped from him a few days later when there was so much stanazolol found in his system it could have powered a small town for a month.

In Brisbane I'd renewed a friendship with one of the Canadian athletes, Angela Taylor. We had known each other for several years — I'd first met her in Edmonton in 1978 at the Commonwealth Games. Back then she had been a third-string sprinter on the Canadian team and had approached me one day at training, saying she admired my career and my style of running. She was young then, and very lithe and small. I chatted with her and then we went our separate ways.

When we met again in Brisbane I couldn't get over the changes in her body. Another of Francis's proteges, she had undergone a remarkable transformation. She had turned into a shapely, hugely muscular and powerful woman — a black Renate Stecher. Her times reflected the changes — she won the 100 metres and on the last leg of that 4x400-metre relay, my final international event, I was unable to chase her down because of her sheer power, and my exhaustion, too.

I knew Angela could beat me, not only because she was younger and stronger, but because she had been given a chemical advantage. She shook her head one evening as we chatted, looked me in the eye and told me that, with my talent, I had been mad not to have given myself "extra help" during my career. "You could have been the dominant sprinter of your time," she said. I shrugged. I'd heard it all before, from a wide range of athletes, both in Australia and overseas. Yet I had never even toyed with the idea. I might have cut my ties with Dad prematurely, but at heart I'd always been my father's daughter when it came to old-fashioned views about the purity of sport.

Angela thought I was stubborn and old for my time. But at least my record stands unblemished. Years after her victories in Brisbane and elsewhere around the world, Angela testified that she had taken drugs.

WHILE RENATE Stecher and I had barely shared a word back in Munich and Montreal, she had become a shadow in my life ever since. It seemed I would never really be rid of her, because I was constantly asked about her, even long after my career had finished. Everyone wanted to know for sure if she had been on drugs. Once the Stasi files were uncovered in 1991 revealing the extent of the East German doping program, I expected to hear news confirming Stecher's involvement. But there was none forthcoming. I got on with my life, immersing myself in my gardening career. The only time I ever dwelt on those days was when I was asked about them. Every year or so a reporter would trudge out to the Victoria

Gardens to write a "Whatever happened to..." story on me. By the 1990s, some of these reporters were too young to even remember the days when I ran. So the story always seemed new to them — Raelene Boyle, possibly beaten to gold by a drug cheat, and then beaten in 1976 by her own mistiming.

But in 1997 everything began to change. For a start, Australian athletics had just made undoubtedly the stupidest decision ever made by officialdom — and I'd seen plenty of them. In early October the sport's governing body, Athletics Australia, confirmed that it had offered East German athletics coach Dr Eckhard Arbeit the position of Australia's national coach. Words momentarily failed me when I first heard the news — I was gobsmacked. I wasn't just disappointed. I was disgusted.

Naturally, my phone began ringing with journalists seeking my reaction. I'm sure they knew what it would be before I even picked up the receiver. "I question their ethics," I said of AA's decision. "They must have a very short memory."

What disturbed me most was that I'd felt Australia had done more than most countries to lead a fight against drug usage in sport. Paltry and insipid as it had been, we had at least been seen to be doing something. But by appointing Arbeit we stood to become a laughing stock. We were going to pay him more than $100 000 a year, with a lot of that money coming straight out of federal government grants to athletics.

It was outrageous. The reaction of Dr Werner Franke, a German molecular biologist who had done more to expose the secrets of the Stasi drug files than anyone else, said it all. "Are they insane?" asked Franke when he heard about Arbeit's appointment. "How can this sit together with Raelene Boyle having had her Munich medals stolen by Renate Stecher, or with your swimmers' strong stance against doping?"

Amid the furore, I received a phone call from "60 Minutes".

Would I be interested in accompanying them to the former East Germany to get to the bottom of the drug controversy and confront my old foe, Stecher? I didn't need to be asked twice.

THAT TRIP became a significant journey. It made me finally realise what I'd missed out on. I wasn't bitter — I had long before shrugged my shoulders and come to terms with the fact that my opportunity to win Olympic gold might have been sabotaged by performance-enhancing drugs. But I came to realise the full magnitude of the hoax that East Germany had perpetrated on the world, and its own people.

The East German leader Erich Honecker had pulled off one of the biggest scams in history. His people, unlike those in many Iron Curtain countries, had never suffered from vital food shortages or wanted for many of life's modern conveniences. Yet what they were forced to endure was just as bad. The East Germans were psychologically abused. Honecker's secret police created a culture of informants: students spied on teachers, workers spied on bosses and even husbands and wives spied on one another. That, to me, was a frightening prospect. This was paranoia on a grand scale. You were under observation, or felt like it, from cradle to grave. Take the case of Werner Fischer, one of a handful of human rights activists who planned and helped to stage a series of weekly demonstrations that played a key role in the fall of the Berlin Wall. A decade later, Fischer read 67 files kept on him by the Stasi and discovered his mother had spied on him for four years. Not only that, but she received a distinguished medal for her services to the state for informing on her son.

Of course, the system was not as blatantly tyrannical as some. Instead of being taken away for torture and ultimate execution, those who showed signs of civil disobedience were broken psychologically. University lecturers ended up sweeping streets or cleaning toilets. One high school teacher, during his mandatory stint with the army, shot dead two people trying to flee to freedom in West Germany. Only later, after reading the Stasi files, did he discover that he had killed two high school students. Just kids. It destroyed his life with guilt. And it was not an unusual tale. Scientists were sent to state dairy farms to hose down the yards. It created a society where everyone was suspect, and in turn it helped make it easier for doctors and coaches to be lured into the sports drug program under the pretext of helping the state and furthering the credibility of communism.

As part of the "60 Minutes" story we arrived at an enormous building that had been the Stasi headquarters. The Germans were determined not to repeat the mistakes of the past. A half century before, in an effort to erase the memory of Hitler, they had destroyed many reminders of the Nazi era. But they were now determined to keep much of the old East Germany intact as a reminder to future generations. Millions of once-secret documents remained here. It was incredible — it was like being on the set of the old television spy show "Get Smart" and going inside the offices of the evil KAOS. Single-person elevators moved constantly from floor to floor. There were acres of bags of material that would take more than a century to read and archive. When the Berlin Wall began to fall in 1989, orders had gone out to shred the documents. When the shredders broke down under the enormous workload, staff had begun tearing them up by hand.

It was an impossible task. After the crew finished filming, and just as we were leaving, Johan Legner, the manager of the files, took me aside. "This Arbeit . . ." he said in his halting English. "He is not a good man."

THE OLD East Germany was everything I had imagined it would be — grey and sombre. Some of the architecture was magnificent, of course — it's difficult to walk a block anywhere in Europe without stumbling across something beautiful preserved after centuries of use. But the overall impression was one of sobriety and stodginess.

To me, perhaps nothing better exemplified the fall of the old East Germany and its sporting dominance than a disused swimming pool we came across. Drained long ago, and fenced off from the general public, graffiti artists had managed to get in and deface the pool walls. Everything was broken and desolate, weeds grew between cracks and voices echoed around the emptiness. The crew weren't supposed to go in, but Richard Carleton, a gung-ho reporter if ever I have met one, was certainly not going to let such an opportunity pass him by. (I think Richard has spent his life seeking confrontations. He should have been an athlete.)

The crew scaled the fence and proceeded to film a compelling segment in this remnant of East German sporting prowess. And then it was the moment we had all been waiting for — a meeting with Renate Stecher.

She lived, ironically I thought, in Jena, the town where the German pharmaceutical company that first synthesised the anabolic steroid Oral-Turinabol, VEB Jenapharm, is based. And it became clear from the start that the only reason she had agreed to be interviewed was because "60 Minutes" was paying her. I'm not sure how much she received, but several thousand dollars to Stecher would have been a godsend, given that she was living in a small flat with her husband and children. I suddenly realised just who had been the big winner out of the two of us. At the end of the interview I would get on a plane and return home to one of the most comfortable lifestyles on the planet. Stecher would remain in drab Jena, eking out an existence as a secretary. Under the old regime she had been given an honorary degree and a job in a leading university. But all that had been lost when the Cold War ended.

She was twitchy from the start. Her arms remained crossed for much of the interview. I sat next to her, but small talk was difficult because she spoke next to no English. Her husband sat just out of the camera's view and he put on a display that should have been filmed — he was obviously going out of his mind when Carleton began questioning Stecher about her drug use.

The key document had first been uncovered by Franke and revealed publicly by Robert Hartman, a journalist with the Munich-based *Sueddeutsche Zeitung* newspaper. It remains unclear whether Stecher was taking steroids at the time of the 1972 Olympics, but the document shows unequivocally that she had been part of the doping program. The document is part of a doctor's report relating to the East German track team, and notes that Stecher and others had declined to take particular drugs, but would consider another program "again" in the future. As we now know from the trials investigating doping in the old East Germany, to represent that country meant taking drugs — athletes who refused point blank to take any drugs were simply dropped and sent home.

"So were you taking anything when you were running?" I asked her.

"I have to say I don't like being addressed in this way with such a quick question right off the bat," she replied. "But to answer your question, no. At no time did I take helpful substances … I tried to train harder."

Richard Carleton then jumped in, handing over a copy of the incriminating document. Stecher was clearly surprised at seeing it, but there was no way she was going to admit any involvement. The doctor who wrote the report was lying, she said. "I wasn't doped."

I was holding one of her gold medals at the time. "I do consider in some ways I deserve one of these," I told her.

"We both fought honestly but I was first," she replied, through the translator. "You have to accept that."

At the end I shrugged. It was clear that my old opponent was not going to admit to anything. We shook hands remotely, just as we had twenty-five years before.

Some people might say they would have found it difficult handling the gold medal that should rightfully have been theirs. But the medal itself, as I've said before, means nothing; it's the knowledge that you were the best. I came away from that encounter with Stecher confident more than ever that in 1972 I had been the fastest non-drugged woman in the world over 100 and 200 metres. And I was going home to a wonderful life.

Lisa Curry-Kenny was also on that trip with "60 Minutes". She would meet up with Christine Knacke-Sommer, one of the East German swimmers who had beaten Lisa in their events in Montreal. For Lisa, it was clearly an emotional journey. She broke down and cried at the end. I comforted her on that final day, and told her not to worry. The things we had seen had only confirmed what we had long suspected. I felt more sorry for Stecher and the rest of the East German athletes who had been used as guinea pigs for so many years. The doping program had become so insidious at one stage that it set athlete against athlete. Marita Koch, the dominant 400-metre runner of the 1980s and still the world-record holder, once wrote to senior officials complaining that the drugs given to her were not as powerful and effective as those given to a team-mate. She demanded equality. Such complaints were not unusual. The East German administrators even had a term for it. "Doping envy" they called it.

IN THE end, Athletics Australia was forced to see reason and Arbeit was prevented from taking up his position. I was thankful when I heard the news, but hardly impressed. How the issue had ever got to the stage it had was a sad reflection on the Australian athletic movement. It seemed to me they had learned nothing over the years. While the swimmers had made a very public stand against drug taking — I often thought they were setting themselves up for a big fall, because how could they ever really know what their team-mates were doing — track and field had been a long way behind.

It was as if everyone had given up the fight, if indeed they had ever been serious about it in the first place. I understood such a view — drugs had completely corrupted international sport by the end of the twentieth century — but to me, that was no reason to surrender. There was an important ethical issue to be addressed when it came to drugs. It was wrong to take them. Simple. There is no moral argument that justifies their use when it comes to athletic competition.

Yet we now live in a time when I believe every athlete is guilty, unless they can prove their innocence. I have grown so cynical and disgusted with the way in which track and field, and the Olympics for that matter, have been polluted that whenever I commentate on races I wonder how many competitors are *not* on something that is improving their performance. I hate thinking this way — it goes against every instinct I was born with. But I only have to look at the shabby way in which Werner Reiterer was treated in the lead-up to the Sydney Olympics to see why no-one really wants to listen anymore.

Reiterer wrote a book in which he revealed that drugs were common in Australian sport, just as they were around the world. He didn't "name names" of course — he knew only too well how strict the defamation laws are in this country. Yet, instead of having been seen to have lifted the lid on a shameful side of Australian athletics, he was attacked by politicians and Australian Olympic officials. The last thing they wanted was a drug scandal so close to the Sydney Games, and they made damn sure none would take place.

When it comes to hypocrisy, Australians are world-competitive. We've had enough athletes already who have returned positive drug samples. But what worries me now is what lies ahead.

We have already seen how an entire generation of athletes can be corrupted by the desire to improve performance using artificial means. Each year new substances appear on the scene, aided by more sophisticated masking drugs. The International Olympic Committee, far too concerned in the 1970s and early 1980s with simply surviving after years of political turmoil, acted too sluggishly when it came to addressing the problem. Growing fat on the billions of dollars in revenue it attracted in television rights and corporate sponsorships, it allowed the drug problem to escalate and get out of control.

Now, how long will it be before we see athletes appearing on our tracks and in our pools who have undergone genetic alterations?

Don't laugh. Genetic engineering, as any medical professional will tell you, is the way of the future. I'm not suggesting that we are about to see teams of cloned Ben Johnsons walking into the stadium under their nation's flag for the opening ceremony. The changes will be far more subtle. If you think what I'm suggesting is pure science fiction, think again. In May 2000, a team of researchers at Pennsylvania State University genetically altered a mouse by injecting it with a synthetic gene that caused its body to produce more muscle, as well as help repair it. The genetically engineered mouse ended up boasting 60 per cent greater muscle mass than a normal mouse, and when it finally died of old age, the scientists discovered it had maintained that mass.

Already there are predictions that within the next two years a human will be genetically manipulated, probably as a method of curing a disease. At a conference held not long ago and reported by the US magazine *Sports Illustrated*, the head of the mouse research team, Lee Sweeney, said every time there was publicity about his mighty-mouse experiment, "my phone rings off the hook with athletes — mostly weightlifters — looking for an edge. The sports world has reason to be nervous."

Don't forget, we already have evidence that one nation — East Germany — embarked on a deliberate mass doping program in order to achieve sporting dominance. There is evidence that China, too, has had some form of state-sponsored doping in place, particularly for swimmers. I've seen some of those girls, been bug-eyed at the size of their backs and chests, and wondered why an Australian football team hasn't signed them up yet to play at centre half-forward. Or, if that fails, why they don't become opera singers. Their voices are at least as deep as Pavarotti's. What I am saying is we should never underestimate the lengths people will go to in order to achieve an advantage on the sporting field. It is, unfortunately, a human trait. In 1904 at the St Louis Olympics, a runner called Tom Hanks collapsed into a coma after winning the marathon. He had swallowed a significant amount of brandy and strychnine before the race in the belief that it would boost his performance. Perhaps it did. But he paid the price.

Athletes have been paying the price ever since. A cyclist died during the Helsinki Games in 1952 from excessive amphetamine and coffee use. The East German Stasi files are littered with tales of tumours and other cancerous growths in a wide range of athletes. Many died. Many of the women were forced to have abortions to rid themselves of unwanted foetuses, the result of steroids increasing their libidos to unmanageable levels.

So what needs to be done? The IOC has to become proactive. It is no good crying that anti-doping control is extremely expensive. Of course it is. But in a movement flush with cash, what price can you place on the purity of your sport? Pay whatever it takes. Send the organisation bankrupt if you have to. But every country needs to have in place a sophisticated, state-of-the-art testing laboratory.

The finest scientists in the world need to be recruited. Instead of allowing the world's chemists to side with corrupt athletes, bring them into the fold.

But most of all, any new initiative must begin by being seen to be serious about beating the drug cheats. No more insipid declarations that "Drugs are bad" and "We want the Games to be clean". The IOC needs to announce a war on drugs equivalent to George Bush's war on terrorism.

I want my faith in sport to be restored. Before I die, I would like to see the athletes of the world engage in a fair and true test of ability. At present, we are in a situation similar to the old days when amateurism and professionalism clashed, when so-called amateurs (myself included) were more than happy to accept cash payments under the table, or in the guise of "appearance fees". In fact, I can sympathise with the plight of athletes who turn to drugs. Sympathise — but not quite understand.

Unfortunately, I've been around for long enough to know that I needn't bother holding my breath for the situation to dramatically change.

Besides, I'm only too aware of the ultimate irony in my life. Steroids have wreaked a tremendous amount of damage in those who have used them over the years. A lot of East German women have suffered terribly.

I never touched drugs. But in recent years, cancer has become my constant companion.

20

Descent into darkness

THE SUN HAS JUST RISEN ON THE DAY I DECIDE TO END MY LIFE.
Everything is coated in the soft, dreamy colours of early morning,
but as I make my way gently down the stairs and then out to the
deck, I hardly notice a thing. Something is calling me, urging me on.

Somehow I sense that it is time to end my pain. Once again, the
mental agony far outweighs the physical hurt I am suffering.
Hasn't that always been the way for me? It's clear there is only one
way I will ever be rid of the darkness. I can feel something guiding
me. What is it? I don't really care. I have never been religious or
even that spiritual, and I am sure it is not the hand of God. Yet
something is pushing me on ... but to what? There before me,
lying still and cool, is our swimming pool. Without hesitating,
without even wondering if this is the right thing to do, I enter it
slowly, one step at a time, creating barely a ripple on its tranquil
surface. And then, without warning, I am in the deep end, face

down and floating, staring into what seems a neverending sea of blue. I am not breathing.

Just drifting away.

AND THAT is how it was going to end. There is no other way of describing it. I was entertaining thoughts of suicide. I was lying in a hospital bed on the Sunshine Coast, more broken in body and spirit than at any other time in my life. This was far, far worse than the breast cancer days of four years before. I was haunted — not only had the cancer come back, but this time it was gnawing away at my ovaries. It had begun to infect my mind, too.

Through the haze of a cocktail of pain-killing and antibiotic drugs, the same recurring dream took place each night when I fell asleep. It scared me because everything seemed so real — the walk down the stairs, the steps onto the deck and then sliding gently into that cool water and drowning myself. Each night the dream happened exactly the same way. When I woke I thought about what it meant. I always came to the same conclusion. Perhaps it was time to turn the dream into reality.

One of the things about depression is that if the right trigger is pulled, you can suddenly plunge into a deep, dark place without even realising it. And then it's too late — the darkness feeds on itself.

Let me explain just how quickly it happened to me.

By the middle of 2000 my old cockiness had returned. It had taken me a long time to recover from breast cancer — much longer than I had imagined. It's a common thing among cancer sufferers. After your treatment you can be plagued by months of physical, mental and emotional exhaustion. The doctors and therapists warn you about this — it's normal and not something to worry about. But what are rarely explained are the long-term effects. You can feel perfectly well one day and then, suddenly, something will trigger a scary thought: has it come back? It might be a small, niggling pain, something that in your previous life you would have ignored or laughed off. But a cancer patient who pulls through and survives never really forgets. You are like that person lying in bed listening to every bump and creak in the night. You listen for the warning signs that an intruder is about. As an elite athlete I had always listened closely to my body. But after breast cancer I was constantly on guard. I had simply replaced one stalker in my life with another. That weird man who followed me, who wrote me his letters filled with incoherent ramblings, was long gone; in all probability he had found some other poor soul to haunt and torment. My latest stalker was always unseen. But its presence was palpable, all the same.

And yet, with the 2000 Sydney Olympics just a couple of months away, I had finally regained much of my old confidence. If anything, I was stronger than at any other time in my life since my athletic career had ended. My sense of humour — always the yardstick when it comes to measuring my mental health — had returned. My diary was full — there was always a fundraising dinner to attend, or help prepare. My breast cancer ladies on the coast were keeping me busy; the dream of funding prosthetics for some of them who had experienced full mastectomies was becoming a reality. And, of course, I had the Games to look forward to.

I hadn't looked forward to an Olympics like this one in a long time. Finally the Games were returning to Australia. I must admit to a small twinge of jealousy — my experiences in Brisbane in 1982 had shown me just how wonderful it was to perform at a big event in front of your countrymen, and how rare it was, too. But I had just received a phone call that immediately triggered an enormous adrenalin rush. Not only would I be commentating at the Games — Channel Seven's Bruce McAvaney had made it clear he wanted me sitting next to him for the track and field events — but I would also be a participant. I was going to be given one last opportunity to play a role in the greatest show on earth.

BY THE time June came around in 2000, I was trying to plan a small holiday and take a break before the Games began. I wanted to throw all my energy at the Games. If I was to be sitting next to McAvaney — the ultimate perfectionist in Australian television, and a man I regard as the most outstanding sporting commentator in the world — then I had to be at my best. I was studying the form from the European season, noting some of the emerging names and examining their times.

One typical day around that time I spent at Mountain Creek High School in northern Queensland. The students had raised $78 for breast cancer projects I was supporting — not a huge sum by the standards of the corporate world, but a terrific donation that to me carried just as much significance. I was involved with several fundraisers for a variety of charities, and at one function I was even introduced to Raquel Welch. I'm no movie buff, but I'm sure even many film critics would struggle to remember some of Raquel's cinematic triumphs. Yet it was obvious why she had become such a legendary figure in Hollywood. This was one woman whom age had not wearied. She was gorgeous — a living testament to choosing your plastic surgeon as carefully as your diet. Simply beautiful. But to an old Coburg girl who used to hate having her hair curled, I was left wondering just how much of her life she had devoted to making herself look that way.

One day seemed to blur into another. But there was one that still stands out and which I'll never forget. It still makes the hair on my neck stand up. It's not every day, after all, that one of your brothers gets to hand the Olympic torch to you.

Like everyone else I had been watching the progress of the Olympic flame around the country, right from the first day when the Aboriginal sprinter Nova Peris — also a hockey gold medallist — had run the first leg with her daughter using Uluru as a magnificent backdrop. One of the things that caught my imagination was how the layers of cynicism and bitterness prevalent in the years leading up to the Olympics had started quickly falling away. No matter how many people tried to put them down, and no matter how suspicious people had grown of the Olympic movement (and by then I was quite disgusted with the behaviour and mentality of many who led the IOC), the Games were doing something few of us could have imagined. They were drawing us together as a nation. As corny and as trite as it seemed, there was a genuine spirit of togetherness beginning to form, and the torch relay had a lot to do with it.

As an Olympian I had been invited to watch the relay in Longreach in outback Queensland. It was a fantastic trip. Here we were in the middle of nowhere and it started to pour — a real Queensland drenching, too. The dirt around Longreach doesn't need much prompting before turning into a thick, sticky clay that seems to attach itself to everything. A lot of the farmers in the district were in two minds about whether to attend the relay; the rain suddenly meant a lot of work, and it also held the prospect of them being cut off from their properties for several days if they ventured into town.

As it turned out, most of them managed to make it in and the emotion everyone generated was unbelievable. And I had a fortuitous meeting with a young breast cancer survivor named Felicity Hay. It was one of the highlights of the relay. Somehow Felicity and her parents had managed to convince the powers that be to allow her and the man who had saved her life — her surgeon — to run with the torch. It was a wonderful sight and incredibly moving. Even if it had not been wet, I am sure there would not have been a dry eye left in town.

But the real highlight of the torch relay for me came much later back in Tewantin near my home.

It had been another wet day, but fortunately the rain had eased off by the time my brother Ron came into view. I swear he was wearing the widest grin I have ever seen stretched across a person's face. He justifiably felt proud, and I don't think I have ever felt prouder, either. For a brother to pass on the Olympic flame to his fellow Olympian sister was a rarity in the history of the Olympics. There was a huge crowd and the noise was amazing. I took the torch from Ron and began running toward the football ground. I barely noticed the mud.

The only disappointment was that Ron and I could not run side by side. I had asked if this could be done — after all, we had been a part of the same Olympic team back in 1976 and I believed that if it was good enough for Nova Peris to run with her daughter, then surely it was good enough for Ron and me. But surprise, surprise. There was nothing I could do when it came to the Games without some sort of thick-headed and stupid response from Olympic officialdom. Sorry, they told me. But we can't allow it. There was no good reason given. Someone was simply having a bad day and had decided to be difficult. As it turned out, Ron still tried to run with me, but a truck wedged between us and that was the end of that plan. I had to leave on a plane shortly after to attend a fundraising luncheon the next day in Melbourne. While I was exhausted when I finally arrived at the airport, I was also exhilarated. If this was a taste of things to come, then I couldn't wait for the Games to begin.

ON 11 July I had a commitment to speak at a function at Sanctuary Cove for the large wine group, Southcorp. They had been strong supporters of mine and I had agreed to be a guest speaker for one of their golf days. From there, Judy and I were going to take a short holiday, driving down the coast and through the Hunter Valley.

I was just starting to think about what I would say at the function — I quite often speak off the top of my head and find it far more comfortable to do that than read from a prepared text — when my mobile phone rang.

It was the secretary to Michael Knight, the Minister for the Olympics and the president of the Sydney organising committee. She asked if I was free to talk, because Michael wanted to discuss an extremely confidential matter with me. My brain started jumping to a thousand conclusions, but almost all of them led to the opening ceremony. It wasn't something I had thought much about. I knew Dawn Fraser was hoping like hell that she would be given the task of lighting the cauldron, but I had been fairly relaxed about my possible involvement. After all, what was I but a silver medallist? I had always seen myself that way. Friends used to say that it had something to do with my insecurities and an inferiority complex. But I knew the score. There was a huge leap between silver and gold and despite my controversial disqualification in Montreal and the drug taking by some of my opponents, one fact remained. I wasn't in the league of Dawn Fraser or Betty Cuthbert. There was a reason why a gold medallist stood taller on the medal dais.

Knight came on the line and said that the Australian Olympic Committee and the Sydney Organising Committee for the Olympic Games (SOCOG) had jointly decided on a list of names to be involved in the opening ceremony, had shared them between themselves and started calling the people chosen all over the country. Would I be interested?

I don't think a second passed before I answered. He then asked if I would be interested in pushing Betty Cuthbert into the Olympic stadium with the torch in one of the last acts before the cauldron was lit. I said I would be honoured to be given such a role, particularly as I admired Betty so much. He then told me that the strictest secrecy provisions were in place. I could not tell a soul; they could not afford their plan to leak to the media. It was to be kept confidential right up until the moment I steered Betty's chair into the arena.

I was ecstatic when I hung up. I grabbed Jude and told her what Knight had said. And then I swore her to secrecy. I'm sure Knight would have killed me had he discovered that within seconds of hanging up from him I had already told another person. But I was human. How could I not tell the closest person to me on the planet?

I managed to get through my speech at the function, although don't ask me what I spoke about. And then Jude and I hit the road for a few days of sightseeing and wine tasting. My spirits were soaring. This wasn't just the old me finally resurfacing after several years missing in action. No, this was a brand new model. My depression was a distant memory. I was feeling healthy and the fittest I'd been in years. I had just turned forty-nine and I was no longer that insecure little girl unsure of her place in the world. Now I knew where I stood in my world. Finally, I was on top of it.

And then, just over a week later, it all came tumbling down.

I HAVEN'T had too many heroes in my life. But someone who comes close to deserving such an accolade is the great Australian landscape gardener Edna Walling. Edna spent the last seven years of her life in a small cottage on Buderim Mountain in the Sunshine Coast hinterland. I never met her, but her legacy can be found in thousands of gardens around the country. Born in England, she moved to Australia as a child and by the 1920s was living in a cottage outside Mooroolbark near Melbourne. She became a household name through a national gardening column. Originally she favoured a blend of European plants and exotics intermingled with Australian natives. These were offset by wonderful winding paved paths, rocks and dry-stone walls. By the 1950s, she dispensed with the exotic flora altogether, devoting herself entirely to Australian plant life.

Edna died in the early 1970s, and her cottage was rented out. A few years later a lady called Paula moved into it. I met her when I moved to Queensland. Paula enjoyed sitting in the sun having a chat. Line dancing was one of her hobbies, and whenever we caught up it was a regular topic of conversation. Paula had been married once, a long time before. But now there was no-one in her life and she struck me as a lonely woman who craved companionship. There was a reason for this, apart from the normal human desire to be around other people.

Paula was dying of cancer.

It was in her stomach and it was clear she was losing the fight. I used to give her a cuddle whenever I saw her. She usually put on a cheerful face, but I could tell she had never quite accepted the enormity of the battle in front of her. Over a period of a few months I watched her deteriorate, both in body and confidence. On several occasions I invited her to a businesswomen's breakfast on the coast, but inevitably a new course of chemotherapy would arise and prevent her from joining me. She was fortunate because several neighbours and friends had pitched in, caring for her, sleeping over in the cottage to make sure she was with someone during the night and making sure meals were cooked and the washing was done.

By the end of June Paula was in hospital and it was clear the end was near. One day I went to visit her and took the torch I had carried during my leg of the Olympic relay. I had it wrapped up so it would not create too much attention when I walked through the hospital. At that stage interest in the Games was growing and the torch was like a talisman. Everyone who saw it wanted to touch it, to hold it and coo and sigh over it. The last thing I wanted was to be sitting with Paula while a large crowd gathered around us chatting and laughing.

She looked very sick. Sometimes when people are dying after a long fight it seems their skin is one of the first things that surrenders to the inevitable. Paula's skin was thin and the colour had seeped from it like a just-finished painting doused with water. But she managed a small smile and when she saw the torch her eyes twinkled. "Thank you so much," she said.

A tear formed in the corner of her eye and fell slowly onto her pillow.

"Are you scared?" I asked.

"Yes." Her voice was quiet. "I don't want to die."

Then she moved her head and made sure she looked me in the eye. "I hope this never happens to you," she whispered. I held her hand and cried with her and promised it never would.

Paula died not long after. Just before she went she managed to dictate a thank-you note to be given to people after her funeral. "Thanks to those who came to feed me," it read. "To Raelene Boyle, the message is: The day you brought the Olympic torch in — that was very special to me. Thank you."

Paula showed remarkable courage toward the end. How many of us can even contemplate what it must be like to know you are about to die, and to write notes to people thanking them? At the end of the note Paula dictated a poem. It read:

God lends our friends to us
Only for a while
We share some time together
A laugh, a tear, a smile.
And then before we know it
A lifetime has unfurled
Then he takes them back again
To another world.
But God is never selfish
He nurses them with love,
Until the day we meet again
In his garden up above.
I'm waiting!
Paula

I don't really believe in an afterlife. But I'm sure Paula found hers. And I damn well hope it was designed by Edna Walling.

ON WEDNESDAY, 19 July, just a few days after Paula passed away, I took Marley, our Dalmatian, out for a walk. Marley can be a grumpy old bitch at times. She has a wonderfully ludicrous smile — yes, it's true, this is a dog that grins. When you call her, she'll turn and look at you and then pull back her upper lip in a bizarre attempt at grinning. But Marley is a smiling assassin. She can be aggressive when she sees other dogs, so she always has to stay on a lead. As we walked down the street I was oblivious to the fact that Marley had spotted an enemy. She took off after it, snapping me around as she strained at the leash. A sharp spasm ripped across my lower back. By the time we arrived home I was in considerable pain.

I was still hurting the following day. I went and saw my doctor, Ellen Mowatt, who is herself a breast cancer survivor and a GP I had instantly felt comfortable with when we first met. I walked into her surgery that day and when she asked how I was, I replied rather curtly, "I've got it in the liver now."

"Oh yeah," she replied. "That's where we all think it ends up."

But I was serious. The pain was quite intense and I knew it was more than just a simple muscle strain or tear — I had suffered through enough of them during my running years to know one when it happened. But after examining me, Ellen quickly dispelled any notion that my liver was in danger. She thought it was worth pursuing, but could not get me booked in for an ultrasound until the following week. I suffered enormously over that weekend — I tossed and turned in bed unable to get comfortable, and spent most of my time in the bath trying to ease the pain with warmth. Because of my worsening condition, Ellen managed to have the ultrasound brought forward twenty-four hours.

The man who performed it on the Monday quickly confirmed my fears. "You've got a mass in here that I suspect is about 9 centimetres," he said. "I don't know what it is. It could be just an endometrial mass." I was booked in to see a surgeon the following day. At that stage I wasn't worrying about cancer; once Ellen had confirmed my liver was not in danger I had pushed the thought out of my mind.

So off I went to the surgeon. He checked me out and said he was pretty certain that there were no indications of cancer. I was going to be fine. It was all going to work out hunky-dory. Bloody marvellous. Fine, fine, fine. Now, where had I heard that before? He was sure there was no connection between my breast cancer and the mass in my abdomen, and he would operate the following day to get to the bottom of the mystery.

I was checked into a small private hospital on the Sunshine Coast. Right from the start my antenna began working overtime. Things just didn't take place the way I expected them to. There was no room available in the wing I would normally have been placed in so I was given a small room in the maternity section. The irony didn't escape me. The surgeon had already told me that because of the position of the mass, he would in all likelihood have to remove my right ovary. I wasn't exactly excited by this news. I had the Olympics coming up and I thought that removing my ovaries would trigger the onset of menopause. Four years before when I had undergone chemotherapy my hot flushes and wildly fluctuating hormone levels had been put down to the treatment. I still thought that menopause was just around the corner for me — at least its major symptoms. Blood tests had shown that my ovaries had begun to function again and had survived the ravages of chemotherapy. So I told the surgeon to try everything to keep at least my left ovary intact and functioning. I didn't want to be sitting in the commentary booth with Bruce McAvaney and experience the discomforting and sometimes extreme symptoms associated with menopause.

That night I lay in bed listening to the cries of newborn babies and wondered what in hell I was doing back in hospital. More than anything, I was annoyed. This visit was the last thing I needed interfering with my schedule. I'm a person who loves routine. I like the way my days pan out — the opportunity to walk the dogs, to drink tea in the sun, to pick and choose the tasks I want to do. Having that routine disrupted grated on me. But who was I to question the benefits of the scalpel?

IT WAS fairly obvious when I regained consciousness that I was losing a lot of blood after the surgery. I spent the rest of the day in a strange, groggy state and when I woke the next morning I felt terrible. I was in pain and I felt like I wanted to die. I had never felt that way after surgery before. The mass they extracted from near my right ovary ended up being 12 centimetres wide. Originally they thought nothing was wrong with it. But after it was sent to Brisbane for tests, those assumptions were thrown out the window.

I had cancer again. The news was broken to me by a doctor telling me: "There is cancer in the walls of the mass, but it's not really cancer. It's not really malignant but not really benign."

Huh? I was still trapped in an anaesthetic fog. I was lurching between despair and anger and now I was utterly confused. What did that mean, exactly? I've always had a black and white attitude toward such things. You either have cancer or you don't. It's like the old line — you can never be just a "little bit" pregnant. Either you are, or you are not.

Despite the vague nature of the diagnosis, it soon became quite clear that yes, I did have cancer. Not only that, but they would have to operate again to remove my left ovary and eliminate any chance of the cancer spreading.

I went into shock. My heart rate leaped to 150 beats per minute and I began plunging down that deep well. There he was, the old black dog, sitting in the corner of my room, back to haunt me for what felt like the rest of my days. When Judy arrived later that day, I broke down and sobbed like a child. It was heavy stuff and I was very scared this time around. My heart was beating so fast it felt like it was banging against my rib cage in an attempt to leap out of my chest. A cardiac specialist was called in to try to slow its rate.

At night I lay, scared and helpless, listening to my heart pound. I was still bleeding from the wound. At one stage I got up and left a trail of blood on the floor. Judy was concerned. She had been keeping a close eye on my charts and became alarmed at what was going on. Every few hours one of the nurses would come in to monitor me. Every time she entered the room I could smell her — the nicotine seemed to trail her like a bridal train. Scientists will tell you that our ability to smell is a powerful thing, even though it is not as sophisticated as it is in many animals. It can trigger emotions and memories. In those nights as I sank further into depression — I had not been able to take antidepressants because I couldn't keep them down — I was taken back to my childhood, back to those nights when Mum would tuck me in, kiss me goodnight and I could smell the tar on her breath.

Around me, babies wailed.

The surgeon went back in on Friday afternoon. He was hardly an intrepid explorer going where no-one had gone before. This was pretty familiar terrain, after all. I had started to think as many people had seen the inside of me as my outside. Barely forty-eight hours had passed since the previous operation, but I was still bleeding internally and my left ovary had to be removed. I woke up in intensive care with a new catheter and nasogastric tubes attached to me. A bank of heart monitors surrounded me. I hadn't been told this was a possibility. After all my previous surgeries I had woken up in a familiar room. The nasal tube was uncomfortable but it was the least of my concerns. What stressed me more was an oxygen mask over my nose and ears — that was how Mum had lived the last part of her life.

I can recall waking at one stage and seeing Judy, Rick and his wife, Tess, looking at me. I thought, "Shit, am I going to die?" They had grim faces, I remember that. No-one was cracking any jokes.

I was back in my own room the following day. Rick came in and asked how I was.

"Shithouse," I replied. He sat there making conversation and I ignored him. He eventually gave up and went home. The next day he rang and said, "Are you the same as you were yesterday?" I was abrupt again. I just said yes. He said fine, he wouldn't waste his time coming in. Obviously, he was trying to snap me out of the funk I was in, but I couldn't see it at the time. I was furious with him. I didn't want people near me, but I craved their presence at the same time. I didn't want to make small talk, I wanted to be left alone. But I was scared, too. I needed company.

That's how it goes. I was sliding headlong into a black pit. My heart was still bouncing around. Ron came to see me late one night. It was about 11.30pm. That was like Ron. I don't know how he did it, but he had always had an amazing ability to talk his way into places when he should not have been there. They were strict about visiting times, but because Ron's job saw him working crazy hours — he was probably jetlagged for a good portion of his life — he always had a logical reason for turning up at the wrong time. Coupled with his charm and gentle nature, it was easy, I guess, to see how he managed to get into places. But it has perplexed me from time to time just how he managed to be a great cyclist. It's an aggressive sport — the testosterone just about spills onto the track. Yet Ron has always been the gentleman.

I woke up to him tickling my feet. He came and sat next to me and held my hand and rubbed my arm very gently. I told him that I had to get well. There was no choice. I had been asked to participate in the Sydney Olympics opening ceremony. But at that stage I didn't know where I would be when the Olympics began — or even if I would be around to care. Ron was ecstatic. Although I didn't tell him what my role would be, that huge grin once again appeared on his face.

"I've got to get well," I said to him, trying to convince myself as much as him. "I really want to be there."

But who was I fooling? I was dreaming of dying and when I wasn't, I was awake thinking about it. The antidepressants that had given me some measure of protection over the years had long vanished from my system, and I was feeling more vulnerable by the hour.

What made matters worse was the constant need of the nurses to draw blood from me. It was important — my blood levels could tell the doctors so much about my health. But I was getting increasingly angry because the nurses kept tapping into my left arm. When you have had breast cancer, and particularly if you have had the auxiliary nodes removed from your armpit, you must protect that arm from infection otherwise the chances of developing lymphodema — a chronic swelling of the arm and hand — increase. I had been vigilant over the four years since my breast operation. At one point, when doctors operated fearing I had an infected appendix, they had wanted to take blood out of my left arm and I had been extremely forceful in letting them know that it was one place they must not venture near.

I reached my breaking point about five days after the operation to remove my left ovary. A nurse walked into my room to give me another round of antibiotics via the intravenous drip.

"I'm not having any more drugs," I told her.

"Come on Raelene," she replied. "You know you need them. You have to have them. Besides, I'm just doing what the doctor wants."

"If you try to put any more bloody drugs into me I'll rip all these tubes out right now," I said. I was deadly serious and the nurse could tell that any further debate was useless.

"If that's the way you want it, that's your choice," she said. Then she walked out, presumably to jot down a note for the doctors that patient Boyle was being difficult. Yet again.

I began telling everyone who entered my room that I was going home. Most of them humoured me — it was far too soon for someone in my predicament to even dream of leaving the hospital. But my mind was made up. The only question remaining as far as I was concerned was whether I would walk with the hospital's blessing, or as an escapee.

When Judy arrived I told her what I planned to do. She was surprised and concerned. "Are you sure?" she asked.

"I know I'm not going to get well here, but I know I'll get well at home. Please, support me on this."

So Judy told the nurses. One of them asked what nursing qualifications she had. "I'm the mother of three and a sensible woman," she told them.

It was hard to work out who they were less impressed with by then — me or Judy. But the surgeon eventually relented. Judy drove me home and immediately I went upstairs into my favourite room. While Judy fixed up a batch of "Jewish penicillin" — a chicken broth a Jewish friend, Pearl, had once shown me how to make — I lay down on the couch.

I barely moved for the next three weeks. I didn't talk to anyone. I hardly ate or drank. When dogs and cats are sick they tend to slink away, find a cool spot under a tree, a shady place out of the way where no-one can disturb them, and they will stay there until they get better, or they die. That was what I had effectively chosen to do. I had found my safe place.

Now I had to decide whether I was going to pull through, or give up.

THOSE WEEKS were, without doubt, the worst of my life. I was sullen, withdrawn and felt completely alienated from everyone around me. I shudder to think what might have happened had Judy and my family not been there to try and coax me out of the darkness. Sometimes I just curled up in a foetal position and lay like that for hours, uninterested in anything happening around me. By then, I had rung my manager, Rob Woodhouse, and told him I was far too sick to do anything and every appointment in my diary had to be cancelled. I also told him to forget the Olympic Games — I wouldn't be there.

Rob assured me he would look after things. But he told me not to make any hasty decisions about the Games. They were weeks away; a lot could change in that time. I shrugged, barely listening. I didn't know if I was going to live or die at that stage and by then I no longer really cared. I was still thinking about suicide and I kept remembering that dream I had in the hospital. I have never been very religious. To me, when a person dies that is it. The party's over. I've never believed in an afterlife or that we are even here for a purpose. But I couldn't shake the memory of that dream. Something seemed to be suggesting to me that it was time to end my life. Something was pushing the idea, selling it to me.

I slept a lot. I couldn't respond to anything, not even my beloved Goldie. By early August I had lost 13 kilograms. The only things I was eating were tiny spoonfuls of mashed pumpkin, or sips of soup. My heart was still out of control. At times it would burst into a rhythmic pounding that frightened me, before slowing to some form of normality. On 16 August I had to force myself to get up and get dressed. I'd had a long-standing arrangement to have my photograph taken for a book titled *Exposure*. It was being produced to raise funds for research into Ovarian cancer through a group connected to the Monash Medical Centre in Melbourne. Ironically, I'd agreed to be in the book long before my own diagnosis. So I got up and tried to put my best face on. Believe me, it was extraordinarily difficult just making small talk with people. When you suffer deep-seated depression such as I was experiencing, one of the first things that vanishes is your interest in the world around you. You become so self-centred and obsessed with your own experiences that it becomes impossible to empathise with other people. I don't mean to sound glib here, but it's like being an insecure teenager again, except a hundred times more intense.

I'd also had a phone call from Bruce McAvaney. Rob had released news of my condition to the media, and this time around there had been little intrusion into my private life. Bruce was concerned about my health and I told him I didn't think I'd be joining him at the Games. Once again, as he always seems to do, Bruce found just the right words for the occasion.

"Boyley, I don't want you to pull out of the Games," he said. "I don't care if you don't say anything. Don't bother doing any research. If you have to say anything when we're commentating, just talk about what you see out there on the track. But I want you to understand this. I just want you sitting next to me at the Olympics."

That conversation made me feel much better. By then I was back on antidepressants and I could feel the darkness slowly beginning to lift. I had turned a corner — a very small one for sure — but a significant one nevertheless. Rozi, my psychiatrist, had been overseas but as soon as she returned she was on the phone, and I was slowly starting to talk again.

One afternoon Judy asked me if it was true that I had been considering suicide. I had mentioned it to a couple of visitors by then, but I had not had the courage to tell her. "I'm sorry," I said. "But I didn't think you needed to know about it. And I didn't know how to tell you."

I was feeling guilty, too. I had been planning a surprise birthday party for Judy in late August. It was going to be a brilliant affair and I had been quite proud of myself a few months before in conceiving and executing the plans. I had booked out the restaurant at Kingfisher Resort on Fraser Island and secretly invited all Judy's friends to come up for the party. The kids were going to decorate the restaurant with balloons and streamers and I had organised for vases of Dutch blue irises — Judy's favourite flower — to be positioned around the restaurant. I had booked a large number of rooms for the guests to stay in overnight. She wasn't going to know a thing until she arrived at the restaurant for dinner.

But while she was doing the books for the café one Sunday afternoon, I went downstairs and told her all about it. I was sorry, I explained, but I just wasn't strong enough to go through with it. She was upset, naturally, but she also seemed to understand. Perhaps it was a sign that I was slowly returning to the normal world, because I felt guilty about letting her down. So a couple of weeks later I managed to pull off a different surprise party. A close friend, Aileen, kindly offered to let us use her house for a surprise dinner party. I had a chef go there and cook all day, and then we invented a pretext for Judy to pop in. She was exhausted by then. It was early September, she had been running the café, running a household and taking care of possibly the worst patient in the world. But the look on her face when she walked in to be greeted by her closest friends was worth it. It also brought a rare smile to my face.

But by then I knew I was through the worst of it. There was no real significant turning point, no grand moment when I woke and suddenly knew that things were getting better. Instead, it had been a gradual, drawn-out struggle. I had found my shady spot. I had withdrawn from the world and fought my own life and death battle. And now I knew that I would endure.

I was going to Sydney. How dare they even contemplate holding an Olympics in my own country without me.

21

Catching up with an old flame

THE OLYMPIC GAMES ARE A LOT LIKE GOING TO DISNEYLAND. REALITY tends to be suspended while you are there. Of course, a few cracks always tend to appear — it seems you can't hold a Games in the modern era without at least one Bulgarian weightlifter being sent home in disgrace. Yet it's the only time when athletes with necks wider than heads get to protest their innocence and claim that their magnificent builds and superhuman performances are due to mothers' cooking and plenty of fresh air and exercise.

But I love the Games, despite my cynicism and the fact that when I was competing they conspired to leave me in second place. When the cauldron is lit and the Games begin, you cannot help but sense a feeling of unity and purpose. It is strongest among the competitors — to be in the athletes village and have the opportunity to mingle with the world's best leaves you with a very special feeling. In Sydney in 2000, however, that feeling extended to the public as well.

I liked Sydney as a city. Having been born and raised in Melbourne I'd always found Sydney a little faster and louder than what I was used to, but I admired the town's cockiness and belief in itself. But when I arrived in the days leading up to the Games I couldn't believe how the city had transformed itself. Taxi drivers were polite. Drivers who normally raised their middle finger at a pedestrian having the audacity to cross a street stopped and waved politely. People everywhere were smiling. At peak hour, as the hordes of commuters were swallowed up in the gaping maws of the train stations, everyone was minding their manners, holding doors open for stragglers and giving up their seats to pregnant women and old ladies. I was stunned, and quite tickled. The entire nation seemed to have turned into a giant gathering of scouts. We were clearly on our best behaviour — a typical Australian trait. We politely tucked all our dirty business to one side, put on our make-up and welcomed the visitors in for a party.

Michael Knight's office had called me just before I left home for Sydney. A voice on the other end told me a fax was about to be sent to me. I must stand by my fax machine and personally receive the letter. Then I should answer its questions and respond promptly before destroying the document. Secrecy was paramount. I could almost hear the theme to "Mission: Impossible" playing in the background. Rather mundanely, the fax requested my measurements for an outfit I would wear at the opening ceremony. I was told I would be contacted again once I was in Sydney.

On the morning of 14 September — the day before the opening ceremony — I was contacted at the hotel in which I was staying. I had to be out the front that night to be collected at 7pm. I was to make sure I was there on time and was to tell no-one what I would be doing. I'd been invited by the rugby league legend Johnny Raper to his city office later that evening. His building had an outdoor entertainment area on its roof and you could see George Street

A ROSE, A HERB AND A ... BOYLE: Swimming great Murray Rose, track legend Herb Elliott and me at the Olympic Reunion Centre opening in the lead-up to the 2000 Games. I was only a month away from emergency surgery for ovarian cancer.

OLYMPIC COURAGE: The Olympic flame inspires more than just athletes. Although riddled with cancer, my friend Sharon McAllister insisted on "running" her leg of the torch relay. Within months she had died.

A HELPING HAND: Marion was one of the first women I helped to undergo breast reconstruction. It's made a world of difference. "But you've got to kiss a lot of toads before you find a prince," she says.

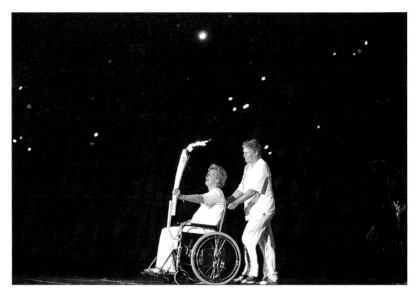

GRAND ENTRANCE: With billions watching on, I steer Betty Cuthbert into the stadium during the Opening Ceremony. All I'm thinking about is … don't trip and spill Betty out of her chair…

LADIES IN WAITING: Dawn Fraser, Cathy Freeman, Debbie Flintoff-King, me, Betty Cuthbert, Shirley Strickland and Shane Gould watch the cauldron rise during the 2000 Olympic Games Opening Ceremony.

Wow!

BIRTHDAY GIRL: Brother Rick gives me a hug on my 50th birthday.

GLAMOUR GIRLS: Janette Howard, wife of the PM, poses with a group of Breast Cancer Network supporters just as the fund-raising 50th birthday party swings into action.

STOP LAUGHING: Professor Boyle at your service. I might have disliked school but the Sunshine Coast University still managed to make me an Honorary Senior Fellow in 2001.

A SPORTING CHANCE: One of the projects of the Sporting Chance Cancer Foundation is to provide the young and sick with support. Here I am with Letitia Hewitt, who is in remission from leukemia, at the launch of the Raelene Boyle Home Care Program.

MAN WITH A GOLDEN TOUCH: Ron Dewhurst showed faith in me when others believed I was all washed up. But he did more than simply restore my self-confidence — his patience, wisdom and advice turned me into a better person away from the track, too.

NEWSPIX/ANTHONY WEATE

CLOSE TO ROYALTY: Swimming great Tracey Wickham and I examine the Queen's Baton, during its journey around the Commonwealth prior to the 2002 Manchester Games.

IN THE PRESENCE OF GREATNESS: Betty Cuthbert never fails to inspire me — from her life as an athlete through to the courage she now displays.

TAKING CHARGE: Former primary school teacher Lyn Swinburne decided to do something to help those suffering breast cancer. Now she's helped change the lives of thousands of Australian women.

MY LITTLE WHITE ANGEL: My assistant out of the black hole, Kimba.

FIELD OF DREAMS: Only by seeing the field of pink and white ladies representing those women diagnosed with breast cancer, organised by Breast Cancer Network Australia, can you truly appreciate the scale and impact of breast cancer each year. I want to be around when a cure is found.

below. Dawn Fraser and several others were due to run up there with the torch and on to the Town Hall before it finally made the 16-kilometre trek to the Olympic Stadium at Homebush the next day in time for the opening ceremony. So I went along to the function and shortly before 7pm I excused myself, telling everyone I had to go to a Channel Seven production meeting.

I was picked up in a limousine back at my hotel and accompanied to Homebush by a SOCOG officer, who either didn't know what I was doing, or simply wasn't allowed to talk about it. At the main stadium, the final rehearsal for Ric Birch's opening ceremony had already begun. I was on my own and had no idea who the other athletes were who would be joining me in the main arena. My task in the rehearsal was simple — I was to practise the role I would play the following night, pushing Betty Cuthbert into the stadium. But there was no need for Betty to attend the rehearsal, so I felt a bit of an idiot pushing an empty wheelchair into the arena. It was a confusing scene — there were power lines running everywhere and blue chalk markings that were supposed to tell us where to stand. I was worried about the power lines — for one horrible moment I had a vision of me hitting one of them, rocking the wheelchair forward and Betty tumbling out in front of the worldwide television audience of more than 2 billion. It would not be a particularly proud moment in my life. How would I handle the situation, I wondered? Would I lean over, pick Betty up and put her back in the chair and pretend nothing had happened? Or would I simply pick up the torch and run on alone, hogging centre stage for myself?

At that stage speculation was mounting about who had been chosen to light the cauldron. I had heard plenty of whispers, most of them to do with Dawn Fraser or Cathy Freeman. I would have loved to have seen Marjorie Jackson — our first female track gold medallist — given the honour. But in the lead-up to the ceremony none of us was in on the secret.

All I knew was that I was extremely fortunate to be out there playing a role. Rob Woodhouse was a smart man and I had much to thank him for. He must have known the Olympics would eventually lure me out of my cave. I was still feeling very weak, and was glad when I discovered I would not be pushing Betty around the track for several laps. But that night during rehearsals, I looked around and knew I was about to have one of the best experiences of my life.

I FINALLY discovered an hour into the opening ceremony who else was participating. We were taken to a room beneath the stands and there we were: me, Betty Cuthbert, Shirley Strickland, Dawn Fraser, Debbie Flintoff-King and Shane Gould.

There was a bit of baggage in that room as well — you can't expect to have so many different sorts of personalities without some of them jarring. A few of us had not seen eye to eye on occasions; my relationship with Shirley had deteriorated over the years to the point where it was effectively non-existent, while my friendship with Dawn had also cooled. But that night all those niggling personal issues were put aside. Shirley still kept pretty much to herself, but there was a genuine sense of unity in the air — we were all Olympians and we shared a unique bond. Yet I was honoured and I guess a little perplexed as to why I had been chosen to be among these gold medallists who would be the last Australians to handle the torch. I'm sure there were plenty of other gold medallists who were wondering the same thing.

It was an issue that cropped up in the media in the days afterwards — who was chosen, who was left out, and why. All I can say is that I obviously had no input in the decision-making process. I'm sure no-one begrudged my role. I can only assume I had been picked because of my longevity in the sport. Perhaps it was some form of compensation because of the drug situation in sport and the fact that I had not won a gold medal because I had never cheated. Perhaps it was because I was a prominent breast cancer survivor. Who knows.

One thing is certain. I was not given a role simply because I had spent my athletic career crawling up to officialdom. I'm sure there were politically correct overtones behind the choice — after all, the Olympic movement was celebrating a century of female participation that year as well. But you had to admit that Australia has always held its successful female athletes in high regard. Our public profile has always seemed to be greater than most of the male athletes; Dawn has long been regarded as a national institution, as have Betty and others.

My fears that I might tip Betty out of her chair were unfounded. When we entered the stadium the magic of the moment took my breath away. Flashlights were popping everywhere — the entire sky seemed to have lit up. People were screaming and yelling, and the adrenalin rush was probably more powerful than it had been when I was an athlete. I was far more relaxed, too. At least this time I did not have the pressure of having to perform in a race.

The opening ceremony itself was clearly the best of its kind. Ric Birch, the ceremony organiser, achieved a remarkable thing — he managed to weave a wonderful story together about the history of Australia without over-dramatising it or making it too obscure. I loved the humorous bits — the outback dunnies, the sudden elevation of corrugated iron into an art form. Whenever I hear people complain that Australia has little culture of its own I cringe. Birch truly showed what it is like to be Australian in that ceremony, without the chest-thumping and corny patriotism you often encounter at such events.

After Betty and I finished our leg with the torch we made our way to the end of the stadium. Eventually, we all gathered together and waited for Cathy to emerge. It was a remarkable moment and despite my earlier misgivings — I'd thought she might be too young for the task and a more senior figure would be more appropriate —

it was instantly clear that the right choice had been made. Cathy was the person for the moment and as she stood there, the flame mixing with the water, I could not have imagined any other Australian being more suited to the role. Certainly, there was no way they could have put someone like me into that white costume she wore. It would have been a horrific sight — particularly with so many school-age children still wide awake and watching around the country.

When the cauldron shuddered to an unscheduled halt we all held our breath. Here was every Australian's greatest fear come to life. If there is one trait we seem to share as a nation, it is one of insecurity. We always expect things to cock up — Australians have come to expect a calamity hiding around every corner. Perhaps it's because of the nature of the land in which we live. Fire, water, wind and dust have long conspired to make life difficult.

We were all supposed to have earpieces and receive instructions from the ceremony's direction unit. But in the rush and chaos of the early moments of the ceremony, someone had forgotten to give them to us. Cathy, as it turned out, was the only one of us wired up and she could hear the frantic cries and profanities of the engineers as they scrambled to repair the small part that had broken and stopped the cauldron from its rise into the sky above the stadium.

She held her nerve magnificently. Once again she showed me how capable she is of controlling her emotions and shutting out external distractions. But it was a long wait for everyone — a 90-second delay that seemed to stretch into minutes. Once again time slowed, just like it did when I was competing. But when the cauldron slowly began to rise again, we all took a breath and relaxed. It was over and the hiccup seemed little more than a dramatic pregnant pause. Now the Games could really begin.

There was one small postcript, however. In the early hours of the next morning as we attempted to get home, some of us discovered that no preparations had been made to get us back to the city.

Marjorie Jackson was there, despite having had back surgery the previous week. She wouldn't have missed the opening ceremony for the world. In a classic example of opposites attracting, I am close to Marj. We are chalk and cheese — Marj never swears and never drinks. But we do share a similar perspective on the importance of sport in our lives and the lives of others. We know it's not the be-all and end-all. I would end up popping in to see her in her hotel room many times during the Games, filling her in on the gossip, although I kept the more salacious material to myself. She, in turn, traded information with me.

Marj managed to get a lift with a policeman, who drove her back to her hotel while she lay flat on the back seat. Judy and I managed to get a lift in a SOCOG staff bus after a long walk out of the stadium through the crowds.

I was exhausted afterwards. But it had certainly been worth it. I was still feeling down from time to time. But my work had just begun at the Games, and I now had something on which to focus.

I SLEPT whenever I could, and the first week of the Games, with its traditional emphasis on swimming, gave me plenty of free time to relax and prepare. I must admit that I wasn't confident in knowing the form of many of those I would be commentating about and so I did my best to catch up. As always, the best way to learn is to use your own eyes and see things for yourself. So I would make the journey out to Homebush, check in at the media centre where Channel Seven had its large series of offices, catch up with the researchers who were compiling statistics and background on many of the athletes and their sports, and then I would head over to the training track.

There, I could sit and watch. You can tell a lot about an athlete during training just by watching. Those who are struggling with their form will often be working on technique — it's one of the first things you go back to when your times are not what they should be. My problem was in getting to the training zone, though had I been fit and well I would not have thought twice about it. Sydney was enjoying glorious weather (even the climate had co-operated with the Games organisers) and trying to thread my way through the crowds when I was recovering from two bouts of major surgery was an exercise that I knew would exhaust me.

I was lucky one afternoon. In what was typical of the mood of the city, a policeman recognised me and offered to give me a lift in one of those motorised golf carts that many officials used to help them move around the Olympic precinct. Not only did he take me to the training track, he then politely asked how long I would be staying there, promising to return and take me to the next venue I wanted to visit. Such service. If the Olympics were like Disneyland, then Homebush had become Fantasyland. Who would have believed it?

By the time the track and field began I was quite nervous. Fortunately, with Bruce McAvaney next to me, I knew I could not get myself into too much trouble. Once again he told me to concentrate on what I was seeing. Having worked with Bruce often, and knowing how professional he is, I knew I was safe. Bruce's commitment to research and homework is legendary in the sports commentating and journalism fraternity. Ever since he was a young kid dreaming of becoming a race caller, he has filled the equivalent of a warehouse with index cards and exercise books noting times and characteristics of athletes from around the world. One day someone will archive the entire collection and discover they have a lifetime's job ahead of them.

The Games, not surprisingly given the money, resources and crowd support, had been a big success for Australia. We had dominated in the pool and several other athletes had performed above expectation. But despite Ian Thorpe's brilliance, everything seemed like a preliminary event leading up to the night of Monday,

25 September. Cathy Freeman was going to try to achieve the impossible — run a lap of Homebush Stadium in under 50 seconds with 19 million Australians sitting on her shoulders.

I KNEW a little about the pressures on Cathy, but only a little. In past Olympics I had gone away — particularly in 1972 and 1976 — with big expectations. But these were different times. Cathy had become so many things to so many people. By the time the Games began it had grown ridiculous. Some had placed her on the same pedestal as Nelson Mandela and Martin Luther King. Not only was she going to win a gold and become our first female track gold medallist since Flintoff-King's win in the 400-metres hurdles in Seoul in 1988, but she was also going to end 200 years of bitterness between black and white Australia, bring about reconciliation and, presumably after that, solve world hunger and end all wars.

It was too much. But once again I had come to believe that if there was one athlete capable of withstanding the strain, it was Cathy. Her effort in Atlanta had already proved that. She had that remarkable ability to close off the world around her. Some thought that having been the centre of attention at the opening ceremony, her form and concentration might have been compromised. They had to be kidding. An athlete spends four years working their way toward the Games and can put up with greater pressure, such as the loss of a relative or a job, and still go on to win. She had also had to endure a very public disintegration of her relationship with her former lover and coach, Nick Bideau, and her former manager Peter Jess. Those two hadn't made life any easier for her — I thought the whole spectacle had turned into a circus. But once again it underlined to me the nature of modern athletics, and how money always seems to gnaw away at even the strongest professional relationships.

Of course, I was tense on the night of the race. I could feel my heart pounding — it hadn't beaten so quickly since my operation two months before. I knew that without the presence in the field of Marie-José Pérec, the brilliant but erratic Frenchwoman who had fled Australia days before, crumbling under the intense pressure of her looming showdown with the local hope, Cathy's job had been made much easier. Across the road from Perec's hotel was a bus stop reserved for the media to help them move around the Olympic precinct. Whenever Perec peered out of her window or walked outside she saw a long line of reporters. In her mind, they were there to watch her every move, all part of a psychological game devised to disrupt her preparation.

In reality, it was just a bus stop. Perec soon left Sydney, never to return, and it seemed Cathy's last obstacle had been removed. But I, as much as anyone in the crowd that night, knew how quickly things could unravel. I had felt fantastic sitting on the blocks in Montreal in that semi-final of the 200 metres. A minute later I was in tears.

I was surprised to see Cathy enter the stadium wearing that one-piece bodysuit. I figured she wouldn't be wearing it unless she felt completely comfortable in it — but I also assumed there would be a handsome dividend awaiting her from her sponsor, Nike.

The stadium was rocking by the time the finalists lined up, but nowhere was the shaking louder than in the commentary booth. Whenever Bruce is nervous he jiggles his legs. This time they were battering the desk and creating a real racket. I was dry-mouthed, and told myself to simply concentrate.

From the hushed silence at the starter's gun, a sudden roar erupted and seemed to push the girls around the track. Everything slowed down once again. But even before the final bend I sensed Cathy had it won. As she crossed the line I saw the energy drain from her and she slumped to the track, sitting there for what seemed like ages, barely able to breathe.

"What a performance, what a champion, what a legend," said Bruce, summing up the contest.

"... what a relief," I added. You didn't need to say anything else. Bruce had taught me many things in the commentary booth, but perhaps the greatest advice was that sometimes the best commentary of all is when you simply let the picture tell the story.

FOR MOST of Australia, Cathy's gold-medal run was the pinnacle of the Olympics. But for Bruce and me and millions of athletics purists around the world, the race immediately after the women's 400-metres final was the icing on the cake. The American Michael Johnson could justifiably lay claim to being one of the genuine legends of world running. When you looked at him he hardly appeared built for speed — he had a low-slung frame and much shorter legs than I would have imagined an elite 400-metre runner would need. There was so much that was deceptive about him — when he ran it looked like he was sitting down. He took far more steps than his opponents, proof yet again of his remarkable leg speed.

But as his race was about to begin, Channel Seven cut to a commercial break. From a business point of view it was perfectly understandable — the businesses that had bought the airtime right after Cathy's run would have paid a premium price. But Bruce, justifiably I thought, was outraged. The air turned blue while we were in the commercial break, with Bruce demanding to know just why, with Johnson making a historic final international appearance, one of the greatest athletes the world had seen was not being paid the sort of respect he deserved.

I don't think I'd ever seen Bruce so livid — he was thumping the table and cursing the decision. I'm sure some of it had to do with the emotion of the evening. His call had been superb but it had also, surely, been an emotionally draining one.

I supported his views. But there was nothing I was capable of doing to change the situation. I wasn't going to mouth off too harshly. This was one Olympics during which I didn't want to become embroiled in any controversy.

By the time the Games finished I was exhausted, but still on a high. On one of my last nights in Sydney I met up with Lyn Swinburne, a good friend of mine who runs Breast Cancer Network Australia. We both headed off to an important function put on by the cosmetics company Estée Lauder. It was one of those official cocktail parties to raise awareness of the disease — one had to watch what one said, and what one drank and ate. But it was tremendously important all the same.

Those sort of functions just simply aren't my style; I become uncomfortable very quickly if I'm out of my tracksuit or T-shirt for longer than a few hours. Besides, I was in the mood to unwind. When I realised that on a floor above the Estée Lauder function was the Foster's Club, I grabbed Lyn and we ended up having a huge party, dancing and carousing through the night. Every so often we would pop downstairs and make an appearance at the cocktail party, before taking the plums out of our mouths and sneaking back upstairs for a few drinks and another round of dancing. We all had too much to drink, and paid the penalty the next day.

But the Games were like that — it was the same feeling you would get on the last day of school before summer holidays, when everyone raced around without a care in the world dreaming about the coming break. For sixteen days straight I lived with that feeling, and like everyone else who was privileged to be there, I was saddened when it came time to leave.

The Olympics, the scene of so many bitter disappointments for me, had proved to be a wonderful restorative tonic. It was with renewed optimism and enthusiasm that I packed my bags and headed home to Queensland. I had a lot of work to do. And Lyn was a woman who had shown me how to do it.

22

My heroes

I MAY NOT UNDERSTAND EINSTEIN'S THEORY OF RELATIVITY. AND DON'T bother asking me about quantum physics or how the universe began with a Big Bang. But welcome anyway to the Raelene Boyle Once-In-A-Lifetime Science Lecture. Today's topic: the butterfly effect (or how two simple phone calls helped to change the lives of thousands of Australian women).

You may have heard of the butterfly effect. It is a theory that contends that even the smallest, most innocuous of acts can have a huge effect on something much larger. It's all about the unpredictability of life. At its simplest, it goes like this. In the Brazilian jungle, a colourful butterfly beats its wings. These tiny movements create the slightest disturbance of air. Eventually, these disturbances create small eddies that turn into slightly larger ones. These, in turn, continue to grow. A few days later, a monsoon hits the coast of Bangladesh, causing flooding and untold damage to millions of lives.

From small things do big things grow. And on a warm summer's day in 1993, the butterfly's wings began beating in a school principal's office in Melbourne when a primary school teacher, Lyn Swinburne, picked up a telephone and dialled the number of her surgeon.

Like a lot of women, Lyn had grown aware of breast cancer and the suffering it had wreaked throughout Australia. Currently, more than 10 000 women are diagnosed with the disease — one in every twelve. A quarter of them die within a few years. She had often performed the routine self-examination, usually searching for a pea-sized lump that could indicate the start of a tumour. One morning she noticed something quite different with her right breast — it was as though a significant part of it had hardened. At first, she shrugged it off. But after mentioning it to her neighbour, and being told to get it checked quickly, she was soon in a surgeon's office being examined. Tests were carried out. The surgeon asked Lyn to call him back the following day to talk to him. "I know you're a schoolteacher, so if you ring at a certain time between classes, I'll make sure I'm there," he said.

So Lyn borrowed the headmistress's office and dialled the surgeon's office. His receptionist answered. "Sorry, the doctor's not here right now," she told Lyn. "But we've got your results and he said it was okay for me to pass them on to you."

Lyn, while surprised the doctor had not been available when he said he would be, nevertheless understood the sudden and unexpected nature of the profession. So she told the receptionist to go ahead, assuming the news must be good.

"I'm sorry, your results are positive."

At first Lyn heard only the word "positive" and figured she had heard what she expected to hear. Then it dawned on her. The tumour was cancerous. She began to think her life was finished.

The receptionist was still talking. "The doctor has a spot available for surgery on Monday, so he'd like you to have a chest x-ray, a bone scan and a blood test before then, thank you. And he's asked me to ask you if you would prefer a room of your own or a shared room?"

Lyn dissolved into tears. Years later, she uses that telephone conversation when invited to lecture medical students. The cold, impersonal way in which she discovered her life was under threat remains vivid. Always remember, she tells the aspiring group of doctors, to understand the vulnerability of your patients at such a time. Show them you care by being there and providing as much compassion as you can. She then goes on to tell them about another phone call.

It came after the surgery — a lumpectomy or partial mastectomy as they are known, when parts of her right breast were removed. She had just been given her first course of chemotherapy treatment and the next day had gone to visit her sister-in-law for lunch. The phone rang. It was for Lyn. But who knew, apart from her husband, where she was?

Her oncologist was on the line, the man responsible for supervising her chemotherapy treatment. He had gone to great lengths to track her down. "You've been on my mind, Lyn," he told her. "I've been wondering how you're getting along with your chemo ..."

When she hung up from the call, Lyn Swinburne felt that she had finally found a medical specialist in whom she could place her trust. She felt extraordinarily lucky. So far, as the mother of a six-year-old boy and an eight-year-old girl, she had been fortunate to have the support of a loving husband. (Tom, her hubby, is a solicitor, but more famously known as the grower of the best tomatoes in the southern hemisphere. Well, at least that's what he'll tell you.) She was well-educated and a confident person who was willing to ask the necessary questions about her condition. She had a wide circle of friends and family (a new freezer had to be purchased just to store all the casseroles everyone was making for her). But what, she wondered, was it like for those who were less fortunate: the single mothers with four kids living in trying conditions on social welfare, the women who spoke little or no English? The system wasn't providing what women really needed alongside the medical procedures. Lyn had been lucky to find a caring and compassionate oncologist who understood and related to her predicament. Many others were not so fortunate.

Those two telephone calls started her thinking. Within a few years she had given up teaching to pursue her new passion — raising awareness of breast cancer and letting its sufferers know they were not alone. Eventually, her tenaciousness led to her, literally, getting a foot in my door.

Getting through to me is a difficult task. As I've said, I'm not the easiest person to get to know, or to track down for that matter. Team Boyle tends to be pretty protective of me and my privacy, and you have to be very quick or extremely persistent to get near me.

In the year after my breast cancer I'd had to decide how I could help the cause. I wanted to do something, but I wasn't sure what. The publicity surrounding my condition had generated an amazing level of interest in my health from the public and many organisations which decided they wanted to use me as their spokeswoman. I did a lot of reading throughout 1997, looking at various organisations and evaluating their strengths and weaknesses. My suspicious nature was working overtime and I had to be sure I would be lending my support to a legitimate group.

The magazine *New Idea* had approached me to help launch an initiative of theirs to raise money for breast cancer research. The launch took place in early 1998 amid great hype at a luxury Melbourne hotel. I was flanked by several advertising executives who looked after me very well, making sure I appeared on time and spoke when I had to. Little did I know that there was a woman lurking in the crowd who was determined to get to me, no matter how difficult the task.

As we left, Lyn Swinburne approached me. She was working in a tiny, cramped office in Carlton that she had managed to secure free of rent. Somehow, she'd also managed to talk her way into scavenging an old computer. She started telling me about her project. It was called Breast Cancer Network Australia and it was something new. Here, finally, was an organisation that Lyn hoped would give breast cancer sufferers a voice when it came to the big decisions made by governments and health bodies. I walked along chatting with her politely. To be honest, I'd found the launch taxing and all I wanted to do was get out of there and have a rest. But this Swinburne woman was persistent. When I got in the elevator, she stuck her foot in the door to prevent it from closing. I told her to send me some information, and got away.

Eventually we caught up and Lyn's passion and zeal soon had me converted. The network, she believed, was a huge opportunity for women to have a say in the way they were treated. It wasn't difficult for her to strike a chord with me — her experiences with cancer had pretty much paralleled mine. We had both endured that sense of being a number, and not a person. We had both experienced that cold and impersonal side of the medical profession. I was amazed, however, at how passionate and enthusiastic Lyn was about the subject, years after recovering from her bout with cancer. "We can make a difference," she said. I believed her.

It was Lyn who came up with the idea of the highly successful Field of Women project. Toward the end of 1998 she had organised a conference in Canberra for breast cancer sufferers that coincided with the official launch of the Breast Cancer Network. It wasn't just one of those let's-all-hug-one-another sessions, where everyone gathers to feel sorry for one another before heading home and forgetting about it. Out of it came a great deal, including a new list of priorities that would help raise greater awareness of breast cancer. But the one with the greatest impact was the planting of 10 000 pink lady silhouettes, and 2500 white ones, on the lawns of Parliament House. The pink ladies represented the women diagnosed with cancer, the white ones those who died each year. I spoke at the launch and found it an incredibly moving experience. Naturally enough, the media flocked to the pink lady exhibition. It was a remarkable thing to have the numbers so starkly represented on the lawns of the nation's legislative capital.

Since then, the Network has become a force to be reckoned with. It has raised and secured millions of dollars in funding and is now listened to by politicians and the medical community. National hotlines have been set up that are staffed twenty-four hours a day, providing women recently diagnosed with cancer with immediate support and information. If they are on their own in the middle of the night, trying to work out what lies ahead, they need only pick up the phone and a breast cancer survivor is there to talk to them. Media awareness of breast cancer has also been heightened, to the point where the Network's success at raising awareness is looked upon as a model by other organisations. A great deal of work still needs to be done, but I sometimes wonder just what would have been achieved had it not been for "Swinny". She has become a great friend, a confidant and an inspiration. She is in demand around the world now, appearing at conferences as well as keeping up with all the latest research in the field. She has a raucous laugh and an incredibly generous nature, and a spare bed is always available for me at her home whenever I'm in Melbourne.

But I have also seen another side to her. There have been days when I have visited the Network's Melbourne offices, or been sitting at the bench in Lyn's kitchen as Tommy pours me another glass of wine and tells me about his latest technique for growing tomatoes, when the phone has rung. Lyn answers it, and the tears well in her eyes. Someone she knows — anyone of hundreds from around the country — has just died after a long battle with breast cancer. That, I'm sure, is what keeps her going at such a hectic pace.

Lyn Swinburne helped to show me what could be done. And she gave me quite a few ideas on how I could personally help change the lives of others less fortunate than myself. It wasn't long before I decided to put those lessons into practice.

By the time I met Lyn I had already agreed to lend my name to a cancer charity called Sporting Chance. Chris Hughes was a young doctor with a large family who had just come home to Australia after a stint working and studying in America. He was a gifted head and neck surgeon who could not believe the gaps and lack of funding available for research into cancer in Australia. He had sent me volumes of information about himself and what he was trying to achieve. One day he rang me out of the blue and said he was coming to see me. He was on the Gold Coast and would drive up to the Sunshine Coast. He showed up with a bottle of Moët and a nice bottle of red. From that moment I knew I was dealing with a man of class, not to mention taste.

When Sporting Chance Cancer Foundation was officially launched at the Opera House in 1997, it happened to fall on the anniversary of Mum's death. I had been asked to speak, and had thought nothing of it at the time. But the emotion of the launch, and the thought of Mum and everything that had taken place the year before, proved too much for me. I broke down and couldn't finish my speech. I felt like such an idiot — a room full of people and here I was unable to even complete reading my prepared notes. Fortunately, sports commentator and identity Graham McNeice was the MC for the event and he managed to finish my speech for me.

Chris hails from a large family of ten, and pretty much all of them are now connected with Sporting Chance in one way or another. Two of his brothers, Tim and Jack, help run the organisation, having taken over from Chris to lighten his burden. Every year a fundraising golf day is held which produces hundreds of thousands of dollars in donations. Out of that money has come a series of scholarships in my name that I present each year to researchers studying cancer and looking for ways to combat it.

It's remarkable how one thing soon leads you into an entire new world. As a young woman I could never have imagined boasting a network of friends and associates ranging from corporate leaders to highly skilled surgeons and doctors. But what is more, after leading the life of a sheltered and, at times, selfish athlete, I have discovered a unique world where people give, rather than take. It's a world that never ceases to amaze me. You wouldn't believe the hours that some of these people give up and the personal sacrifices they make — the time they could have spent relaxing or making money — just to improve the lives of people they may never meet. It's a sad reflection on the current state of modern life that I guess I find this so extraordinary. But stop and think. When was the last time you genuinely gave up something in your life, or even gave blood, to help a stranger? I now understand why many people do it. It's addictive. Even given the small role I have in raising awareness, the people I meet keep me going back for more.

One of the things I am most proud of is a project I became associated with not long after my work began with Sporting Chance Cancer Foundation and the Breast Cancer Network Australia. I was approached by a surgeon on the Sunshine Coast and told about a number of local women who had undergone breast removal procedures, and could not afford to have prostheses fitted.

Let's face it. We live in a breast-dominated culture. Western society is obsessed with tits. You see them everywhere — from roadside billboards advertising everything from icecream to cars, through to movies and shopping centres. Breasts and their cleavage are one of the dominant images of modern life. And in this image-conscious society in which we live, women are constantly having the idea reinforced that breasts equal femininity. To lose them can deliver a savage psychological blow. So many women feel inadequate after undergoing mastectomies and feel as if their womanhood has been taken away from them. And because breast cancer often attacks women in middle and later age groups, some of them are separated or divorced and believe any hope of securing a new relationship has ended. What sort of man would want a woman with no breasts, they think? This is not a stupid question because I have seen both sides of this dilemma. A great friend of mine saw her husband disappear when she was diagnosed with breast cancer. He decided it was time to end their marriage. This is not an uncommon occurrence. Many men cannot cope with the idea that their partner is sick and facing death; they just don't like confronting "health issues". It scares them. It's something they don't — and won't — try to understand. It's the same reason we see soaring prostate cancer rates in this country. Of course, there are just as many men, if not more, who are prepared to stand by their partners and offer them every possible support. I hate stereotyping more than most people. But in the years since I first began learning about the disease, I have seen and heard enough stories to know that, apart from its physical nature, cancer has an ability to inflict mental and social scars that can be just as devastating.

You can argue the rights and wrongs of body image until the cows come home. The reality is far more important to deal with. Here's the bottom line: a woman who has lost a breast to cancer has endured a traumatic and life-changing event. We should do everything we can to help improve her state of mind and her self-esteem.

And that's what happened. I had already begun staging my own fundraising dinners at Twin Waters resort on the Sunshine Coast. Using the lessons I had learned from Lyn Swinburne — plus a dash of her perseverance complemented by my unique streak of stubbornness — I hit the phone and began calling business people and other community leaders I knew and put them on the spot. "I'm holding a fundraising dinner for breast cancer and I'd like you to buy a table," I'd tell them. Some have been terrific, others less so. But I have found my strike rate to be quite high, and having a public profile has obviously been an enormous contributing factor. I am also fortunate to live in a caring community.

Not long after my first dinner, I was approached by Justin Darcy, a surgeon who has performed many mastectomies over the years. He told me how difficult it was for women who had lost their breasts to have them replaced with prosthetic devices. It was a complicated and costly procedure — each prosthetic is worth about $5000 and there is no medical rebate available because the government classifies the implantation procedure as plastic surgery. How ridiculous! But a problem just as great was securing the services of competent surgeons and hospital time in which to perform the procedure. The surgeon and hospital issue was quickly resolved by Lee Brown, a talented plastic surgeon. The money for the prosthetics was my responsibility.

One of the first women we helped was Marion. She had been forty-eight when, in 1996 and using a self-examination sheet published by the *Australian Women's Weekly*, she had discovered a lump in her breast. She had always suffered from an inverted nipple, and doctors say any variation is something that needs to be closely examined. Both her breasts were removed and she underwent chemotherapy. The scars left behind were sizeable, although Justin Darcy had done a remarkably clean and polished job. For months afterward Marion avoided looking at herself in the mirror. Her marriage also broke down, which didn't help her state of mind. She suffered from so much anxiety after splitting from her husband that she was prone to bouts of vomiting. The loss of her breasts compounded her loss of confidence. "It affected my notions of being feminine," she says now. She would wear an external prosthetic — "fake boobs" — that had the unfortunate habit of falling out of her bathing suit whenever she took her grandchildren to the beach and bent over to help them build a sandcastle.

Marion is one of those women whom I always marvel at — somehow she managed to keep a sense of humour despite her predicament. "I tell everyone I was quite attached to the boobs I had," she often says. But she was determined to have implants and planned to use her superannuation to pay for them if she had to. Marion was a classic candidate for internal breast prostheses. Because of the mastectomy, she had not been required to undergo radiation therapy. Radiation tends to toughen and deaden the skin, reducing its elasticity. For an implant like the one Marion received, a silicon sac is inserted into each breast area, and over three months is regularly expanded, allowing the skin to stretch with each injection of a saline solution. Then the initial prosthesis is taken out and a permanent one replaces it.

Now she has regained much of her old confidence. Her bubbly personality has returned and she is on the lookout for a new partner in life. "But you've got to kiss a lot of toads before you find a prince," she says.

SOME WOMEN, just like some men, find it difficult to come to terms with their illness. They feel as though they have been branded on the forehead with a mark that lets the whole world know about their affliction. Meet Michelle, another gorgeous friend of mine, who at times has struggled to accept what has happened to her.

I can't say I blame her. She is an extraordinarily pretty girl with a vivacious personality. A primary school teacher, she was diagnosed with a rare form of breast cancer in her late twenties.

Whooosh.

Hear that sound? That was the noise her then boyfriend made as he decided it was time to set a few land speed records and get out of her life as fast as he could.

Because of the rarity of her condition, the doctors were initially flummoxed when it came to treating her. In the end, in the space of just a few short years, she would undergo a remarkable ten operations. I've often said I regard the scalpel as my friend. But Michelle knows it more intimately than anyone else I've met. It has been a tortuous road for her. She finds it difficult to talk about, even now. During her sickest times she invented excuses and refused to go out in public, in case she was seen and other people learned of her plight.

She is fortunate because she has found an extremely supportive boyfriend who looks after her and does all he can to ease her fears. But like a lot of cancer sufferers, Michelle often wonders whether it really is all over. Will it come back in another form? She dreads the idea of going back to hospital. One of her worst experiences was lying in her hospital bed one morning and being approached by a group of doctors. If you've ever been in a public hospital I'm sure you know the drill. Senior doctor takes group of medical students or recently graduated doctors on the rounds of the wards. Michelle lay there — and no-one acknowledged her presence — as one of the doctors began spouting off about her condition. She felt like an animal in a zoo, a test subject who was to be observed, poked and prodded, but not regarded as a fellow human being. Like a lot of us, she spent years searching for a compassionate bedside voice.

I was introduced to Michelle through some of her friends I had met at a gym where I was working out to help my recovery from breast cancer. They were concerned that she wasn't coping well, and that it might be good for her to talk about her condition with someone who knew a little about what she was experiencing. Since then, we've become very good friends. Slowly, I've been trying to encourage her to come out of her shell more and accept what she has been through.

Her state of mind wasn't helped when she had her remaining breast removed in late 2002. Confronting cancer is going to take her more time. But I'm sure she will have plenty of that.

SO MANY people. So many survivors. And so many who finally succumbed. Quite a few of my friends often express amazement at the large number of people I know. It's a reflection, I guess, of the varied phases of my life — the athletic career, the gardening and, now, my work as a community ambassador for organisations like National Australia Bank, the Blood Bank and various other charities I also work for.

But it is the people who have suffered similar illnesses to me with whom I most identify today. I know what they have gone through. "Having breast cancer is massive amounts of no fun," wrote an American cancer survivor called Molly Ivins. "First they mutilate you; then they poison you; then they burn you. I have been on blind dates better than that."

We all know what she means. Ivins was found to have advanced cancer, and like many in a similar position soon discovered that people around her had suddenly turned into football coaches, spewing forth strings of cliches like, "You can beat this; you can win; you're strong." But as Ivins observed, "I suspect that cancer doesn't give a rat's ass whether you have a positive mental attitude. It just sits in there multiplying away, whether you are admirably stoic or weeping and wailing."

The only real way to deal with it is to get on with life, to accept the chemotherapy and the rest of the bloody awful drugs that make you look like a washed-out ghostly image of yourself. It's a lesson I've learned a little late, particularly given all the wailing and weeping I did in that dreadful year. But it's never too late to learn.

Yet there is something I suspect I will never quite get over. And that is the anger. Sometimes it can come out of nowhere, a thick bile inside me that leaves me feeling livid and red with rage. The worst thing about cancer is the unfairness of it all. It doesn't care who it strikes — young or old, fit or unfit. It's a cruel, insidious disease and I often wonder how so many people can believe there is a gentle and caring God behind life.

I only have to remind myself of Sharon McAllister to see the unfairness of it all. I lived shoulder to shoulder with Sharon as cancer metastasised throughout her body, ravaging her bones and limbs. She had contracted breast cancer in her mid forties when she and her husband ran a hardware store not far from my home. The cancer must have been pretty aggressive when it was diagnosed because she underwent a radical mastectomy where one breast was effectively gouged out of her chest. She had an incredible resilience, however. She showed enormous strength during chemotherapy by forcing herself to walk four kilometres on most days to stay fit.

Sharon and I would often sit in the sun at the local bus stop and swap tales of twinges in our bodies, places where we imagined the old enemy was starting a fresh attack on us. We talked about our fears and we shed a few tears — me more than her, of course. Sharon was tough. She had written a letter to the Sydney Olympic torch relay authorities saying she badly wanted to represent breast cancer women in the area. By the time she was handed the torch she was riddled with cancer and it took all of her energy just to walk her leg of the relay. But she did it. I still don't know how.

She would often lament to me that she wished she and her husband had spent more time with each other, taken more holidays even when they probably couldn't afford it. The ironical thing was that they finally got around to selling their hardware store in the belief it would give them that valuable time together. She had a course of chemotherapy on a Wednesday morning. That afternoon she and her husband did the final stocktake. On the Friday settlement was reached. The following day Sharon died.

That's what gets me angry, that cancer can take someone's life, like Sharon's, when she deserved so much more. Some people can explain it away, saying at least we have the memories of a fine and courageous woman. Well, that's a load of crap. I'd rather have Sharon alive, doing all those things she should have done with her husband.

REMEMBER SUE Eddy? She was that fourteen-year-old swimmer I had played a prank on during the lead-up to the Mexico Olympics. I had told Sue that she had failed her sex test and for a moment she had believed me.

I hadn't seen her for a long time until I wandered into a bar in Southbank in Melbourne one night back in the early 1990s. All Australia's Olympians had been given a badge to indicate they had represented their country, and this badge gave you free admission to the bar. Naturally, it was a bit of a magnet for me. There were a lot of Olympians who met there regularly, and on this night Sue was one of them. We had a good chat and she ended up telling me how she had contracted breast cancer in her early thirties. She'd battled her way through it, however, was a single mum and was running an interior design business.

Sue rang me when news broke about my breast cancer battle, and she was a wonderful support. She had been there, knew exactly what I was feeling, and her words were a great comfort to me. But our paths didn't cross again until 1999 when I received a phone call out of the blue. Her partner, Craig, was on the line. Sue was dying, he told me. Her cancer had returned. She was in Box Hill hospital in a room with three other patients. I went into an absolute spin. I'd always hated entering hospital and luckily, because of my hospital insurance, I had always managed to secure a private room. I thought Sue deserved at least that. So I rang the

Victorian Olympic Committee, told them Sue Eddy, who had represented her country, was dying and that it would be a nice gesture for the Olympic movement to ensure she had a private room. At least there her death could be awarded some dignity, with friends and family around her, rather than in the stark environment of a four-bed public ward filled with strangers. Of course the same applies to all patients facing death in multi-bed wards which afford precious little privacy.

No-one seemed to be very interested. It was all too hard. Despairing, I called a friend of mine at the Freemason's Hospital. Sometime earlier I had performed some radio publicity for the hospital free of charge and now I was determined to call in the debt. But as arrangements were being made for Sue to be transferred to a private room at the Freemason's, she died.

Her death upset me greatly. And it also angered me.

I was angry because I never had the opportunity to say goodbye to her. I was angry that I could not even help her when she needed it the most. I was angry with a system in which those who had represented Australia in sport, particularly in the era when there were no financial incentives or rewards, disappeared from the radar screen and were simply forgotten.

And I was angry that cancer had claimed another victim. This fight against breast cancer means much more to me than my Olympic career ever did. But I see it in much the same terms. And I hate it when we lose.

23

Surprise, surprise

MY HEART WAS RACING. A THIN LAYER OF SWEAT HAD BEGUN TO APPEAR on my brow. I couldn't sleep. I couldn't eat. Who can when they constantly live with terror? My fiftieth birthday was approaching.

There was a prospect that I might have to wear a dress.

Fear ruled my life.

It has always perplexed me that the rest of the world has not yet caught up with my fashion sense. But sooner or later — and it certainly appears now that it will have to be much, much later — I am sure that the name Boyle will grace the catwalks of Paris and Milan in the same way that Versace and Yves Saint Laurent do now. In fact, if I close my eyes I can see it all laid out in front of me — supermodels like Kate Moss and Elle Macpherson parading up and down the catwalk wearing a signature range of Boyle clothing.

The crowd sighs and coos, in raptures over the latest fad in world fashion — shorts and T-shirts. Running shoes optional.

It had always been one of Mum's greatest disappointments in life —
her inability to keep me inside a frilly dress. But a dress had always
felt more like a straitjacket to me. Perhaps it had more to do with my
rebellious streak than anything to do with fashion. Whatever the
reason, classic feminine wear and me have never quite gone hand in
hand. Comfort and practicality has always come first.

But my fiftieth birthday wasn't far away and I knew there was no
way of avoiding the prospect of dressing up.

Or was there?

AT THE end of 2000 I had gone to Melbourne for a board meeting
of the Breast Cancer Network. Ever since my bout with breast
cancer four years before, I had always vowed that if I made it to
fifty I would celebrate the occasion with a big party. There would be
nothing insignificant about it. I wanted the whole world to know I
was still alive and I was in the mood to make a big song and dance
about it. In fact, that is what I planned. However the party turned
out, it would have to have plenty of dancing and real partying.

The year before, the singer John Farnham had turned fifty and
had marked the event with a national tour. It was a successful
concept and it provided the spark of an idea for me. What if I
turned my birthday into more than just a celebratory party — into
an opportunity to raise funds as well? At the end of the board
meeting I mentioned to a couple of the directors that I was
thinking about using my fiftieth as a chance to stage a fundraiser.
"We've already thought about that," they said. "We just haven't
talked to you about it because you've been too busy."

It was time to get down to serious work. Fortunately I had
already made a few preliminary plans. I'd asked John Farnham if
he would be available to appear and at the time he'd been
confident he could, but unfortunately circumstances prevented him
from getting there. And I'd asked the head of Australia Post,

Graham John, a great supporter of mine over the years, if he would be willing to help. As usual, he was more than generous, promising me $1000 for every year I was celebrating.

That gave us $50 000 immediately that we could start working with to plan the party. Like I said, I imagined this party being slightly larger than the traditional barbecue in the backyard on a Saturday night.

Events like these are extraordinarily difficult to organise. Because it was a fundraiser for breast cancer, I wanted it to be as successful as possible and that meant getting as many bums on seats as the venue allowed. We chose Melbourne's Crown Casino because the more planning we did, the more obvious it became that we might be able to reach the magical crowd figure of 1000. As it turned out we went slightly better than that. With the money from Australia Post we were able to hire a project manager to assist with the planning, giving me the opportunity to get out and make sure there were no empty chairs on the night.

I did what I always do — jumped on the phone and began putting people on the spot. Could they come along to my party? It would cost them $185 each, and all profits would go toward breast cancer information, support and advocacy. It didn't take long for the acceptances to start rolling in. One good friend who couldn't make it made the wonderful gesture of buying several tables and telling me to use them for my closest friends and family.

One of the keys to conducting a successful fundraiser is having a range of quality auction items and one of the few things that never seem to lose their value is sporting merchandise. Cathy Freeman organised one of only three Nike bodysuits given to her for use in the Sydney Olympics to be made available. I had a T-shirt which I had managed to have signed by all the women who completed the torch relay inside the stadium during the opening ceremony — and that fetched almost $30 000. I rang my friends at Nissan and for a nominal sum they provided us with a Renault car to auction. I had learned over the years that when you hold that sort of auction it's better to have a few higher-quality items rather than a neverending range of mediocre things that do not attract much interest and allow the auction to drag on interminably.

I had also spoken with the prime minister, John Howard, at a Sports Hall of Fame dinner the previous year and he had promised me he would make it to any party I staged. With his name, and that of his wife, Janette, on the guest list, there was never going to be a problem filling the hall.

All that remained was figuring out what I would wear.

I WASN'T nervous on the night. So much planning had gone into the event that I knew it would turn out all right. Outside the main room a silent auction was conducted during the evening, with goods like refrigerators, washing machines and dishwashers on offer.

The dinner began with a small jazz band acting like Pied Pipers and leading the crowd into the room. There was a group that sang songs from the 1960s through to the 1990s and the atmosphere was tremendous right from the start. Eddie McGuire, the football and television personality, donated his time to compere the evening and, as usual, he was incredibly professional.

But before all that came the moment everybody had been waiting for: the unveiling of my evening attire.

I'd suggested that we open the evening with a video on a big screen. Everyone seemed to think it was a good idea. It showed me being taken down to Brighton, one of the more prestigious bayside suburbs of Melbourne. There, I was followed around by a camera as I went shopping for a dress. We ended up at a dress shop called Aspirations, and followed the usual trauma and travails of a

Raelene Boyle shopping expedition. I tried on several dresses. Some of them I couldn't even fit over my shoulders.

The video showed me becoming more and more frustrated. Was there nothing that really suited or even fitted me? Surely something could be found on the rack that screamed out for me to wear it? Then, just as we were about to walk out of the shop, someone came up with a glittering gold tracksuit. At last, my perfect evening costume!

As the crowd laughed, the video finished and I magically appeared on stage wearing the gold tracksuit personally styled by Trent Nathan, the doyen of Australian designers.

It was a great moment — I absolutely enjoyed it and I could tell from the audience reaction that it had set the perfect tone for the night.

From there it turned into one of the most wonderful evenings of my life. The prime minister described me as "an authentic Australian hero who won the character contest". I would have been happy for him to occupy the microphone for the entire evening. Modesty be buggered. When someone says things like that about you — particularly the prime minister of your country — you could very easily sit back and keep listening all night. John Landy, the newly appointed governor of Victoria, was also in the audience. One of the dominant middle-distance runners of the 1950s, John had been the second man in history to break the four-minute mile. Always the gentleman, John hosted a reception for me at Government House a few days after the birthday bash.

It was close to 4am when I finally managed to put my head on a pillow. It had been an enormous night — when the figures were finally tallied a few days later it turned out we had raised more than $360 000 for breast cancer support.

But just as comforting to me had been the extraordinary atmosphere of the occasion. I couldn't help but feel good about myself. A year before I had been as low as I had ever been in my life, contemplating suicide while shrouded in a thick mist of depression.

Now I was back on top. I could feel my old strength returning. My mind was sharp and full of possibilities. I wanted to get out and meet people once more. I wanted to confront the world as I had when I was younger, to take charge and once again have the final say in my own destiny. I listened to my body all the time, taking note of every creak and strain. I heard nothing that worried me.

I had finally taken the microphone at my party and thanked a long list of people who had helped me over the years. Emotional as always, I'd had to fight back the tears when I listed some of my battles and those who had helped give me strength to get through them. And I also told the audience that I had learned enough over the years to know that the future was always unpredictable.

"There is a moment in time before a race when an athlete is confronted by destiny," I said. "I live with that day by day. I don't know what tomorrow will bring. But I'm here to have a good time and to have fun while it lasts."

It was true. I had no idea what tomorrow would bring. But it would not take long to find out. Inside me, another tumour was growing. Silently, as they always do.

24

Encore

A YEAR HAD PASSED SINCE THE SYDNEY OLYMPICS AND IF I HAD learned something over those twelve months it was this: no matter how difficult your circumstances, things always improve. You could spend months feeling blue, and months seeing red because life just didn't work out the way you thought it should. But destiny was a funny thing. It never quite allowed you a full say. I still wasn't feeling completely 100 per cent, but I was enjoying far more good days than bad. My fiftieth birthday had made an enormous difference and having raised such a large amount of money (and yes, being feted by so many people had certainly done no harm to my ego), I had begun to regain some of my old confidence.

It seemed that a clear pattern in my life was now firmly established. I was destined to forever ride a series of peaks and troughs. That was the nature of my depression. I could be excited and enthusiastic one moment, despondent and withdrawn the next.

My body had also decided to follow a pattern. It seemed that every few years I was doomed to face another life-threatening crisis. What didn't seem fair was that the gap between them kept shortening.

In September 2001, I underwent my regular ultrasound check-up. It had been fourteen months since my ovarian cancer operations and I was feeling better. My body, however, had been lying to me. Hidden inside was another cancerous mass, virtually in the same place as the first one, near where my right ovary had been. Once again the nightmare began. I just didn't need this. I thought I had regained a lot of my mental strength, but when the doctors told me I would have to undergo surgery once more, the same old shock set in.

The tests revealed that the mass this time was about 9 centimetres wide. The surgery would be performed by John Allen, a surgeon at Wesley Hospital in Brisbane. I was upset, but at least on this occasion I was given the news straight. It was worse than the previous year's brush with cancer. John told me it was possible I would lose part of my bowel; I might wake up after the operation with a colostomy bag as my latest fashion accessory. I shuddered when I heard that, but John said it might be reversible. They would wait until the bowel healed and then I might be well enough to lose the bag. He was also concerned about other organs — there was an obvious danger that the cancer might have already spread to several of them. If that was the case I might have to undergo chemotherapy again. That, naturally, really upset me. Once again I could taste the metal in my mouth, the constant feeling of nausea and exhaustion.

For one of the few times in my life I became stressed about the prospect of encountering the scalpel. John said he would give me a vertical incision this time and would have to remove the omentum, a membrane that acts like an apron on the inside of your stomach, covering many of your organs.

Hello darkness, my old friend. I was back in that black pit. That night Judy and I had dinner with some friends, but I was my old morose self. Plunged back into shock, I was scared witless. And yet, even though I had withdrawn once more, going quiet and not wanting to talk, I fell asleep easily that night. Once again I had a dream. This time, though, it contained no visions of ending my life.

Instead, I took myself back to the Victoria Gardens. The sun was out, the gardens were in full bloom and the neighbourhood dogs were scampering and cavorting about the place. Mal Dean was also there with me, sharing a joke and turning the sprinklers on all the lovers in dire need of a hosing down. I used to tell Mal that I was his "day wife" back then, while his real one, Karol, could put up with him at night. He was one person I could listen to all day. It probably had a lot to do with the fact that I admired his courage to make decisions about his life that many others would not. He came from a large Catholic family of sixteen kids, had travelled the world, had worked in offices, but had chosen to take a lower-paid job because he loved horticulture.

The dream was another of those realistic ones — I could reach out and virtually touch the plants. Clearly, my subconscious had decided to take me back to a safe place.

Once again I went through the ritual of cancelling upcoming events in my diary. The only scheduled event I attended was an anniversary celebration for Cathy's medal win. She had helped organise the day to raise funds for a foundation she had set up to provide support for Aboriginal kids with a talent for sport. I felt obligated to go. If there was one person who could put a smile on my face it was Cathy. She has a gorgeous innocence which many mistake for vagueness. During one of my illnesses she had regularly rung me from overseas to leave giggling messages on my answering machine.

I thought the mass in my side was going to explode as I sat on the plane on my way to Cathy's function. I don't know if my mind was playing tricks on me, or if I was experiencing a real physical symptom. But it scared the living hell out of me.

I flew home immediately after the function and the next day I dropped in to see an old friend, Nene King, in Noosa. Nene and I had been mates for many years. I had met her while she was a journalist in the 1970s, long before her many editing stints that turned her into one of Australia's legendary women's magazine supremos. We had a lot in common. She tragically lost her husband, Patrick Bowring, the same year I had breast cancer, and we both suffered from depression. Don't get me wrong. We didn't sit around the table crying into our salad. But it's always therapeutic to chat with someone who knows or at least has an inkling of what you are experiencing. Nene knew my fear of being alone and she understood it.

I wasn't due to be operated on until 1 October. Judy had planned to go away on a holiday for the ten days leading up to the surgery, but she cut it short to be back in time to accompany me to hospital. Team Boyle also began gathering again. Rick and Tess had come and stayed and Karen, a friend from Melbourne, had flown up, all to be sure that I wasn't alone in Judy's absence. I felt safe with someone in the house with me. It's ridiculous. I'm a burly woman in her fifties who remains petrified of the dark.

I was busy right up until the day of the operation. Lyn Swinburne had me working as usual — in another life I'm sure she was one of those whip-cracking bosses who kept the slaves in order below decks. She made me ring Frank Sartor, the Lord Mayor of Sydney, and ask a favour for an upcoming cancer awareness event she was planning. Frank had lost his partner to cancer not long before, so when I told him I was sick again, naturally, he offered to do anything he could.

And then I found myself back in hospital. All the usual secrecy applied. Each time I went in under an assumed name, or was given the strongest possible privacy protection. It was one benefit of having a well-known name. But then, if I did not have a public profile I would not have required the extra assistance. I was suffering a bit of a hangover that day; I'd decided the day before to have a few drinks, because, quite frankly, I was sick of always doing the right thing and it getting me nowhere.

The medical staff were concerned about my heart — it had never really settled down since running out of control the year before. But they decided I was well enough for the surgery to proceed. I was wheeled into theatre at 6pm after a long day of waiting and anticipating the worst. I remember being trolleyed down the hallway and Judy following. She was crying and I had tears falling from my eyes and trickling down to my ears to the point where it felt like I was underwater. Even the nurse with us, who had been a fan of mine during my running days and had asked to be allocated the shift so she could be there, was teary.

I wished everyone luck and told them I would see them when I woke. And then I drifted away into anaesthetic heaven.

I WOKE the next morning in the cardiac unit and instantly felt relieved. I knew where I was and I could feel no pain. Even better, I groped my way down the side of the bed and could not feel a colostomy bag. Right then I knew the surgery had been successful. We had nabbed the cancer early again. I was up and out of bed quickly, moving around my room the next day and doing circuits of the corridors the following morning. There was no pain. No depression. No vivid dreams.

The only thing that set me back took place one evening as I rested in bed watching the television. There were two cancer stories on the news. The big one was that Belinda Emmett, the well-known actress, had suffered a recurrence of her breast cancer. I was stunned. Every woman who has had breast cancer feels a bond; you become part of a web of fellow sufferers who share war stories. I had met Belinda a couple of times. Obviously we had decided to take different paths: I had taken on a public role in raising awareness, while Belinda had decided — and I agreed with her given her age and the demands already on her — that she should get on with her life and career. That she was once again confronting the illness left me feeling sick. The second item on the news dealing with cancer was that I was back in hospital undergoing surgery for a recurrence of ovarian cancer. It was only a brief item, and I was thankful for that. The news editors around the country were probably tiring of running headlines about me being sick again. And I was sick and tired of it, too. All I wanted was to get out of hospital and get home. After five days I did just that, with the blessing this time of my doctors.

Of course, once again I had forgotten the First Rule of being Raelene Boyle.

Whatever Can Go Wrong Will Go Wrong.

On that first night back at home I endured the worst night of pain I could remember. I kept vomiting I hurt so much. I would sleep for a few minutes, then be woken by sharp pains that left me doubled over and unable to settle. A neighbour who is an anaesthetist came over and gave me a pain-killing injection that dulled the ache but did nothing to stop the waves of nausea I was experiencing. That injection wore off after a few hours and I was back in the same predicament. Eventually Judy rang Ellen, my GP, and she came around at 5.30 in the morning. She gave me another pain-killing injection and stayed for a couple of hours watching over me until, eventually, we had the pain under control.

And that was it. I began the long recovery period leading up to Christmas. Once again the house resembled a florist shop — well-wishers were sending bouquets by the dozen. But even more remarkable were the letters. They poured in from across the country and overseas.

Ever since my bout of breast cancer in 1996 and my very public fight against it, I had become the recipient of countless letters and faxes. The outpouring of concern was touching. That so many people took the time to write to a woman who had only ever returned from the Olympic Games with a silver medal amazed me. Of course, I knew it wasn't my background as an athlete that really stirred them. Many of them were fellow cancer sufferers and among them was a predictable group of well-meaning churchgoers. I appreciated their thoughts and prayers, even though I had strong doubts about God's existence. Let's face it. Given what I had been through, I figured that if the big fella really did live upstairs, then he was one sick and sadistic individual in dire need of treatment. I even knew the perfect psychiatrist he could see.

The other group of letter-writers I could always rely on were the extremists peddling every known cure — and some largely unknown ones — for cancer. Some would extol the virtues of certain vitamin tablets, while others let me in on special herbal concoctions that would heal my body and mind.

The worst, however, was one from a person advising me to place my first urine of the day in a glass and then drink it. It got worse. After that, they said, I should cough up my morning mucus and drink that as well. I was disgusted. It might have been a wonderful cure for all I knew. It could also have very easily brought on a heart attack.

THE DIARY was cleared once again as 2001 drew to a close. But there was one more appointment I had to keep. Marjorie Jackson, the "Lithgow Flash", was inaugurated as governor of South Australia and there was no way I was missing this. Another triumph for one of the country's golden girls. I felt extremely proud of Marj — she had known tremendous disappointments in her life and yet she had always come out on top.

What a wonderful runner she had been. She had set four world records in 1950, and then went to the 1952 Olympics in Helsinki and absolutely blew away the field, winning the 100 metres by three metres to her nearest opponent, and the 200 metres by five metres — an unheard of achievement, particularly for a young girl who had trained in the fog at Lithgow with the track lit up by car headlights.

After retiring at the age of twenty-two, she married Peter Nelson, an Olympic cyclist. When he died of leukaemia in 1977, Marj began campaigning for funds for research into the illness and ended up raising millions of dollars. To see her become governor of South Australia was a wonderful recognition, not only for her services to her fellow Australians, but as a tribute to one of the warmest and most humble people I have ever met.

While in Adelaide Judy and I stayed with Bruce McAvaney, his wife, Annie, and their two kids. After the inauguration ceremony we caught up with many old friends, including Australia's first female equestrian gold medallist, Gillian Rolton, who had ridden Peppermint Grove to an almost perfect ride in Barcelona in 1992. We had lunch with Gillian down in the wine country of McLaren Vale, visited the gold-medal winning horse known lovingly as "Fred", and as the days passed I could feel the weight lifting from my shoulders once more.

I felt good enough by the time we arrived home to begin working with the National Australia Bank and a program of theirs supporting research into the early detection of ovarian cancer. I knew from my breast cancer experience that having someone with a public profile helped promote the cause, and it seemed only natural that I should join the fight against my latest enemy.

Early detection is one of the biggest problems with ovarian cancer. Because it is often diagnosed too late, survival rates are not great. Only about 30 per cent of women who contract it live beyond five years. The rate of survival is more than double for breast cancer. I'd been lucky — I had a mad Dalmatian that had triggered the original pain in my back that sent me off for an ultrasound. But often the woman of the house will put herself last on the list of those who need a check-up. Too often, she is simply too busy running little Jared to the football or Ashleigh to netball or ballet, cooking dinner, maybe juggling a full-time or part-time job as well, to keep an eye on her health. Her needs can wait. But can they?

I've heard it said that research into breast cancer is remarkably well-funded these days, and the disease enjoys far more prominence and publicity than male-related diseases such as prostate cancer. It's true. And you know why? Some time ago women decided to stand up and make a noise. They began lobbying governments and health bodies to take notice. Women like Lyn Swinburne took up the cudgels and committed their lives to ensuring that the message got across. Now ovarian cancer is becoming more and more recognised as a secret killer, and the more noise we make the more attention it will be given.

Somewhere in there lies a lesson for the men of Australia.

25

Sometimes beaten, never conquered

I WANT TO ATTEND MY OWN FUNERAL.

Well, to tell you the truth, I don't really care what happens at my funeral. I'd just like to stage it before I die.

It won't be happening any time soon. I'm going to be an old woman when my time on this earth comes to an end. I've already decided that. And given my stubbornness I think I can pull it off.

But I would like to have plenty of advance warning. That way, I can stage my own farewell. I want all my friends and family around me; I want a big table heavily stacked with drinks and good food. The wine and beer will be cold. I want there to be laughter and plenty of jokes. And bugger modesty and humility. I want to hear everyone say something nice about me.

I might even be in the mood to say something nice about everyone else.

It will be a crowded room, filled with all the old familiar faces. All my old mates from my running days will be there. Family and other friends will also fill the room. But by far the biggest majority will be the people I have met in the years since I first contracted breast cancer — the doctors and specialists I have come to admire and those people like Lyn Swinburne and others who helped show me that there is something more important than myself ... other people.

There won't be any medals or trophies on display. I don't want an audience standing around admiring a piece of metal that no longer means that much to me.

Instead, I might show them my scars.

SO NOW you've seen mine. A new, very small one was added in 2002 when I underwent heart surgery. For months I had found it difficult to even walk down the street. I was constantly out of breath and my heart seemed to jump about wildly, just as it had after my ovarian cancer operation.

By entering the femoral artery in my groin, the doctors were able to restore my heart to a regular rhythm. It was just another slight setback; the post-operative drugs were the biggest pain. Each day I felt as though I was suffering from the worst hangover of all time — and I hadn't even had a drink. But it wasn't long before I began to feel like my old self. The lethargy that had dogged me for some time had lifted, and there was none of that fear in the back of my mind that had haunted me for years.

In fact, I could feel plenty of my old emotions returning, including that ability of mine to grow angry.

I often remember the day back in 1998 when the Breast Cancer Network was launched in Canberra. It was the same day we planted the 10 000 pink lady silhouettes on the lawns of Parliament House to represent the number of women who are diagnosed each year with breast cancer.

There was a silent march that day as well to commemorate the hundreds of thousands of lives already lost to breast cancer. It was an emotional event — many of those marching were crying, others were clenching their jaws and swallowing hard, fighting back the tears. I was walking with a small group of Aboriginal breast cancer survivors. Overhead, the sky hung grey and lifeless and a light drizzle was threatening to turn into a heavier downpour.

"It's going to be a pity if it rains on us," I said to the Aboriginal woman marching alongside me.

"No," she said, quick to correct me. "It's not a shame at all. It's a sign that the gods are crying with us."

I'm tired of the tears. I'm tired of the toll and the anguish and the grieving that cancer leaves in its wake. I'm angry about the way death and its bastard child, depression, have hovered on my horizon over the last few years, taunting me and never quite falling from view.

And yet it is a battle I know I must face and fight every day for the rest of my life. More often I win. But there are hours, sometimes days, when I lose. The key, though, is to never surrender. It's a message I passed on in 2002 to Cathy Freeman and her husband, Sandy Bodecker. I was in Melbourne one day and felt the urge to call Cathy and see how she was faring. The Manchester Commonwealth Games were just a few months away and I was wondering how her preparation was going, given the considerable lay-off she had enjoyed after the Sydney Olympics, as well as a few injuries that had hampered her training.

When I arrived at Cathy's home she was drawn and exhausted. Her eyes were glazed, the telltale sign that someone is having difficulty coping with a crisis in their life.

"Sandy's got cancer," she said.

She had only just learned that Sandy was suffering a rare form of throat cancer and the emotions were raging inside her, all of them competing for attention. She couldn't sit down and so we moved from room to room, engaged in a conversation that was all over the place. She wouldn't be able to make it to Manchester, she explained. There was no way she was leaving Sandy.

I tried to explain to her the chemotherapy that lay ahead for Sandy, the good and bad days to come. I'd always marvelled at Cathy's resilience and her ability to cope with enormous pressures. And I knew that she and her husband would need to draw on every reserve of strength over the coming months. There would be times when both of them would feel down and out.

Relax, I told her. It gets better.

THE SCALPEL has performed wonders for me over the years, but it cannot entirely remove the blackness that occasionally envelops my world.

The medical profession still does not fully understand what causes depression. Countless studies have been conducted in the finest laboratories of the world and yet science still skirts on the outer edges of the illness. We know it is linked to levels of the brain chemical serotonin, and that some drugs and tranquillisers can have a calming effect. Until recently I had been taking Prozac for several years. While it seemed to improve my mood, I had also grown tired of living as if my mind was wrapped in fog. So far I have been doing well, and the knowledge that I can combat depression without Prozac has boosted my confidence.

But I am aware that the fight must go on. Depression tends to be an overwhelmingly long-term illness. One in two people will suffer a relapse within nine months of experiencing a significant depressive episode, and four out of five usually experience some form of recurrence later in life. My lifeline over the years when it has come to my psychological health has been my psychiatrist, Rozi. And Judy. And a huge array of other friends and family who make up Team Boyle.

None of them allow me to fall down too far. Besides, I have discovered a "cure" for depression of my own. I keep myself occupied. I take on projects, and lately two more have been keeping me busy.

A year ago, not long after the death of my beloved golden retriever, Goldie, I bought a new retriever — Kimba. Dogs have always been very important to me. They love me no matter who I am or what I am. I trust them, probably because they seem to place an enormous amount of faith and trust in me. My dogs have never questioned me. And they never demand too much.

Why have I always been attracted to animals? I've been to Africa several times and it's hard to explain the anticipation and eagerness that comes over me once I take my seat in the plane that will take me to Johannesburg. I don't go to Africa to see the people or the countryside, even though the landscape is capable of taking your breath away at times. No, I go to see the animals. They fascinate me, particularly those big cats. One afternoon I was privileged to see them out hunting and chasing down their prey. Their power and grace as they moved across the grassy plains excited me. But it was their sheer speed and fluency that really captivated me. Being able to move quickly across the ground — now that's an art I can appreciate.

So not surprisingly, one of my most prized possessions is my French blue WRX Subaru. Strange, though, the finger marks in the dashboard on the passenger side. For some reason visitors get a little nervous when I take them for a drive up one of my favourite mountains. There's a section of a steep hill where I drop it into third gear, the turbos kick in and the acceleration forces you back in your seat. Of course, I always try to drive according to the rules. But I love that part of the hill. My friends seem to like it, too. The experience always seems to leave them speechless.

Which brings me to a second project. High up on that

escarpment of my favourite mountain, overlooking a lush green plain filled with sugarcane fields and bush that eventually leads to Noosa, is a small block of land that Judy and I recently purchased. A new home is going to be built there, our idea of a dream house. Large windows and a sweeping deck leading to a pool will offer the sort of views I only dreamed about when I was a little girl growing up amid the concrete and bitumen of Coburg.

This is going to be my ultimate sanctuary. I'm going to sit on that deck every night, sip a cold glass of wine and soak in all the perfumes of the garden. This will be my reward to myself. After a life in the fast lane, I'm really going to concentrate on slowing down.

Except when I'm in that car.

And perhaps while I'm sitting there one night, looking out over the ocean and the burning cane fields to my left, I'll raise my glass and make a toast to what I regard as my greatest achievement in life: my ability to keep coming back.

DID SOMEONE mention comebacks? Is athletics staging one of its own?

I noticed a funny thing at the Manchester Commonwealth Games in 2002. Very few world records were broken, but something far more heart warming seemed to be taking place. Out on the track I saw more "pure" performances of courage and stamina than I've seen in a long time. More athletes seemed to be concentrating on personal best performances and worrying less about doing just enough to impress their sponsors. Maybe, just maybe, I thought, the decades-long era of drug abuse, and the subsequent corruption of athletics, is nearing an end.

It won't ever go away, I know that. There will always be someone trying to discover the next best thing to give them an advantage over the rest of the field. That's a human trait. Just like greed. But perhaps there is still a place in sport for the athlete who continues to believe in such old-fashioned notions as fairness and doing the best with what you were born with.

I came away from my stint in Manchester as a commentator for Channel Seven with one extra vivid memory — Cathy Freeman's effort in the 400 metres relay. I was glad she went. Her husband, Sandy, had recovered to the point where he had urged her to go, and it was especially good to see her competing, even though she was not at her fittest. Her effort in the second leg of the relay was courageous. To have travelled so far, with so little preparation, and yet still play a vital role in a gold-medal winning team showed once again the enormous reserves of tenacity and self-belief Cathy always carries with her.

I hope to see that grit and talent on display again at the Athens Olympics in 2004. And then it will be back to Melbourne for the 2006 Commonwealth Games, and then to Beijing for the 2008 Olympics ...

Meanwhile, a more important contest will continue — the fight to make life better for cancer sufferers. And most importantly, my breast cancer girls.

One day a cure will be found to end the heartache and the enduring pain suffered by the individual, their families and friends. I couldn't imagine anything better than being there when that day comes. The drinks would be on me. So hurry and find that cure. I want to hear about it before I, too, become one of those pink ladies in heaven.

My name is Raelene Boyle.
I've been beaten. But I've never been conquered.

I am proud to be able to support the
following organisations:

BREAST CANCER NETWORK AUSTRALIA is the informed national voice of Australians personally affected by breast cancer. It seeks to empower them and improve their care through advocacy, the provision of information and targeted support, for the benefit of the whole community.

As the peak, national umbrella organisation, Breast Cancer Network Australia links together and represents 97 member groups and over 7000 individuals across the country.

To receive the free, quarterly newsletter, *The Beacon* or to find out more, ring 1800 500 258 (freecall) or visit the website at www.bcna.org.au

THE SPORTING CHANCE CANCER FOUNDATION started when a team of outstanding Australian sporting personalities united to establish this unique charity. The Foundation's founding members are Mark Taylor, Rugby League's legend Reg Gasnier and AFL triple Brownlow Medallist, Bob Skilton.

Named after Raelene Boyle, the scholarships enable skilled young doctors to devote a year of their surgical training to work side by side with the nation's top cancer research scientists.

The Sporting Chance Cancer Foundation fills an acknowledged void in medical education, providing adequately financed scholarships to encourage our future doctors and scientists to develop creative ideas to better fight cancer.

The contact number is: 1 300 36 300 1 or visit the website at
www.sportingchance.com.au

THE OVARIAN CANCER RESEARCH FOUNDATION (OCRF) has been established to foster research into ovarian cancer — a disease that in Australia claims the life of one woman every 10 hours and often remains undetected until in its advanced stages.

A collaboration between Monash Medical Centre and Prince Henry's Institute for Medical Research in Melbourne, the Foundation is headed by Gynaecological Oncologist Associate Professor Thomas Jobling.

OCRF aims to:

1. Improve the mortality rate, management and long-term survival of women with ovarian cancer;
2. To develop and implement an early detection program;
3. To raise community awareness of the symptoms and importance of early detection.

For further information, please visit www.ocrf.com.au
or telephone (03) 9296 2040.

Index

Knight, Michael, 246, 262
Koch, Marita, 191, 235
Kunkel, Ted, 69

L
lactic acid, 142–143
Lamy, Jenny, 109
Lancman, Mark, 198–199
Landy, John, 293
Lannaman, Sonia, 179
Lawlor, George, 42–43, 53–54
Lawrence, T.E., 149–150
Legner, Johan, 232
Liberal government, 31, 191
libido *see* sex
Long, Billy, 176
Longreach (Qld), 244
looking back *see* controversies
lumpectomies, 50, 242, 275
lymph nodes, 50, 51
Lynch, Andrea, 168

M
McAllister, Sharon, 286–287
McAvaney, Annie, 302
McAvaney, Bruce, 242, 251, 258,
    268, 270–272, 302
McGuire, Eddie, 292
McKenzie, Sue, 103
McMahon, Peg, 178
McNeice, Graham, 279
McWilliams (wine company), 204
Mahony, Marg, 201–202
Maltese population, 90
mammograms, 33, 35
Marion (friend), 282–283
mastectomies, 50, 242, 275
Mathews-Willard, Marlene, 135,
    142
medals, RB's
    1968 Mexico 200-metres silver, 3,
        68–69, 108–109, 223
    1970 Edinburgh 4x100-metre
        relay gold, 115

1970 Edinburgh 100-metres gold,
    115
1970 Edinburgh 200-metres gold,
    115
1972 Munich 100-metres silver, 3,
    133–134, 222–225, 234–235
1972 Munich 200-metres silver, 3,
    139–141, 223, 234–235
1974 Christchurch 4x100-metre
    relay gold, 152
1974 Christchurch 100-metres
    gold, 152
1974 Christchurch 200-metres
    gold, 152
1978 Edmonton 100-metres silver,
    179
1982 Brisbane 400-metres gold,
    201–204, 205
media
    Arbeit appointment, 230
    Brisbane Commonwealth Games,
        200, 202–203
    drug cheats, 225
    head-swivel controversy, 112–113
    Montreal Olympics, 163, 173
    Moscow Olympics, 187–188, 190
    RB and cancer, 62–63, 300
    RB and Robertson, 151–152,
        178–179
    Wimmera championships, 118
medical profession *see* doctors
medication *see* drugs
melancholia *see* depression
Melbourne Cricket Ground, 75,
    224
men and health issues, 281
Mengele, Josef, 145
meningitis, 115
menopause, 76
menstrual cycles, 196–197. *see also*
    endometriosis
Menzies, Sir Robert, 59
Mexico City, 96, 103, 110
Michelle (friend), 283–285